**Modern Poetry in Trans**
New Series / No.19

# Iraqi Poetry Today

Edited by Daniel Weissbort
Guest editor Saadi A Simawe

M A

Published by
KING'S COLLEGE LONDON
University of London
Strand, London WC2R 2LS

Modern Poetry in Translation
No. 19, New Series
© Modern Poetry in Translation 2003
ISBN 0-9533824-6-x
ISSN 0969-3572
Typeset by WM Pank
Printed and bound in the US by BookMobile.

Editor:
Daniel Weissbort

Manuscripts, with copies of the original texts, should be sent to the Editor
and cannot be returned unless accompanied by a self-addressed and
stamped envelope or by international reply coupons. Wherever possible,
translators should obtain copyright clearance. Submission on 3.5" disk
(preferably Macintosh formatted, in MSWord or RTF) is welcomed.

Advisory Editors:
Michael Hamburger, Tomislav Longinović, Arvind Krishna Mehrotra,
Norma Rinsler, Anthony Rudolf
Managing Editor: Norma Rinsler

Modern Poetry in Translation is available in North America through
Zephyr Press and Consortium Book Sales and Distribution
www.cbsd.com

Subscription Rates:  (two issues, surface mail)
UK and EC          £22.00   post free
Overseas           £26.00 / US$40.00  post free

Sterling or US dollars *payable to King's College London*
Send to:
MPT, The School of Humanities,
King's College London,
Strand,
London WC2R 2LS

Represented in UK by Central Books, 99 Wallis Road, London E9 5LN
Orders: tel +44 (0)2 0845 458 9925, fax +44 (0)2 0845 458 9921.
email magazines@centralbooks.com

# Contents

## Essay

## Review

# Introduction

This special issue of *Modern Poetry in Translation* on modern Iraqi poetry was conceived when Daniel Weissbort and I were translating Palestinian and Israeli poetry some two years ago. We hoped that translating poetry might contribute to the appreciation of other civilizations and even to peace in the Middle East. It seems that our dream has failed. Our hope for peace in the Middle East has all but disappeared after the horrors of 11 September 2001. Daniel and I shared our disappointment when we spoke in London, Iowa City, Grinnell, and in numerous phone calls and email messages. Then our third and inspiring partner, Professor Norma Rinsler, co-editor of *MPT*, fell sick in November 2002 and spent some time in hospital. Norma has been instrumental in these two projects on the poetry of the Middle Eastern people.

In spite of these international, national and personal challenges, our faith in poetry abides. We continue to believe in its ability to represent the best aspects of human culture. I felt, as I once told Daniel, that translating Iraqi poetry and publishing it in English had become for me a desperate effort to save what remains of Iraqi humanity and culture in the face of a brutal dictatorship and war. As the drums of war clamoured throughout the Islamic world, I could not help feeling like the Chinese student who, in 1989, stood in the path of tanks in Tiananmen Square, exemplifying Ernest Hemingway's belief that human beings can be destroyed but not defeated. Although I lost faith in politics long ago, I still believe in the power of the word, and especially in the power of translation.

The globalization of capital threatens to extinguish the spirit of each culture, but one positive change has come with this movement. It has shed light on the importance of translation. Translation can, of course, be seen as a tool that facilitates the globalization of capital and thus contributes to the overall deadening of cultures, but when poetry is translated, it works against these effects. The particularities of one culture, expressed through poetry, can be appreciated by readers of another because of translation. My work on translation from Arabic into English and vice versa has thus been immensely spiritually rewarding, for in the process of translating, I have discovered and rediscovered many aspects of my own native culture.

My work has also been intellectually challenging, for in order to translate certain words, idioms, phrases, and cultural significations from Arabic into English, I have to transmute myself into an English-language reader. That experience frequently provides me with a unique double perspective on both the Arabic and English languages. Therefore, I have begun to realize the importance of collaboration between native speakers of the source language and native speakers of the target language in any effective translation. More specifically, translating poetry requires not only familiarity with the two languages, but also knowledge of the poetic sensibilities of the peoples and literary traditions of those languages. Hence, most of the poems translated here have been read and emendated by American poets working with near literal translation. This collaboration, when successful, results in "Arabic" poetry that is transplanted into English without losing its particular Arabic signification. Since absolute translation is a myth, and since the literal translation is spiritless if not meaningless in most cases, such collaboration is essential in establishing a linguistic and cultural conduit between the two languages. Even if the translator has mastery over both languages, the translated work should be reviewed by experts in the two languages. Of course, even the best translation is inevitably the outcome of one particular interpretation, which accounts for the existence of multiple translations of classic texts such as the *Iliad* or the *Arabian Nights*.

In this issue, the selection of Iraqi poets who write in Arabic and Hebrew is mine. The Iraqi Kurdish poets were selected by Muhamad Tawfiq Ali. As a society and culture, Iraq is ethnically and religiously complex. Some of the Iraqi Arab poets are ethnically Kurdish, Chaldean, Jewish, and Sabean (or Mendaean). Although there are some 40 Iraqi poets in this anthology, it hardly includes all the poets of the twentieth century. Due to space and time limitations and the difficulty of finding major sources of Iraqi poetry since 1980, when the series of wars began, we could not include some of the important poets, such as Ali Ja'ffar al Allaq, Sargon Boulus, Abd al-Amir al-Hussairy, Hassab al-Shaikh Ja'ffar, Ma'ruf al-Rasafi, Hamid Sa'id, Ali al-Shibani, Abu Sirhan, Abd al-Rahman al-Tuhmazi, Tariq Yasin, Abd al-Razzaq Abd al-Wahid, Jamil Sidqi al-Zahhawi, and many others, especially the new generation of poets who began writing under sanctions and do not have access to publication.

Sometimes we wonder what the value is of rendering Iraqi poetry in English at this historical juncture. As Daniel Weissbort indicated in his introduction to *MPT* 17 (Non-English Language Poetry in England, published last year), whether we like it or not, English has become the world language, and thus has come to belong to people of all nations. Hundreds of the poets who live in exile have lost their audience and have begun either to write in English or to get their poetry translated into English or the language of their host country. The outcome of this hybrid poetics has become an important feature of Western modernism: a phenomenon that has not yet been significantly explored. Some of the reasons for this neglect may have to do with the fact that major critics in the West are not familiar with, and some not even interested in, the languages of the colonized. Further, some academics resist teaching literature in English translation, arguing that translation is not pure English (as if ancient Greek and Roman literatures and the Bible were written in pure English). Hence, the value of translation, for political and cultural reasons, has not yet been recognized. And very few people are ready so far to accept translation as creative writing. Once translation is seen as creative, not an inferior literature at the margins of the imperial culture, then critics and academics, and of course publishers, will be encouraged to appreciate it.

A majority of the poets translated here live in exile in the West. Five still live in Iraq. We have arranged the table of contents alphabetically, rather than chronologically or thematically. Although this is not the place to discuss the literary history of modern Iraqi poetry and the historical factors that have shaped it, a quick glance at the development of modern Iraqi poetry and its main characteristics may illuminate some of the crucial aspects of the poetry in this issue. In broad terms, the movement of modern poetry in Iraq between 1900 and 1945 began with the ancient traditional form inspired by neoclassical themes under European influence. In the early 1950s, the pioneer poets, *al-shu'ara'a al-ruwwad*, Badr Shakir al-Sayyab and Nazik al-Mala'ika, stimulated by their reading of Western modernist poets such as TS Eliot and Edith Sitwell, began what is termed now *al-sh'ir al-hur*, free verse, free, that is, from the confines of the traditional two-hemistich line. This poetic revolution, which began in Iraq and spread through the Arab world, introduced new imagery, new metrical patterns and a new sensibility. In the 1960s, Iraqi poets, like poets all over the world, obsessively experimented with new stylistics and new philosophies. Many of them, rebelling against traditional thought, embraced existentialism, iconoclasm, and nihilism that introduced the aesthetics of ambiguity and solipsism. During those dynamic and sometimes chaotic years the prose poem, *qaissidat al-nathr*, was born and faced fierce resistance, even from the practitioners of free verse. Although the battle against the prose poem is not yet over, one can clearly see that prose poets, like Fadhil al-Azzawi and Dunya Mikhail, have successfully proven in their powerful lyricism and intricate rhythms that prose poetry is legitimate and cannot be considered just prose.

My selection of the poets and their poetry is guided by several factors, which include representation of major poetic styles in Iraq from traditional to modernistic to experimental, and representation of the major themes such as love, war, fascism, sanctions, torture, prison, exile, communism, Sufism, nationalism, feminism, homeland, exile, colonialism, and selfhood. I have urged the translators to stay within the spirit of the originals. For example, one of the most challenging experiences was the translation of Muzaffer al-Nawwab's 'The Bridge of the Ancient Joys'. Because the poem, like most of al-Nawwab's poetry, is disseminated throughout the Arab world on cassettes and because of the poet's habit of improvising as he performs, for more than a year Carol Bardenstein and I spent many days, and much time on the phone, transcribing, comparing the taped texts with some unauthorized printed texts, and finding the equivalents for the many allusions to the Quranic text, to Arab and Islamic history, and to classical Arabic poetry. Though we were reluctant to burden the translated text with too many footnotes, we ended up using some for the most crucial lines. Translating Iraqi vernacular poetry, *al-shi'r al-sha'abi*, presents another challenge. Poet Chuck Miller, who fortunately lives in Iowa City, and I spent long hours trying to convey the whispers, the convoluted images, and the visceral metres and rhythms in Shakir al-Samawi's three poems.

I hope readers and teachers of Arabic and Middle Eastern literatures and cultures benefit from this collective effort. I appreciate Daniel Weissbort's invitation to guest edit this issue, his and Norma Rinsler's patience and their attempt to make me meet the deadline. I would also like to express my special thanks to Vicki Bunnell and Linda Price, our academic support and technical support assistants at Grinnell College. Without Vicki's meticulous work on the manuscript, her insightful editorial suggestions, and her passion for publishing this issue at this particular juncture in world events, publication would have been long delayed. Wendy Pank at King's College London efficiently and patiently oversaw the final production of the project. When we were faced with financial difficulties, Russell O Osgood, President of Grinnell College, and the Oded Halahmy Foundation for the Arts, Inc (New York) were both enthusiastic and generous in their support. Many other individuals have contributed time and energy. Kay Wilson Jenkins, Grinnell College's curator of the art collection, made many sensitive and helpful suggestions for early versions of the translations. I shall not forget our Library Assistant for Acquisition Kim Gilbert's brisk help in obtaining many of the Arabic sources I needed for the project, as our Burling Library is not equipped for serious research on Middle Eastern literature. With Kim's abundant help, our college library has now some of the basic Arabic encyclopaedias, directories and dictionaries. My work with the poets and translators has been a pleasure. My thanks to all of them. I should love to collaborate with them on future projects.

*Saadi A Simawe*

*MPT* gratefully acknowledges the support of Grinnell College – Iowa, King's College London, International Writing Program – University of Iowa, and the Oded Halahmy Foundation for the Arts, Inc.

# Kurdish Poetry

## by Muhamad Tawfiq Ali

### Poetry v Prose

a) Rhyme
b) Rhythm
c) Meaning

An Arabic definition of poetry is "meaningful speech which has rhyme and rhythm". In other words, the absence of any of these three specifications, particularly rhyme, renders the speech as prose, not poetry.

a) Rhyme is the key attribute of poetry, rhythm and meaning being its other major attributes in common with prose.

The latter is often referred to as 'Free Poetry', its written form being vertical, recognised by a single column; real poetry's written form is horizontal, recognised by twin columns.

If that were the case, all press writings would be classified as poetry and newspaper columnists as poets. The proof of the pudding is in the eating.

A litmus test to distinguish one from the other is: if suitable as lyrics for a song, then it is poetry, if not suitable it is prose. And a prose by any other name is just a prose!

A comparison between the poetry of Goran (Abdula Sulaiman Abdula Beg) and Bekes (Faiq Abdulla Beg) demonstrates the change which Kurdish poetry has undergone since the middle of the 20th century. The former was its pioneer, the latter carried on regardless and didn't even get a chance to change as he died too early.

b) Rhythm: As is the case of the rest of the Muslim peoples, Arabic influenced not only their culture, language and literature, but also the form of their poetry. The classical Arabic poetry rhythm of 'rudh' prevailed over the indigenous 'haja', or metric. This common rhythm amounts to five syllables, a pause and another five syllables in each half of a verse.

Goran was the pioneer who rediscovered and adopted this rhythm. Simultaneously, he also reverted to using plain Kurdish and reduced the number of words copied from Arabic and other languages. This is what endeared him to the Kurdish intelligentsia, which is predominantly nationalist. The irony is that Goran was an internationalist and a socialist.

Bekes, although a nationalist through and through, is frowned upon by fellow nationalists as an embarrassment. Because they didn't approve of the form of his poetry, they abandoned him and the contents of his poetry. Although they didn't approve of Goran's ideology, they admired the form of his poetry which they adopted in all written Kurdish, interpreting it as an expression of nationalist separatism. But Goran's choice of words has not been at the expense of either rhyme, meaning or grammar in a single verse, which is more than can be said for the hijackers of his innovation.

The stark irony is that the proletarian poet wrote in the social dialect of the bourgeoisie, whereas the nationalist poet wrote in the dialect of the working class and peasants. This is further evident in their stylistics. Goran's poetry is formal, indirect and subtle: Bekes is informal, direct and popular or simple.

### Published poems
A typical book of poems by a Kurdish poet of the era comprised the following chapters:

1. Nature / scenery
2. Patriotic / nationalist ballads
3. Romance
4. Lyrics for children
5. Food for thought
6. Conscience
7. Satire, quizzes
8. Social / cultural

Goran is almost unique in having a chapter dedicated to plays, in this case eight short sketches of political satire. Another feature of his is a chapter of translations from other languages, Arabic, Persian, Turkish and English into Kurdish verse, but not conversely. His professions include teaching and journalism. He has written three operettas, the most famous being *The Blood Red Rose*, music composed by Abdul-Wehab Muhamad and sung by the tenors Omer Dizayi and the late Qadir Dilan. The other two are the *The Monster's Dungeon* and the *The Gorgeous without a Name*.

Bekes's only acknowledged translation is a poem entitled 'Change' by the English poet E Wilcox. This was in response to a request from Goran who sent his Kurdish translation of the poem to Bekes, attaching an Arabic translation of the same, published in an Egyptian magazine. There are also two which have not been acknowledged, whether "translated from" or simply "inspired by". One is 'The Barman' from the Persian poet Hafiz Shirazi and the other is 'Oh moon' from the Egyptian poet Lutfi Ali-Menfeluti. A translation of the latter from Kurdish has been produced by my colleague, Salah Baban.

In another poem, 'Complaint', Bekes uses broken colloquial Arabic as a form of comedy. In 'Bilingual' and two other poems, Bekes alternates verses in Kurdish and in standard modern Arabic as complementary in meaning, rhyme and rhythm.

Bekes is acknowledged as having reached the pinnacle of his poetry of revolutionary fervour and social liberalism in 'Freedom Tree' (not included here) which I have translated.

My colleague, Salah Baban, in retrospect begs to differ with the poet on this issue. So much so, that he composed a few verses in Kurdish and translated them into English there and then. I should add that both of us are admirers of the poet as we were schooled in his nationalist ballads.

I have selected poems from each of the two poets, Bekes and Goran, as the models for the old and new schools of rhythm, respectively. A poem each by a few more out of a score of poets will also be incorporated as further examples, in the interests of fairness and variety of styles.

So much for the synchronic variation of Kurdish poetry in the first half of the 20th century. As for its diachronic change, further comparison is provided in the selected poems of some of the multitude of 'modernist' poets of the latter half of the last century. I take Sherko Bekes as the model for the new school of rhythm. His strongest literary attributes are expressive and oratory skills. Furthermore, as the son of the late Faiq Bekes, he has the credit of saving the Bekes literary dynasty from extinction.

As a tribute to another departed Kurd, I am incorporating the translations of poem by Goran by the late Mr Abdul Kadir Said Ferhadi, who was Head of the Department of English Language at Salahedin University, Erbil.

# Mahdi Muhammed Ali

## Translated by Salaam Yousif

### An Upside Down Picture

Not a homeland,
That which is faraway
Armed to the teeth
And cruel desires
That which is sleepwalking,
Dragging a whole people
To desolation.

Not a homeland,
That which is far away,
That in which I know not how to look for
What I am losing these days.
Is it under the ruins of memories
Or the ruins of war?

Not a homeland,
That which is shrieking in the wilderness of death
Whereas I want nothing
But to hear the rustle of my curtains,
Feel the roundness of my mirror,
And laugh with the neighbours' kids.

Not a homeland this exile,
This which is nearby
Devoid of the rustle of my curtains,
The roundness of my mirror,
And laughing with my neighbours' kids!

[1987]

## Condition

When the city becomes a vast prison
You ought to be
    Cautious like a sharpened sword
    Simple like a grain of wheat
    And patient like a camel.

*[1979]*


## Homeland

O thou little tree which I planted a few years ago,
Does the grass in our yard still remember me?
And the crack in the fence,
Is it still filled with children's eyes, peeping?

O thou young woman for whom I became lost,
Is my room still lonely,
Wallowing in the silence of the homeland,
The homeland which is writhing on ashes of war,
The war which is devouring memories?

*[1981]*


## Flight

He was carrying only
His papers,
His caution,
A friend's farewell,
A suitcase too small to be seen,
And his misgivings of what the road might conceal.

*[1979]*

## Heritage

They were nil.
All of a sudden they assumed a glory,
Which extends back to the dinosaurs.

*[1979]*


## Expatriation

What an abyss
Filled the distance between me and my mother
That parting which was done without farewell
As if I were going for a drink of water
Or to dry my hands!

# Sinan Anton

Translated by the poet

### A Prism: Wet With Wars

this is the chapter of
devastation
this is our oasis
an angle where wars intersect
tyrants accumulate around our eyes
and in the shackle's verandah
there is enough space for
applause
let us applaud

another evening climbs
the city's candles
technological hoofs crush the night
a people is being slaughtered across short waves:
but local radio vomits raw statements
and urges us to
applaud

with a skeleton of a burning umbrella
we receive this rain
a god sleeps on our flag
but the horizon is prophetless
maybe they will come if we
applaud
let us applaud

we will baptize our infants with smoke
plough their tongues
with flagrant war songs
teach them the bray of slogans
and leave them beside burning nipples
in an imminent wreckage
and applaud

before we weave an autumn for tyrants
we must cross this galaxy of barbed wires
and keep on repeating
HAPPY NEW WAR

[Baghdad, March 1991]


## Phantasmagoria

blue rain
addressing a silent orchestra
in a distant morning
the maestro
cannot read
the foggy notes
butterflies
bloom
from your vocal chords
and colonize
my memory


## A Prisoner's Song

*(for the POWs of the Iraq-Iran war . . . on both sides)*

from the distant fog
after communiqués had withered
and canons stopped spitting
he returned
wet with the "there"
his silence an umbrella under our ululation
he passed by us
through us
to his old room
. . .
the 'oud was still there
its strings in their wooden exile
yearned for his rainy fingers
but he never touched it
what language could explain
that eight years
had gnawed . . .
ten fingers?

[Baghdad 1989]

## The Milky Way

her nipple
is a rounded decade of
strawberries
my tongue
is a tribe
of motherless fingers
climbing
the marble dome
of an atheist temple
angels wail for asylum
i swim in a fountain
of undeciphered languages
BUT
it's a temporary galaxy
the next morning
her bra
strangles my metaphors


## Wars I

when i was torn by war
i took a brush
immersed in death
and drew a window
on war's wall
i opened it
searching for
something
But
i saw another war
and a mother
weaving a shroud
for the dead man
still in her womb

# Fadhil Assultani

Translated by Saadi A Simawe, Raghid Nahhas,
Melissa L Brown and the author

### A Tree

I remember now, in my forties,
a tree
next to my home
beside a brook.

I remember now our secrets:
how she used to spread her shadows under me
bend her branches around me
and slip into my clothes
putting me on
as I put her on
together entering the brook.

I remember now, in my forties,
my stories to the tree about the gardenia
and about the girl
who left us
only shadows over the water.

And I moved away
how far did I move away?
But I still see her
stretch her branches towards me
in order to lift me – to heaven.

*[SAS]*


### Van Gogh

Go away!
How many times should I see you
dangling from the ceiling of hunger
from the nineteenth century till now
I see you every night
hanging from the ceiling of hunger . . . and I weep

as if I were your brother, though not born to your mother.
I look at your empty chair
and feel guilty for not sitting in it,
I look at your yellow corncobs
and feel guilty for not picking them,
I look at your whore
and feel guilty
for not marrying her.
Go away!
I am the stranger coming from another land
a land you have not heard of.
Aren't you satisfied with a whole nation?
Take your empty chair,
your field of yellow corn,
your whore,
take even your cut ear, for who would need it?
And go away.
I am satisfied with my empty chair,
my field of yellow corn,
and my sun with its throat cut
since birth.


### That Thing

Strange and mysterious
was that thing
like your laughter breaking now in your throat

Strange and mysterious
was that thing
like your coat melting now in the ice

Strange and mysterious
was that thing
like my face disappearing now on a road of no return.


### Morning

Good morning ... morning of losses
as you collect me
and spread me
over your balconies ... a killed bird.

Morning of the dead stranger
Beautiful morning
Morning of a city crossing me
to the others
And I read
*al-Fatiha*[1]
at every bend
and corner
and a street hastening its steps, behind that street.
Slow down a little
for after a short while,
we shall ease a mast
and sail . . .
enter a river
and drink sweet waters
or . . . let me go fast
open a gate and enter . . .
little by little shall we calm down . . .
then sleep
long . . . long

[RN]

1   Al-Fatiha is the opening chapter of the Koran, often recited as a prayer.


## Incomplete Anthem

What will Iraq catch as she travels by sea for a thousand years?
Water in the veins? The peals of sons
sinking to the depths of the sea?
The world has returned, and Iraq has not.
No limits appear while she is travelling – what will she catch?
Will it be fish swimming in the sea?
Some oysters?
Shoes thrown overboard by people?
Shoes and papers roaming the sea for a thousand years?
The veins of the dead are her nets
our bodies with their necks cut are her fish-hooks

What will Iraq catch?
An ounce of sand, a basket of Euphrates' water.
On the other bank creatures are sleeping, and life is born
God is in the mosque and life is between the thighs,
while she travels the sea – what will she catch?

Basra misguided her land, and sold her Negroes.
A world collapses under a shout from the poet al-Mutanabbi,
A brick from Caliph al-Ma'moun's ruined house could rebuild it again

Her sons are in the water and sky,
dead and alive who are dying
while she travels the sea.
What will she catch?
A sperm and a piece of clay drifting in the water
A sperm and a piece of clay longing for life?

From my distant chair I see the dead rising
shaking off their sleeves the dust of graves
as if it were the day of Resurrection

Have the dead risen
to draw something on the sand
and returned – to sleep?

Return, Iraq! You are not the master of the ship
nor prince of the sea.
There is no tower there,
no dam to keep back the tide.
You are naked like the waves.
There is no cloud to shade the caravan
and no tiny star to look down from your sky
no harbour calling you, and no *houri* to sing to you

Everyone has returned
but you have been in the middle of the sea for a thousand years
There is a dress of canes you spread out as a sail
and the wind rolls it up as tiredness envelops you
Are these your hands? Or two wooden boards?
Where did you throw the tower of Babylon?

Which god bought it?
Where did you hang the cities of gold?
On which neck have they become – necklaces?
Where is your first engraving?
Where is your first obelisk?
Where is your beloved Ishtar?
In which bed is she sleeping now,
to give birth to the legendary terrifying beast?

Iraq has come
and Iraq has gone
in her peace and in her war.
The water gulps her down
and the wind plays with her robe – it imagines it is a sail
sometimes, and sometimes it takes a rest
in her heart.
Delusion, delusion
all the times have passed you.
We knew you as a deity and wild beast
a house and a bier.
You were the obelisks high up, and the water-moss from Babylon.
A bed of Babylonian water-moss?
A bed of Sumerian stone so as to take rest?
A bed of love because the earth is narrow?
You have the sea, expansive like life
the columns of cities which have departed from you for the sea?
Pillows of books which have departed from you for the river?
Will your face return again?
Two steps to Astarte
two steps to the kingdom,
will you enter there?
You will reach it and die.

A bed of Babylonian stone?
A bed of obelisks high up?
A stair to go up?
Two steps to an apartment in heaven.
Will you enter it?
You will reach it, and return.

*[FA with thanks to Richard McKane]*


### My Mother, in memoriam

You are here in my little room,
the closest point in the universe to the heavens.
All night I hear your last prayers,
I touch your forehead as it bows to God.
Your spirit, here in my little room,
the closest point in the universe to life.

## RS Thomas*

Like you, I too
hear in silence
barking in Babylon
and sometimes I see in the dark
vultures tear apart my corpse which was thrown on to a Baghdad street.
But like you, I too sometimes hear the fluttering of swans in an
unknown sea
and the breaking of the waves on a distant shore.
And I see fish breed and the sea drifts them to the coast
to enter the net of eternity.

Sometimes, like you, I hear
in the middle of night tenebrous music
and a voice summoning me,
and I leave my home
hoping to see a voice I am familiar with:
No voice is there.
Who is, then, calling you or me all night?
No one.
Wandering voices in the wilderness?
Who was, then, behind the door,
listening in on Death's voice,
creeping on the walls of the room?
Was it you, or I?

*[SAS and MLB]*

\* *This poem was written one month before RS Thomas's death in September, 2000.*

# Fadhil al-Azzawi

Translated by Saadi A Simawe and Ralph Savarese,
Salaam Yousif and Melissa L Brown, and the poet

### Crossing the Valley

This desolate valley is crowded with thieves
but I'm crossing it alone.
I'm afraid of no one,
for I have neither gold nor silver in my saddle.

This desolate valley stretches before me
dotted with stones that shimmer like mirrors in the sun.
I drag my mules behind me and sing happily to myself.

Often rain pours down in this valley.
But there is no cave to shelter me
and I don't have a tent.
If the flood comes and water is everywhere
who will save me in an ark?
Yet , I go on without a miracle,
sheltering in my hand my heart's ember,
hoping to set fire to the world's dead wood
and to feed the ghosts that regularly dine at my table.

Alone I cross this valley
and the wind diligently follows me.

### A film in a railway station

In a train station in winter,
I am returning from a long journey
when I somehow find myself at a theatre for travellers,
watching a movie I cannot understand,
for it started long before I got there.
The movie seems endless.
It does not matter when you begin watching it;
its events are repetitive:

thieves don heroes' masks;
armies crawl through heavy snow to invade a city;
and clowns walk in front of carriages,
dragged by tired horses;
men wearing wings made of wax fly
under burning suns,
(insects on their strange paths toward distant planets),
someone finally finds a pearl, only to lose it.

And we bleed on our bed-sheets
in a cheap one-night hotel.

Dead spectators and living spectators in the theatre around me.
Someone enters, another leaves.
The hall is always dark
and our movie goes on without end.


### Leave the earth behind you!

Leave the earth behind you! What are you looking for here in a planet
overcrowded with corpses, where lost ancestors swing between trees,
chased by apes descending from distant hills? Daytime is in one conti-
nent, and night in the other one. Flocks of sand grouses hover like huge
bows in a sky crossed by wind-driven clouds. We can hear the noise of
screeching tyres in the streets, and we impulsively catch a ride to
nowhere.

There is no promised land here. No one but blind men with black glasses,
coming out of their ancient caves, carrying birdcages over their heads.
No sign of death in their faces, for they could never have died, nor scars
of time over their skins, for they could never have lived. No promised
land whatever here. They are simply walking through the forests of the
world, feeling with their sticks their dark ways between trees. If you
follow them, they will lead you to the last tavern in the village of thieves.
Tunnels infested with rats scurrying around, unaware of your presence.
Rivers, countless rivers. Islands and oceans. Towns and villages. Hima-
layas and the snows of distant Siberia. Clouds that do not rain. Cities and
streets. Robot-soldiers and robot-workers. Birds and trees. And travellers
are always on the road. A spider weaves its web and a dove lays eggs at
the opening of a grotto. Night and daylight. Men and women. Rocks
everywhere. Sand and dust as well.

Having left the earth behind you, you are going ahead through the most primordial nebulas. You will meet spaceships, driven by angels of mercy on a tour. The universe unveils itself for you, azure-blue like hidden music. Marvellous explosions go on forever. Mars thunders in its loneliness and Mercury throws shadows upon its frosty moons. On a distant star I see you now walking in a garden under falling purple meteors. Look! The polar dawn glow is drawing its wild bears across the River Lethe, while devil hunters are setting up their traps between galaxies.

Oh, don't be afraid! Farewell, go in peace! We will never forget you.


### For Everyone His Own Tree

The desert was drifting its sands
in front of me,
and my horse was neighing wearily
in the stable.

Hence, I carried my meagre belongings
and went away to the farthest valley in the future
and sowed my seeds.

Never say to the leave-taker: Come back!
What he has left behind is enough.

The eye lights up with the foam of the sea,
while a cloud veils the moon.

Someday, everyone will find his own tree.


### On a Dying Planet

The air is foul in the room,
but no one opens the window.
We carry our books in our left hands,
but no one asks us for forgiveness.
The corpse is lying in the cellar,
but no one cries.

We have to discover fire again
so that we can light our reactors.

We ought to pay our outstanding bills
before we give birth to our baby
in laboratory tubes.
We should have consoled our Neanderthal grandfathers
before we drove them away
to the mountains.

No hope of returning again
to the lost forests of our happy days.

Aliens in a UFO
are waving to me
from behind their glass.

Since the dawn of history, countless planets and murky galaxies
have been awaiting
my arrival.

Then, what am I doing here?


### Shipping Out

Who would be waiting for us
on our unknown island?
All we knew is that  fate alone
would be our captain; a seaman,
who has secret maps
of distant straits and mysterious seas.
So we went on board after paying
all of our worldly debts.

Unexpectedly we found ourselves
in the middle of a raucous party:
men and women were dancing on the stage,
robots in silky aprons and with beating hearts
coming and going, serving the guests
cocaine-spiced caviar dishes
and hotdogs from the angels' dining tables.
I sat among strangers,
reclining in folding chairs at sunset,
and ate to the full.

As they threw their fishhooks into the water,
I threw mine,
contemplating the sunset
and anxiously dreaming of good luck ,
which brought me a drowned princess
whom I took in my arms.
But as she opened her eyes,
she trembled like a fish
before she surrendered to me

and vehemently wept,
yearning for the sea.

I didn't know what to do.
I think I fell in love with her.

So I carried her to a room,
guarded by a statue standing at attention,
stretching a hand to all of the passers-by
to clear them one by one.
We shook hands with him
like old friends,
before we slipped away into a long corridor
resounding with music,
hoping to return from where we came:
– No escape!

We were standing alone in the dark,
lured again into the same trap.

Suddenly, I saw a globe in the room,
and excitedly I pointed my finger at it:
– Here's where I live.

I didn't think she understood what I said,
for she smiled bitterly
and pointed to her heart.


### The Song of the Slave Girl

After they threw me in a cell and locked the door
a slave girl came out of the wall.
She sang her life story,

gave me the golden key to her heart
and disappeared,
leaving her hopeless kiss
on my mouth.
I forgot about that key.

Years, long years passed
before I opened my eyes again
and saw the key in my hand.
Hopeless, I tried the lock,
and the door opened.

At the door I saw her
standing in the rain
still waiting for me
silently.


### The Lion and the Apostle

If you are an Apostle, whose name is engraved on the Tablet of Martyrs,
then I am the devouring lion, poised in front of you in the ring.
Dream as you wish of the Gardens of Paradise
as I am gnawing your limbs to the bone.
Oh, do not curse me; you know very well
that we both have to do
our duty together as destined in the world.
Ascend then joyful, victorious to Eternal Heaven,
while I, the lion of the forest,
continue to roar on this earth,
and to devour all the saints.


### The Poet

Once I met a poet who spent his life
among the dead.
Discovering that I was alive,
he named himself Fadhil Al-Azzawi, my very name, and began
publishing poems – my poems – under his own name
to bamboozle his enemies.
Then he came and asked me to join him
in his holy war
against the devils of the world.

"Together, we could defeat
all the soldiers of death
with our poems",
he would say
and I believed him.
So I sat and wrote
      poem
   after
      poem
about a poet who wrote
      poem
   after
      poem
against all of the death in the world
so he might stay alive.


## The Night with the Vampire

Once in a bar in Transylvania –
it was evening –
I met a tall skinny man in a top hat
and a black silk robe.
He said that he went by the name of Count Dracula
and had just left his plush coffin
to hunt for beautiful young girls
who'd be coming back home late at night
from discos.

Though I didn't believe him,
he invited me to his cellar
for a glass of red wine
in honour of his Irish creator,
Bram Stoker.
When he took off his hat
and looked at me grimacing,
I saw that spiders were roaming freely in his hair
and that his teeth were dripping blood.

I don't know how I escaped him
and with the help of what stick
I drove off his wolves,
which chased me along the desolate streets!
Was it Professor Van Helsing

who hurried to rescue me?
Probably someone draped
garlic lace around my neck?
Or was it the lovely Lucy
who took the form of a black bat
and lured him away
to the city's ruined graveyard
wrapped in fog?

All I remember now is that
when I woke in the morning
after such a long night of horror,
I found myself in a foetal position
on the sofa in the living room,
as Dracula was still searching for me
and howling on TV.

But then, suddenly – thank God – the sun shone
through the window
and set him on fire.

[SAS and RS]


### The Self-Defeating Poem

They will never come, neither from here, nor from there
They will never come, neither from here, nor from
They will never come, neither from here, nor
They will never come, neither from here
They will never come, neither from
They will never come, neither
They will never come
They will never
They will
They

[F al-A]

## Political Prisoner

Behind a locked door
In a locked prison
In a locked desert
Of a locked homeland,
A human being is kept in chains:
None of us knows him.

The torturers might kick him,
The cops might mock him,
Even his companions might deny him.
He might grow a beard to pass the time.
The yellow journalists might vilify him,
Not even mention his name
Or post it at night
On Satan's wall.

But as he faces his executioners,
Shackled in the darkness of his cell,
United with the revolution
Which approaches like a mysterious song,
He can destroy all the world's prisons
And free us, before it is too late,
From the legacy of fear.

Though he is bound and wounded tonight,
Tomorrow he will rise up
To set forth his history.

*[SY and MLB]*


## Every Morning The War Gets Up From Sleep

*1*

Every morning the war gets up from sleep,
Afflicted with purifying fear,
Leaving its memory in the mud of history.
There is nothing between the beginning and the end,
Except for one who is wounded, and who crawls, leaning on his rifle;
Except for prisoners of war singing an oppositional song
Except for angels busily transporting this one or that one to Paradise,
Exhausted, working 24 hours a day

Without overtime pay, or even a word of thanks.

Every morning the war arrives,
A woman who places a kiss on the mouth of the man
Who has been waiting for her.
All is well.
The slain fill the wilderness and the guns howl forever.
The soldiers urinate on the tanks.
A corpse grows on all sides, which the crowds enter, shouting.
A corpse wearing a clown's suit at a soirée
Cries to an enemy, who is squatting on a hillock
With a pair of binoculars in his hands
Watching a caravan of desert Arabs
Coming from another, distant, Qadisiyya.[1]

    O thou enemy! O thou enemy!
    Come and spend the night with us,
    For perhaps tomorrow we'll die together.

**2**

Every morning the war gets up from sleep,
A bridge rising between the fire and the ashes
A scaffold we climb by chance, one rung after another,
Like false prophets in a circus.
A dawn's childhood, which extends its neck far away
And sniffs the rear of a tank sunken in mud.

    O thou enemy! O thou enemy!
    Get out of your nocturnal hideout
    For we've grown weary of the wait!

**3**

Every morning the war gets up from sleep: two Qadisiyyas of elephants and blind-folded horses ambling from the right, with desert Arabs, brandishing swords, jogging along behind, their robes fluttering in the wind. From the left emerge Centurion tanks which cross a lake of booby traps covered with dead fish. The guns bombard the second tent to the left, where the commander is sipping a cup of coffee with eternity. The missiles whizz by, bombing mud-built Yathrib, perhaps Beirut, or perhaps Cairo. Airplanes, airplanes; airplanes soar above the sea by an abandoned quay, and the confused Ma'dan[2] in their boats shake their heads at the strange sight.

O thou enemy! O thou enemy!
Put out your fire,
For we all hate Zarathustra!


## 4

Every morning the war gets up from sleep:
    A Militant escapes from Nuqrat al-Salman prison at night.
    The wolves chew him up as he makes his way into History.
A vampire sits at Qasr al-Nihaya prison
And smiles, gazing at my face.
A dark coup d'état, spitting out blood on the red horizon,
Crawls like a mythical beast out of Langley, Virginia.[3]
I used to smuggle to Hamza Salman in his solitary cell a slice of meat
        and bread
Before he was taken in chains like a captive king to his death.
Military courts are guarded by tanks in al-Rashid and al-Washshash
        camps.
Young soldiers stamp our heads with their boots.
The IPC[4] shoots bullets at its workers in Gahwarbaghi
While its Director General, Mr Tisseau, stares at the eternal fire.[5]
Children are raped in prison
While Arab radios chirp about morality.

Every morning the war gets up from sleep:
A slave trader purchases poets wholesale.
Eunuchs play on the tambourines
At the wedding of the Minotaur.
A train is full of corpses –
The wolves sniff their smell
And follow them from one village to another.
A decrepit donkey lies down, exhausted, in a field.

O thou enemy! O thou enemy!
Put your weapons aside
And call me a brother!

This is war, then.


## 5

One Qadisiyya, two Qadisiyyas – whence is the third? A Qadisiyya that
is farther away than a sky cast on a desert, farther than Baghdad stabbed
in the back, washing its wound with the flame borne by invaders a
thousand years ago, shackled in chains, dragged into exile. Over its
imploded chest the birds hover, clad in that darkness which has no

name, clad in the pride of the dead who fight from street to street, from house to house, and from room to room.

O thou Conqueror, dazzled by his whip, leave your scarecrow in
   your field and listen to me!
O thou Conqueror, returning from the past, fold your flag and go home,
Where trumpeters blow for the wind and priests chant prayers to a
   different saint who plays chess with his fate.

Qadisiyya of sand and storms at Nuqrat al-Salman, where the Bedouin patrol stands on time's passageway. Flocks of sand grouse soar farther away, and the sad mothers gaze at the flagpole which is wetted by the sun. Stars forever. Stars at night. Under the walls, wolves howl like a conscience that has been flogged. A Qadisiyya of jeeps transports putrid corpses in August, where policemen, their faces covered, urinate on the camel's thorns.[6]

O thou war! Open your gates so the Leader can enter his castle, so the Conqueror can bless his captives, so the slain can chew their memories.

Far away is this exile, still farther is the dream which gets up from time's essence, where a mother bids farewell to her son who will be hanged in the morning in front of her house at Shaterloo in Kirkuk. O thou child, playing on the tree over there, do not close your eyes, ever! For to your right stands al-Hallaj,[7] leaning on his tree, birds licking his blood, and to your left the shepherd rises up from his nap and goes back to the fields.

### 6

Arabs and Kurds, Assyrians and Nestorians, Yazidis and Turkomen stand on a hill and wave to me. We are all mingled with the dust of tanks and the powder of guns firing at ghosts. We are all mingled with the thunder of airplanes, which come and go, paying us no heed. We enter life through its lost caves, then we sit on a rock and gaze at time passing in front of us like a secret song recited by soldiers crossing from one mountain to another.

Every morning the war gets up from sleep:
Like a sad widow, it enters the Cavalry Squadron jail in Baghdad, sleeps at the General Detention Centre, gets beaten at the Fifth Castle prison and is slain at Hilla prison. O thou war! O guardian of the ancestors! O resurrection without a resurrectioner! What should we do with you? Glory no longer has its glitter, nor the sea its clamour! Here I, the conqueror, fling my dreams to the dogs and my jewels to the thieves. O thou war! What should we do with you? O tyrant branded with fire! O

corpse moving from one map into another! Year by year you grow inside our conscience like a cross raised by Magians[8] descending from the Torah with thorns over their heads.

Every morning the war gets up from sleep and presses its fingers on my palm.

### 7

Ah! This is Baghdad: I move through it every day, to and fro,
While I squat in this cold exile. I look for it
In the demonstrators who move along Rashid Street carrying banners,
In the strikes of textile workers,
To whom we throw bags of bread and political tracts.
At dawn, carrying paint, we spray the walls with our slogans:
"Down with Dictatorship!"
In the coffee-houses extending along the river on Abu Nawwas,
In the fishermen by the bridge,
In the monument of Jawad Selim[9] which is riddled with bullets,
In Majid's coffee-house, where the geniuses and informers sip tea,
Where a poet expelled from college gazes at a window
Behind which three Palestinian girls gaze down the street forever.

Ah! Every morning the war gets up from sleep.
So I place it in a poem, make the poem into a boat, which I throw into the Tigris.

### 8

This is war, then.
It spills its blood in Basra, hides among the palm-trees, behind sandbags in the trenches flooded with water. The ships are sunken in the river over which the guns thunder. The airplanes are spraying poison on history, and the statue of Badr Shakir al-Sayyab[10] is trembling alone, terrified. Sinbad leaves his island, and the Abeed quarter[11] dances in the middle of the night, spraying the ashes of its dead on the soldiers who are on their way to the front line.

This is war, then.
I see it in the courthouses that move between Baghdad and Basra.
I follow it on a train used for animal transport, handcuffed to a prostitute, the two of us guarded by a policeman who curses the morning. "Look at you, Fadhil, a rat in Satan's church!" On the way back, I ride inside a wooden bus tied to a mad leper, who is forever falling into a well.

This is war, then.
It crawls with a thousand and one legs across Amara's mud houses,
coming from the ruins of Alyashan,[12] from the hideouts in the marshes
where swine and army deserters roam.

Here it is emerging from Qasr Shireen,[13] like a stupid dragon, climbing
the Himreen mountains which are traversed by a thousand rainbows
and which overlook Diyala's green plains, marching behind
Nebuchadnezzar[14] as he watches an unfathomable star. On the outskirts
of villages, Alexander's Macedonian soldiers hear the howling of jackals
which are spying on their own fate, where during the night an Arab rebel
hurls his hand grenade at eternity.

Between one Qadisiyya and another Qadisiyya the earth is scorched
pitch black, and on these crossroads I stand and wait for him who comes
with an axe in his hand. There is no time between one Qadisiyya and
another, no passage between the mountain and the sea, no blood
between the wound and the knife. Our camels are weary. Let's now
dismount by the water source, for tomorrow morning the desert will be
awaiting us at its distant barracks.

> O thou, the Impossible!
> Let's enter
> Your last dwelling.

**9**
Between one Qadisiyya and another Qadisiyya
I see a dictator atoning for his sins,
Desert Arabs purchasing concubines from a souk,
And kingdoms devoured by fright.

Between one war and another war
Our exile grows bigger, our homeland smaller.
Angels are on the run from one city to another,
From Paris to London, from Berlin to Stockholm,
From Rome to Aden, from Detroit to Sidney,
From fire to ashes, from ashes to fire,
From refugee camps to coffee-houses for drugs and prostitutes.
– Allow me, please? Are you an Arab?
– Who knows this, O Sir? Who knows?

Between one Qadisiyya and another Qadisiyya
I see a man fling his passport into the sea.
Consuls of wax provide us with documents,

Which we forge every time
Or fling into the fire.
From one city to another,
I see the intelligence services of the whole world chasing us:
From one airport to another,
From one park to another,
From one coffee-house to another,
While on the radio naïve singers mix Virtue with soda,
Unity with poison, Socialism with hunger, Liberty with blood,
And present them on a silver platter
To men whose heads are pecked at by birds.

### 10

This is the enemy who has just come out of his cave, sitting there
under the moon, calling up his memories.
The enemy who has no name is wandering amidst the palm-trees.
The slain enemy lies down on the hillside
Like a fallen tree
In spring.


This is war, then: All is well.
The missiles bomb the cities, and the airplanes bid the clouds farewell.
It is nothing but a corpse which grows and stretches
Between Kirkuk and Isfahan,
Between Baghdad and Qum,
Between Irbil and Tehran,
Between time and time,
Between blood and blood.
All is well.
Except for this spring approaching from afar,
Except for these birds flying between one front and another,
Except for those who await their death in silence,
Except for this mother whose cries I can hear from afar.
Ah! I saw eyes glowing amidst the branches,
A monster running on a sea-coast
Gliding down from my heart.


Peace to you, O Iraq!
Peace to springtime, coming forth from the fissures of the earth!
Peace to Baghdad, redeemer and redeemed!
Peace to Basra, to its burnt palm-trees!
Peace to Kirkuk, to its red sky!
Peace to Amara, to its marshes mined with dynamite!
Peace to the fourteen provinces!

Thus does the war get up from sleep.
A man takes it to a hillock
And leaves it in History.
Then he wipes away his tears with a rose
Which he hurls at a hazel bird,
Which rises up from its ashes
And soars far away.

*October, 1987*
*[SY and MLB]*

**Notes**

1    The Battle of Qadisiyya, fought between Persia and Arabia in CE 637, was a major victory for Arabia, and led to the fall of the Persian capital. It is also the name given by the Iraqi government to the Iraq–Iran war (1980-1988).

2    Arabs who live near the marshes in Iraq.

3    Location of the CIA headquarters.

4    The Iraqi Petroleum Company.

5    Reference to the ancient Iraqi belief that the fire rushing up from the oil underground was the "eternal fire".

6    A desert plant.

7    The great Sufi poet executed in CE 922 for blasphemy.

8    The Magians were followers of the cult of Zoroaster in ancient Persia.

9    Jawad Salim (1919-1961) founded The Baghdad Modern Art Group in 1951.

10    Iraqi poet (1926-1964).

11    The area of the city where East African slave labourers called Zanj lived in early Iraq

12    Mythical, ancient city in Iraqi folklore which is considered another paradise. Its location is believed to be in the marshes in southern Iraq.

13    City on the border between Iraq and Iran destroyed by the Iraqi army.

14    The name of one of the two Republican Guard divisions presently deployed in northern Iraq to reinforce the regular army stationed there. Nebuchadnezzar was also the most powerful Chaldean king who ruled from 605-562 BCE and defeated the kingdom of Judah in 586 BCE.

### The unknown man

Forever we abandon
our days,
throwing them at night
like pebbles into a well.

Forever an unknown man climbs up, dripping,
sits down on the edge

and gives us back
what we have lost.

## In a magic land

We have tales full of tragic knights,
who descend upon burning horses
from distant skies
like meteors at night.
We have many sleeping dinosaurs, which we have tied to rocks
in green meadows full of singing birds.

Then the world was just born,
the gods were our neighbours,
and we believed in wonders.

One day, we went to help them in their work,
but they unleashed all the bloody beasts upon us,
slipped away down the valley
and headed towards another magic land.

What traitors!

[SAS]

## The Last Iraq

Every night I place this creature on my table
And pull its ears,
Till tears of joy come to its eyes.
Another cold winter, penetrated by airplanes
And soldiers sitting on the edge of a hillock,
Waiting for history
To rise up from the darkness of the marshes
With a gun in its hand,
To shoot angels
Training for the revolution.
Every night I put my hand on this country,
It slips away from my fingers,
Like a soldier running from the front.

[1987]
[SY]

# Abd al-Wahhab al-Bayyati

Translated by Farouk Abdel Wahab, Najat Rahman, and Carolina Hotchandani

### To Naguib Mahfouz

Sultan of Light Years at Café Riche
around the treasures of his world
gather grandchildren of present generations
and generations yet unborn.
All the seats of the Café –
even the waiter and the government spy –
listen, intent
when he laughs out loud,
or looks at his watch,
seeing time sprinting away.

When the Sultan is not there,
it means he has taken the Café away with him,
leaving the grandchildren orphaned,
waiting for the spirit to return,
and the warmth of the Song of Songs.

*[Amman, 15 April 1997]*

### Who Owns the Homeland?

Who owns the homeland?
The hired killer and the jailer, my lady,
or the rainmaker?
Nazik, al-Sayyab, and al-Jawahiri?
Or those who steal bread, medicine,
and the homeland?

### I am Born and I Burn in My Love

1

Lara awakes in my memory, a Tatarian cat, lying in wait for me,
stretching, yawning, scratching my feverish face, robbing me of sleep. I
see her at the bottom of the hell of polar cities, strangling me with her

braids and hanging me like a rabbit on the wall strung on the thread of my tears. I cry: "Lara" and the startled wind replies: "Lara". I run after the wind and after the night trains and I ask the waitress at the café. No one knows. I walk under the falling snow, alone, crying over my failed love in all the cafés and bars of the world.

2

In the paintings in the Louvre and the icons,
in the sorrows of the eyes of queens,
in the enchantment of adored women,
Lara dwelled under the golden mask of death and under the rays
of the light bathed in the paintings,
would call me; I bring my face closer to her, feverishly crying,
but a hand reaches out, erases all the paintings and hides all the icons,
leaving over the golden mask of death a glimmer of light for a day that
has died.

3

"Lara has left,
"Lara's taken her own life,"
the doorman said, her neighbour said and intensely cried.
Another woman said: "No one knows. Not even the devil."

4

I toss a bomb under the night train loaded with autumn leaves in my memory; I crawl among the corpses, feeling my way in the mud of unploughed fields, asking the night watchman for help to stop in my memory this blind marauding love, this black light; feverishly I cry under the falling rain. At dawn I shoot myself.

5

Exiled in my memory,
a prisoner of words,
I run away under the falling rain.
I cry: "Lara!"
And the startled wind replies: "Lara!"

6

At the Alhambra,
in the rooms of the king's blonde harem,
I hear an eastern lute, a gazelle crying;
dazzled, I approach the haloes of Arabic letters braided with a thousand flowers;
I hear sighs.

It is Lara calling me; I bring my face closer to her, fiercely crying. But a hand reaches out and hurls me into the well of darkness, leaving on the carpet my guitar and a glimmer of light for a day that has died.

### 7

"She left no address," said the manager of the theatre, slurring the words.

### 8

Leaves fall in the forest of the Black Sea,
lights are extinguished and lovers depart.
I remain by myself, looking for her, deeply crying under the falling rain.

### 9

I cry: "Lara!" and the startled wind replies: "Lara!" in the fisherman's hut.

### 10

I paint her picture on the snow, the green, dark amber colour of her eyes burns, her warm cherry mouth comes close to my face, the hands cleave together in an eternal embrace, but a hand reaches out, erasing her picture, leaving on the slain colour a glimmer of light from a day that has died.

### 11

The sun of my life has set. No one knows. Love is a blind and lonely existence. No one in this exile knows anyone. Everyone is alone. The heart of the world in this exile-kingdom is made of stone.

*[26 October 1974]*

## Love Under The Rain

### 1

Waterloo was the beginning; all the bridges of the world led to Waterloo and embraced it, seeing two strangers meet at the lamppost, smile, stand, point to the lightning flash and the peals of thunder. Once again, the two strangers waited and smiled. Her eyes said: "Who are you?" He replied: "Me? I don't know" and cried. She came close to him, placed her hand in his. They walked under the falling rain until dawn. Like a child she sang, jumping over the small puddles, running away, then coming back. London's streets heaved deep sighs. The dawn on the wet pavements in her eyes hid in the leaves. He replied: "I don't know," and cried. She said: "I'll see you tomorrow." He embraced her, kissed her eyes under the falling rain. Like the ice of the night she melted lovingly under the kisses.

### 2

He embraced her again and they separated under the dawn's bare black sky.

### 3

Inside him sobbed his childhood years of loss and need.

### 4

For many years, he sees her often in his dreams; her picture fading when he woke or called to her. With a lover's fever he looked for her everywhere. He saw her in all the eyes of the women in all the cities on earth, covered with flowers and the reddish leaves of lemon trees, running barefoot under the falling rain, beckoning him: "follow me." Madly he would dash off, lamenting his years of exile, the agony of his fruitless search for her, and their partings.

### 5

Inside him, a battle broke out among women he adored: one died before love, one after love, a third in-between and another under the rubble.

### 6

The revolution of my death was an earthquake.

### 7

"Follow me" remained, in the naked flesh of the years,
And the blood of assassinated love,
An open wound and a fatal longing.

### 8

He saw her in all his travels
In all cities of the earth, among people,
And invoked her in all names.

### 9

She hid in lemon tree leaves and apple flowers.

### 10

Waterloo was the beginning ; and all the bridges of the world used to lead to Waterloo, seeking to meet strangers.

**11**

Under the lamppost they met, smiled, stopped, pointed to the flash of
lightning and to the peal of thunder and they embraced.

**12**

He secretly practiced black magic: "She'll come; she will not come?
Who knows?" He was crazy.

**13**

In his hand was a wax doll, which he pricked with a pin of fire.
"Love me," he said to her, and his eyes lit up
with a spark of grief that rose from the heart of the tragedy.

**14**

Pale as a rose by the lamppost he saw her. She came before the
appointed time. She was wearing her blue raincoat. He kissed her on
the mouth. They walked. She said: "Let's hurry up!" They laughed.
They went into a bar. They ordered two drinks. She came closer to
him, placed her hand in his. His eyes said to her: "Love me." Lost in
a dream, he saw her and she saw him in another land burned by the
desert sun. They smiled. They came back from the land of the
dream. He showed her his picture in nomadic Bedouin garb. She
said: "Who are you?" He replied: "I don't know" and he cried. It
was a red desert that extended endlessly to cover the map of all
things.

**15**

He embraced her and kissed her eyes. London heaved deep sighs
and the dawn on the wet pavement in her eyes was hiding in the
leaves.

**16**

"Aisha is my name," she said, "and my father is a mythical king who
ruled a kingdom that was destroyed by an earthquake five thousand
years ago."


### The Nightmare

A ghost in the dark hunts the author of "The Little Man",
sniffing out old books on the shelves of the bookstores at
                    Sa'adoon Square and Sari Souq.
Defeated, he goes again to the coffeehouse,
doesn't find those he'd hunted only yesterday;

they had flown, like flocks of birds,
into exile.
No more big catches:
tombs and prisons are full.
The carnival of death after their departure
has reached its apogee.
Ishtar is now a blind she-wolf,
feared by all.
She's now the soul of the city,
taken captive
after the invaders have deflowered her.
In her other mirror, besieged,
Ishtar is an old mother in rags,
crying the night away, forlorn.
Hungry, she goes to bed to dream.
Instead, she is assaulted by nightmares.
She cries: who's there?
Nothing but the wind going through the trash,
or the steps of the ghost in the dark,
hunting the author of "The Little Man".

[Amman, 13 April 1997]


## Shiraz Moon

1

I wound my heart. I give my poetry its blood to drink. A gem glistens
at the bottom of the human river. Red butterflies fly. From my poetry
is born a woman bearing a Shiraz moon in a wreath of braided gold. Her
eyes glisten with the glow of forest honey and the sadness of eternal fire.
In the night, wings sprout on her and she flies to awaken a sun asleep in
the beads of pearly sweat on the brow of the lover, in the sadness of the
colours hidden in paintings. A woman bearing a Shiraz moon, flying in
the night, besieges my sleep, wounding my heart, giving my poetry its
blood to drink. I adore her, and I see cities sunken at the bottom of the
river springing from her eyes. A glowing, honeyed charm kills anyone
who draws near, gazes or swims against the current. I see all the women
of the world in one born from my poetry; I possess her, I live in her, I
worship her. I cry in the face of the night but my wing breaks on the
colours hidden in the paintings.


2

Crazed by the river springing from her eyes,

by the fiery honey glowing in the river of fire,
I swim against the current.

### 3
I write the history of rivers.
I begin it with the birds of love and with the river with golden trees.

### 4
With my blood lovers wash,
and with my poetry strangers build
Shiraz in exile.

### 5
I possess her. I live in her.
I worship her.
In her plumage I paint virtuous cities where poets worship.

### 6
Crazed by the river springing from her eyes,
by the indomitable torrent and the flood,
by the ravenous flames,
I swim without reaching the shore; I drown, drunk.

### 7
I spread my wings and fly to her in the middle of the night. I see her
asleep, dreaming of the green Shiraz moon over the stone gates. Crying,
the moon climbs down from the branches of her garden, alone, worship-
ful. What was is. My life on earth has been an absence and a presence
filled with loneliness, travel and ghosts of the dead. You, of cheeks
where red berries rest on white mountain roses, be my sustenance on this
journey, be the last exile, the last homeland where I will worship, live
and die.

### 8
Lady, say "yes" to love or say "no."

### 9
Lady, say: "Leave" and I will leave at once.
Say: "I love you,"
or say: "I love you not."

### 10
Two gold lanterns your eyes are;
your hands two sails.

**11**

I hide a disaster behind the mask of words; I say to my wound: "Don't heal," and to my grief: "Don't abate"; and to lovers I say: "wash in my blood."

**12**

Fire devours fire, and the grief of the nomad lovers in the desert of love abates. Shiraz remains and we keep travelling to it in the night, burned by the eternal fire of grief. We sprout wings at dawn and we fly. But before we arrive there, we possess it, live in it and return.

**13**

They found me at the springs of light, slain, my mouth dyed with red berries and white mountain roses and my wing planted in the light.


## The Dragon

A dictator, hiding behind a nihilist's mask,
has killed and killed and killed,
pillaged and wasted,
but is afraid, he claims,
to kill a sparrow.
His smiling picture is everywhere:
in the coffeehouse, in the brothel,
in the nightclub, and the marketplace.
Satan used to be an original,
now he is just the dictator's shadow.
The dictator has banned the solar calendar,
abolished Neruda, Marquez, and Amado,
abolished the Constitution;
he's given his name to all the squares, the open spaces,
the rivers,
and all the jails in his blighted homeland.
He's burned the last soothsayer
who failed to kneel before the idol.
He's doled out death as a gift or a pledge.
His watchdogs have corrupted the land,
stolen the people's food,
raped the Muses,
raped the widows of the men who died under torture,
raped the daughters and widows of his soldiers
who lost the war,
from which, like rabbits in clover fields,

they had run away,
leaving behind corpses of workers and peasants,
writers and artists,
twenty-year-old children,
carpenters and ironsmiths,
hungry and burned under the autumn sky,
all forcibly led to slaughter,
killed by invaders, alien and homegrown.
The dictator hides his disgraced face in the mud.
Now he is having a taste of his own medicine,
and the pillars of deception have collapsed,
his picture is now underfoot,
trampled by history's worn shoes.
The deposed dictator is executed in exile,
another monster is crowned in the hapless homeland.
The hourglass restarts,
counting the breaths of the new dictator,
lurking everywhere,
in the coffeehouse, the brothel,
in the nightclub, and the marketplace.


2

From the Caribbean to China's Great Wall,
the dictator-dragon is being cloned.
When will you do it, St George?
When will you slay the dragon?


### Transformations of Aisha: Aisha's Birth and Death in the Magical Rituals Inscribed in Cuneiform on the Nineveh Tablets

1

Ashurbanipal fell in love with me.
He built me a walled city
to which he drove the sun in chains
and fire, and slaves, and prisoners, and the Euphrates, river of Paradise.
He fell in love with me while half his heart was imprisoned
at the bottom of the well of the world, enthralled;
the other half was in Ashur,
being eaten by eagles.
A storm he was and an axe in fate's hand,
crushing skulls of kings, forts and towns.
He fell in love with me, but I, alas, was not in love with him:
so the trees died

and the Euphrates, river of Paradise, dried up;
the city disappeared,
as did the fire and the magical rites.
In their place rose a cock of stone,
that crowed when the iron knight returned from death's kingdom,
atop the twin steeds of wind and rain,
looking for my face and my braids in the cities of magic,
and in the talismans of the priests in the temples of dusk,
awaiting my birth at the bottom of the well of the bewitched world,
as a gazelle, running after the chariots of exile in Ashur.


### 2

The slave trader is selling me in the slave market as I lie, lovesick,
dreaming of red carnations in the gardens of the Euphrates,
covering my body possessed by death and by life,
as the shrieks of a bird of prey, dying deep down,
taking its own life, its beak stabbing the body of things.


### 3

The sorcerer, poet, and warrior fell in love with me;
he made an offering, built an obelisk
on which he inscribed his spells,
the movements of the wind and the stars
and the fragrant breezes.
He wrote down the names of the flowers of my faraway homeland.
He cried over my grave and sprinkled the blood of a slain youth.
He kissed me and, naked in his arms, I cried;
the red moonlight in Ashur
dyed my face and my hands and covered the tomb;
colour came back to my cheek and the blood coursed through my veins.
With the words of his black magic, he brought nature's corpse back to
          life,
and the roots.
He unleashed the clouds and the lightning,
so the night sky of the world thundered, lit up, and rained flowers;
the hand of the wind combed my hair,
and a sparrow hungrily hovered around my breast
and landed on my stunned body,
looking in the garden of vision for rubies,
fire, and the spring.
He said,
as I was pushing the sparrow away from me and my braids, "O cypress,
O Ishtar,
mother goddess of sunny days and rain,

born of the earth's blood
and Tammuz's tears,
over the Euphrates,
let's run away tonight across these mountains
dressed like shepherds."
He didn't finish; the troops trampled him underfoot
and plucked out his eyes.
Awaiting them was Ashurbanipal, bathed in light,
combing his beard in the hall of mirrors.


### 4
A slave girl, sold in the markets,
in the cities of the East swept by whirlwinds,
I am awaiting labour pains.


### 5
To the chariots of exile in Ashur,
to the king of the world, to the sun, to the rich green fields,
to the sacred bird imprisoned
in the nether world under the bewitched mountain,
to fire and rituals,
to the body of the earth, annually resurrected by summer's kisses,
to the Euphrates,
I came, bearing the lash marks of captivity
in the kingdom of the Lord,
and the kingdom of man,
looking for Tammuz in poems and tablets,
braiding a crown of red carnation,
in my wanderings,
for his severed head.
I sleep in a shell with pebbles, and light
and goldfish, and weeds
at the bottom of a river in a deserted star.
I write on the tablets
a prophecy that solves the riddle of the essence that overcomes death
            and matter.
I embrace the frightful and the beautiful.
On the shore I see
an eagle perched on a gazelle.
I see Ashurbanipal
thrusting with his spear the setting sun.  I see
prisoners on gallows,
strung up in the frightful dusk of twilight,
and a priest chanting the prayer;

"The Lords of hosts,"
says Jeremiah the Prophet,
"thus will I make the commanders,
and the princes drunk and they shall sleep forever."
Thus says the Lord of hosts.
What could I, the captive, say to my death?
What has fate hidden
tonight under the foot of the monster lurking at the gate of the unknown?


### An Elegy to Aisha

When a shepherd dies, his death is no different from Galen's;
Orpheus eats the disk of the sun;
Ashtaroth cries over the Euphrates,
she looks in its water for a lost ring and a dying song,
she mourns Tammuz.
O boats of smoke,
Aisha returns with winter to the orchard,
a leafless willow, sentinel to the dead,
crying over the Euphrates,
making of her tears
a crown for a love that has died.
In the night of the locks of her hair, rats roam,
on her face legions of worms crawl,
eating the eyes.
Aisha sleeps in the in-between,
headless on the throne.
O Queen,
I had a vision: there was thunder in the sky,
the earth's response was a cloud of fire,
an eagle without talons,
that choked me and stripped me bare,
covering my hands with feathers and shells,
my hand became a bird's wing, an oar;
I reached out and the eagle led me to the sentinel to the dead,
where crowns stripped from the heads of kings were piled up
and where there were no doors
to open or close, where the lion of the dust
fed on mud and waste.
The priest of that netherworld, sharpening the knife, cried:
Who brought this poor man here?
Aisha has returned to her distant country,
a poem on a tomb, a piece of ancient wisdom,

an orphan rhyme,
a leafless willow weeping over the Euphrates,
making of her tears, sentinel to the dead,
a crown for a love that has died.
A cloud of smoke rose and the day was gone,
and a third one and a fourth and the fire
was my sickbed and the stones.
And here I am dying after this vision on the couch,
just like you, my queen,
writing on the leaves of the willow
on the Euphrates with my blood what the soothsayer has said
to the wind, and the sparrow, and the ashes.
I die every night, drunk
and sober: O dearth of sustenance.
I pass through Babylon alone, in the house of the dead,
alone in the ruins of the Euphrates,
talking to the clouds,
clawing at the dust,
crying from the tomb of my waiting,
desperately crying.
I tell the willow
what the soothsayer said.
Aisha has returned to her distant country,
let the poem mourn her
and the wind, and the ashes, and the dove,
and let the cloud mourn her,
and the priest of the temple, and the stars, and the Euphrates.
On the deathbed I laid you down, Ishtar.
I cried in Babylon until the walls melted.
What good did it do me, O griffon?
I returned to the Euphrates, a virgin wave,
a hearth that goes out when it is cold, and a door that cannot keep
          the cold out.
I returned, a book of faded letters,
read by lovers,
sold by copyists
to one and all, to every new reader;
I returned, an old bone, a poisoned hope.
Aisha returned to her distant country;
let the poem mourn her;
let the Euphrates mourn her.

## Writing On Aisha's Tomb

O, Traveller to Najran, convey to my two companions, when the
        day breaks,
when the fire horses storm the city of the dead,
when visitation is not attainable,
that there will be "no more meeting or reunion."
Cry over my childhood in front of the silence of the tomb,
stop by the ruins of this heart
offering prayers to the Lord.
For it is from here that I came
and from here I departed
in the chariot of the dawn,
carrying to the grave my rags,
and the sorrow of the land
whose pale brow no rain has washed at daybreak,
whose lips have not tasted the sweet, red, earthen kisses,
and whose nakedness no one has possessed,
for here she stands sentinel to the dead forever.
On the rocks of her grave grass grows
and the crow caws.

[FAW]


## Three Ruba'iyat[1]

**1**

In my sleep I saw
my beloved, naked, dancing in a glass of wine.
I wanted to drink it, but I drowned in the glass and the darkness;
I was a bard to His Majesty, the Sultan.


**2**

I wanted to embrace the children on the streets;
I wanted to kindle a fire in my poems,
but I drowned in my silence and the dark deep well of my life.
I was a bard to His Majesty , the Sultan.


**3**

I placed my heart in a basin. I placed my sword in another.
I took my beloved, her lips flowing with wine;
I burst forth in song;
I slayed the majesty of the sultan.

[Stalino, 14/1/1960]

## To TS Eliot

No wandering poets
no lovers
no martyrs
no drop of water
or a mill
in this cursed land
land of the last judgment
land of mute prayers
land of the dead, of strangers
and villains.
Venture
where the rags are
where the poets are
the living martyrs,
in the real cities of the poor
in the gutters
in the trenches
they burn
they wait
with sad eyes
in the blazing plazas.
Venture
where there are men
who wait,
burning
to light cities on earth
and proclaim liberties.

## Nine Ruba'iyat

1

The Messiah has sold his blood to the imbecile king.
The noble warriors were defeated;
the world sank in mud,
and the masks of impostors fell in disgrace.

2

You sparked a fire in the bed where I love;
you left me broken and aging at their doors;
you set me on fire and blew my ashes,
and you slept like a python in the wall.

### 3

The knaves cut the cords from words.
They fell in the darkness of the well,
while circus artists on ropes
melted like phantoms of the night in daylight.

### 4

Oh, Socrates, to find meaning
we must leave the cradle,
we must be decisive.
The goat must be sacrificed, the phantom annihilated.

### 5

Hired politicians are chopping wood for the coffin
while you are in exile, neither living nor dying.
You wait, embattled,
adorned with snow and stars and sapphires.

### 6

We must choose
to capture the wind and fill the zeros
to find meaning in life's absurdity,
for having to live in this orbit eternally is suicide.

### 7

Rome must collapse
and fire must blaze from this ash;
lightning must burn the trees,
and from this dead foetus, warriors must be born.

### 8

We may or we may not return
to our motherland, which carries hope in its loins
and grief and the glitter of promises.
Around our fire, the butterfly of life continues to hover.

### 9

The living dead are without provisions and a homeland.
They are blowing like ashes
so that Nisapore, like a snake,
may shed her mourning robes and break the chains.

## Two Poems for my son, Ali

My sad moon
the sea is dead; its dark waves engulfed the sails of Sinbad.
His sons no longer shriek with the gulls, "He's returned,"
nor do they hear the hoarse echo of their call.
Ash has shrouded the horizon.
So for whom do the Sirens sing?
The sea is dead,
and on its face, grass floats with our golden days,
the memory of which returns when the singer sings.
Our golden days are drowning and singing is turning
to weeping.
The larks have fled, my sad moon, and
the treasure is buried in the stream,
at the end of the garden, under the lemon tree.
It was hidden there by Sinbad.
It is hollow.
Ash, snow, darkness, and dead leaves bury it.
Fog has veiled the earth.
Is this how we die? In a wasteland,
watching the candle of childhood shrivel in the sand?
Is this how the sun sets?
With no fire in the hearth of the poor?


2

Cities sleep without dawn.
I beckoned your name in the streets, and darkness replied.
I begged the wind, wailing in the heart of the void;
I saw your face in mirrors and eyes,
in windowpanes of that elusive dawn
and on postcards.
In cities without dawn,
even the birds deserted the churches.
So for whom do you sing, my heart? The street shops have sealed
their doors.
For whom do you pray, my broken heart?
The night has passed
and carriages
laced with frost
returned without horses.
The riders died.
Is this how the years pass?
With pain tearing the heart?

We move from exile to exile and home to home
and wither like lilies that never bloomed.
Poor, we die, my son,
and our train forever passes us by.

*[NR and CH]*

**Notes**
1    Ruba'iyat: Quatrains or poems of four lines.

# Bekes (Faiq Abdulla Beg)

Iraqi Kurdish

## Translated by Salah Ahmed Baban and Abdul Kadir Said Ferhadi

### Oh, Moon

Oh, moon, you and I have something to share,
We are wanderers who observe and stare.
You are lonely, pale in our vast sky,
As I am, a tramp of towns with no care.

Oh, Moon, my refuge, Mecca of lovers,
You are the healer of all wounded hearts.
I feel so lonely and dismal tonight
And no one but you may solace my heart.

I ask you to swear by Love and Beauty,
By the dawn breeze, to tell me the truth,
What troubles  you, what is your story?
Your reply may soothe
My sad misery, set my mind at ease.

Please tell me,  Moon, what caused your sadness
And silent sorrow on your lovely face? I can only guess.
For God's sake, tell me how many you've seen
Deprived young couples tormented in love?

How many tyrants and heroes have you seen,
How many nations, countries and towns,
How many unjust wars of aggression,
Awful bombardments of Kurdistan towns
And how often have you gazed
At scarlet shrouds of youthful martyrs?

How many grieving mothers and widows have you seen;
Eyes red, full of tears,
Miserable orphans in pain, fearful,
How much misery, how often have you seen it?

Oh, Moon, you've seen so much of this world,
Witnessed injustice, hypocrisy and lies.
That is why you are so sad, so pale
With silent sorrow on your lips and eyes.

I know the reason for your sadness, Moon.

[SB]


## I Who Have Nothing

When I am deprived of your touch, what is the point of living?
What can I do with fame and fortune, soul and religion?
You are the delight of my heart, my eye.
Without you, what good is the world of inheritance?
I who have been endowed with the beloved soil of Kurdistan,
What do I do with the continents of Europe and Asia?
I who have delicious grape syrup and grape juice
do not want champagne. What do I do with ginger wine?
I was born to serve you, not just sit.
If I don't struggle for the homeland,
Why do I need strength of mind and body?

[Bekes wrote this poem when in exile in southern Iraq in the 1930s.]


## Bright Star

You bright star of the space
About you I am in a mess
I watch you but cannot guess
Who's set you in that place?

*


At night as I come to the roof terrace
I see you are in the heavens
In the beautiful azure space
Twinkling till the day breaks.

*

That's why you're gay and joyous
Unstrained, so lofty and marvellous
Always so sure and luminous:
Because earth is at a distance.

*

I wish you could converse.
Explain to me the penniless:
are you a rock, a tree, of the human race?
With gold, diamond or silver lustrous?
I'm your captive full of distress,
Please make haste, please be terse.

*

This was the response:
I'm a celestial sphere in space
By god's strength and ordinance
Suspended on heaven's face.

[A-KF]

# Bekes Jr (Sherko Faiq)

Iraqi Kurdish

## Translated by Muhamad Tawfiq Ali

### Picture

Four children
a Turk, a Persian
an Arab and a Kurd
were collectively drawing  the picture of a man.
The first drew his head
The second drew his hands and upper limbs
The third drew his legs and torso
The fourth drew a gun on his shoulder

[1979]

### Love

There is many a country
more elegant than Kurdistan
more delightful than Kurdistan.
There is many a country
more starry-eyed than Kurdistan
more adorable than Kurdistan.
There is many a country
sweeter-sounding than Kurdistan,
more colourful and adroit than Kurdistan.
But, my Kurdistan
there is no country
more lovable than you.

[1985]

## Separation

If they remove the flower
from my poetry,
one of my four seasons will die.
If they remove the beloved,
two of them will die.
If they remove bread,
three of them will die.
If they remove freedom,
my whole year will die,
and I, myself, will die.

[1988]

# Mahmoud al-Braikan

Translated by Saadi A Simawe with Ralph Savarese and Ellen Doré Watson

## Meditations on a World of Stones

### I  Desert Stone

It is a great sundial in the desert,
a  sign for the sands of the labyrinth,
an answer to the search for water,
a tombstone of an immense grave
whose names are totally effaced.

### II  Inner Life

Mysterious things
happen in the interior of stones:
their well-concealed crystal,
their invisible beams,
their surfaces, their lines,
their geometry –
who knows the alphabet of stones?

### III  Sea Stone

Naked in its green body
without the splash of the sea,
it is calm when the wind works
its chisel and the rain bathes in light
the tiny shells under its shadow.
While the waves dance for the moon,
the melancholy of eternity dwells inside the stone.

### IV  Creation Stone

At first glance:
the balance of matter.
At second glance:
a fierce bust exploring the horizon.
At third glance:
the very poem of creation.

### V  Mountain Stone

It has the dull red colour of iron
and lines of antiquity.

A goddess of a forgotten world
had cracked under the reverberation of thunder
and sucked the shapeless lightning.

### VI  *Fellow Traveller's Stone*
It stretches its hand with ultimate succour
for the tired traveller.
A friend of passengers, this pleasant sage;
a guardian of delight,
a bearer of the lamp in the dark.

[1971]


### An Empty City

In one of my travels,
I suddenly find myself
in a silent city –
not a trace of life anywhere.
The doors of the houses are locked,
the wind plays in the squares.
But the city's windows shine all night.
Who switched on the lights?
I saw in gardens all kinds of flowers
bending their heads.
And I saw a ruined playground.
I knocked at many doors,
I shouted:
Are they all dead?
Emigrated?
Turned with what magic into invisible creatures?
  . . .
Then, suddenly, I saw the shadow of a woman
stirring on a marble pedestal,
trying lazily to arise from her ancient hibernation,
and I said: "Do you know who I am?
It's me, Adam."
But she did not know language.

[1990]

### The Face

It's the same face, again and again, hovering near the window.
The same face, painted behind the window pane
during the tedious nights when the rain falls.
That ghost with a halo,
his lips atremble while mumbling something –
what, a secret prayer?  a silent rattling in the throat?

The same face appears when storms blow in,
cloaked in leaden darkness,
framed by flying hair,
hurling glances of horror and torment
through the glass.
And then the wind erases it again.

That same face appears
when the rain pours
in the middle of the night.
Like the face of somebody drowning, it taps at the window,
rippled by the surface of the water,
aflame with all kinds of lightning –
on its cheeks
flow tears and rain.

[1989]


### The Monkey's Journey

In a wood box
in the back of a barred truck,
a monkey squats
and very calmly examines its surroundings:
the earth rapidly rolls underneath,
sights run away from him,
and the truck speeds up
on the highway that turns but never seems to end.
The monkey is disturbed
but regains his composure
and resumes his staring at the things that pass him:
green, yellow, and dusty pastures
under the daylight,
palm trees, rocks, women, children,

houses, graves, hills, valleys,
villages, cities.
Then darkness falls and the moon rises.
Under the moonlight the monkey dreams of the distant jungle
and its natural swinging.
The morning rooster breathes
and the landscapes appear bright.
The truck enters a cloud of dust,
the monkey sneezes
and wipes a tear
and resumes his staring.
The landscapes tremble. The sun jumps over the horizon.
The monkey feels anxious for a moment
but then goes on staring. The mile markers accumulate.
One horizon disappears and another emerges.
Astonishing sights speed by,
colours keep changing:
the monkey's journey seems an endless enchanted adventure,
and the monkey examines all that his stare captures.

The monkey does not know anything about the laboratory:
the equipment room,
the microscopes, the scalpels,
where from his white small brain
many specimens will be taken for experiments.
From behind the bars of his box, the monkey
casts on everything a sedate glance.

[1979]


### The Possessed

Lured by a summons he does not
understand,
taken away from the kingdom of earthly joy,
alienated even from himself,
he slowly steps toward a door.

Leaving behind
a faceless woman
and a child,
he dreams in bed
and like one whose soul has been snatched
he steps slowly toward a door.

Leaving a dog who perplexes him
and a library he has not read
and bills he has not paid,
he steps like a robot
toward a door.

He walks toward the open door,
staring into darkness
as the darkness stares into him,
listening to a whisper no one hears but him,
and without delay
steps through.

[1992]
[SAS and RS]


## A World of Lightning

A blue world,
bursting out of black nothingness,
radiating into the abyss of night
A curving horizon,
flash of sword sharpened by cold flame
A lone tree,
long branches
drooping into stretches of emptiness
A minaret,
dome defined by glow
Roads erupting
like beams into the heights of heaven
Clouds burning as they collide,
sky cutting sky
Thunder caving in,
fraying at the edges of the universe

The pleading of a frightened dog
The shaky hand pulling the curtain

[1992]
[SAS and EDW]

# Goran (Abdula Sulaiman Abdula Beg)

Iraqi Kurdish

## Translated by Abdul Kadir Said Ferhadi

### A Lover's Song

Under the azure sky,
By the snowy peak,
I searched all over Kurdistan,
Every valley and ravine.

\*

Neither in city nor country
Did I see anyone
As graceful as you!
It's only you, no one else,
A Kurdish lass,
Who gladdens the heart
As a fairy of a heavenly host!

\*

Neither slender nor stout,
Neither youngish nor elderly,
Eyes not too dark-coloured
Nor too wide,
But as to the sweet figure:
I saw none as vigorous.
It's only you: no one else!
Whom a moonlit-night smile befits
Such a neat figure
And a quail's demeanour!

\*

From the day I saw you
Love has taken root in my heart!
When one hour you are away,
A flame will burn me away
Since my hand can't get at you!
My heart can calm down

With no one: except you,
Refuge of my hopes and dreaming,
Sweet hope of my living being!

\*

Then, when I hadn't met you,
Hard and bitter was my living:
Without joy or tolerance,
Without hope, diminishing,
Living life marginally,
I had no one to command:
But for you: only you,
Leader to my way of relief,
Easing the hardships of my life!

\*

You elder daughter of Zeus!
Beauteous sister of Venus!
I worship you and
That's why I am so drunk!
For my creed
Some people seek:
Let it be known;
It's only you: no one else.
You're the Kiblah[1] of my belief!
Goddess of my young heart's paradise!
Restless seeker of the place of hope
Neither the Zaza[2] nor the Kirmanj,
I toured Kurdistan:
Garmyan[3] and Kwestan,
Neither in cities nor the country,
Did I see anyone
As beautiful as you are;
It's only you: no one else,
A Kurdish girl like a flower
Who is Kurdistan's riches!

**Notes**

1   Kiblah: direction towards which a Muslim turns in praying.
2   Zaza and Kirmanji: two northern Kurdish dialects.
3   Garmyan: the southern part of Kurdistan; Kwestan:
the northern part of Kurdistan

## Woman and Beauty

In the sky, I've seen
Celestial bodies
From spring gardens, I've picked
Many blossoms
Dewdrops of trees
Have sprinkled my face
I have watched twilights
Over many peaks,
A rainbow after torrential rains
Bending before the sun's rays,
The sun of Newrozôt the month of May,
Have come and gone
By night and day . . .
The roar of forest falls
Of silvery foam,
Radiation in the haze
Are a thousand ways,
Ripe garden fruits,
Yellow and red,
The chirping and peeping
Of the mountain wood
From the flute's throat
The violin's cord
Have often risen
Sweet tunes so good
They are all so sweet
And such beautiful
Illuminators of life's way!
Yet nature is ever and ever
Lightless but for
The smile of the beloved:
Tuneless it is
Unless the wind
To my ear brings
Her tender voice
How merry, I say!
What bright star
What mountain bloom
Matches her cheek?
Her nipple? Her lips?
What blackness can match
That of her eyes? Her lashes?

Her flowing plait? Her brows?
What height's so lovely
as her tall body?
What light can match
That of her eyes?
What longing
What waiting
What attraction
Is so mysterious
As that of affection?

# Gzar Hantoosh

Translated by Saadi A Simawe and Ellen Doré Watson

### The Happiest Man in the World

Lushly I walk, like flowers under the bitter orange,
towards my friend the poet.
A handful of beans and lentils will satisfy the stomach,
al-Saigh Yousif 's crystal verses will feed the soul,
and I have sorrows that get me
drunk for free.
And won't my pocket be full,
with a checkbook from al-Sayyab's Bank of Gold?*
I walk under a thundering sky
under God's tears
under the people's compassion
under white birds
angling for a safe haven.
. . .
Lushly I walk toward the other side.

* al-Sayyab: Iraqi poet Badir Shakir al-Sayyab (1926-1964),
who died in poverty and left a wealth of intensely lyrical poetry.

### Take Me, Loneliness

I won apples out of season for her.
For her I wrote poetry on a fig leaf.
For her wearing clay horns I battled angry bulls.
I stole a shawl from al-Gharraf's* green moon for her.
And still she left, she left me
heart-stricken like a lantern
sharing secrets with a muddy river
and the wind raging.
She left me like water shooting through the limbs
of the pomegranate tree.
I jump out of my unholy anger.
When the salt in the earth gives blossom, please
come, and come if the sun turns green,
and if the elder Hantoosh comes
back from the grave, come.

How many times al-Diwaniyah, my city
took me to the river
and brought me back thirsty.

[1979]

*Al-Gharraf: a town in southern Iraq. Al-Diwaniyah
is the poet's city, also in southern Iraq.


## A Glass of Ancient Wine

Many years from now
the days will catch up with us
and we'll grow old.
It's not in our power
to prevent this disaster!
One day, we'll meet by chance
dragging our tired feet among vain
and merry youth,
our solemnity, their arrogance,
passing each other by.
We'll meet by chance
when the fig in our hearts is withered.
It could be Midan Square or the Writers' Union,
Sa'adoon Street or a 21st Century bar.
I'd extend my hand to you
and you to me.
You'd let loose your tears on my shoulder
and I mine,
and in a blink of lightning
we'd be attuned once more,
light years thundering inside,
cloudbursts and fresh winds of compassion
washing us clean.
Then we'd fly like two old eagles
straight for the singing beside lavish orchards
and blooms of loving people.
Hold up memory like a diamond, I say,
and you say: no one should deny one of his own.
For this seedling is Iraqi, which water will not forget,
nor soil deny.

Many years from now
we'll shake hands, and clink glasses at one another
at the Bar of Forgotten Poets.

[1992]


## Celebration

A woman wandered
like a penguin through the city
until Haroon Street led her to al-Bab al-Sharqi Square.
People there were astounded
and electric wires trembled.
The woman wouldn't have cared
if her wool stockings burst into flame
or one of her sons
suddenly rose like a phoenix
from the rubble of bombing.
She walked on, slowly like a penguin,
until Freedom Monument
where she threw her head scarf to the myrtle
and her fateful aba'ah *
and stood very, very still
and all at once began dancing, dancing
to the music of the spheres.

[1992]

*aba'ah: traditional cloak-like wrap worn by some Muslim women,
much like the Iranian chador, but in Iraq it is usually black.


## Love in the Time of Cholera

One morning I'll come home
with a name and calendar of sleeplessness
in my left hand and daisies in my right.
And you'll hurry to the door:
a young woman in her fifties
with voluptuous breasts.
I'll hold you heart to heart
until our souls trade places,
bury my nose in your fragrant hair

and say: take me like a cat from al-Diwaniyah,
melt between your delicious lips
my seven souls.


**Poems for Rasmia**


*1*

Lead me like a lost sheep
to your green season,
let me graze in your orchards.
You are pure mud
and I am water,
let's mix until we're thick as country cream.
  . . .


**2**

For a long time, I've been crumbling
like a timeworn building.
As you gathered my shards
from among thorns and friendly grasses
one of my days fell like a clay brick
into your delicate hands.
Like a potter
inspired by the forest
you shaped me;
in your leafy hands
I'm a bundle of flutes.


*3*

For twenty years, I've been sniffing after you
like a police dog.
Nothing escaped my nose,
not even the navel of the Iman's daughter.
And at last . . .
  . . .


*4*

If not for Fayruz's songs
and Baghdad
and Rasmia
a frog would have been my wife,

goats would have covered me with their droppings.
I would have been
a car without fuel,
without wheels.

    5

Oh love, soul of sorrel,
how delicate you are.
I worry that one morning I'll wake up
to find you dew on a flower,
a sparrow in the palm tree,
I worry that I'll awaken at dawn
to find you a scent on every woman.
Oh love, soul of sorrel,
how delicate you are.

# Bulland al-Haydari

## Translated by Hussein Kadhim and Christopher Merrill

### The Will

Barefoot except for my skin
Like a shoe with a hole it carries me
From a land that was my country
To a land in search of a country for me.

Oh son
Change the colour of your shoes
Free your history from my fetters
From the step of a man no longer searching
For a promise
From my eternal death
Who knows. . . ?
You may be born under a sun
Even smaller than my hand is wide
Under a sun
That one day may shine
A promise of dawn rising on my country.

### The City Ravaged by Silence

Baghdad, that captive, forgotten
Between the corpse and the nail.

Baghdad was not besieged by the Persian army
Not seduced by a mare
Nor tempted by a hurricane nor touched by fire.

Baghdad died of a wound from within
From a blind silence that paralyzed the tongues of its children.

That captive was not a homeland
It was just a prison
Wrapped with black walls and guardrails
It was not a night beyond which we say day lies
Baghdad, that captive, forgotten

And ravaged by the silence
Only a desert inhabited by death
Known only to the stones.

One day it almost became . . .    at a certain time
A thing in secret
A secret restlessness in the stillness of a room
It almost became a promise in two eyes
A vow in blue films
In which we almost lived a dream
Paper boats borne by the air, flowing
Lightly, seeking no anchor,
No mooring on a bank.
We wished it would turn into lightning, revealing desire
but . . .

– Listen . . . listen
And so I listened, and listened closely
But I heard nothing
– Listen . . . listen.

And I laughed . . . Here's the meow of the cat in the neighbour's house
There . . . A rustle of small leaves
Pay no attention . . . It's only the meow of the cat
Only the rustle of the trees.

A hand knocks on the door four times
The anxious heart pounds a thousand times
– Listen . . . Don't you hear? Don't you see something. . . ?
I see a shadow lurking behind the window
I can almost see in the dark of its eyes. . .  yes
In the dark of its eyes. . .  yes. . .  my tear-streaked face
For tomorrow the report will be prepared
The grounds will be prepared for killing you inside us, with us,
        Oh Baghdad
We must confess, we're the corpse and the nail
And you, forgotten between the corpse and the nail.

– You were awake until the wee hours
– We were awake until the wee hours . . . but we
– What does it mean . . . ? What does it imply . . . ?
On the chair with two broken legs
Above the black table
Near the flickering lantern

There were white papers, yellow papers like pus
There was an open book
Like an exposed secret
And the remains of two pens
What does it mean that you read . . . that you write
That you stay up until dawn
What does it mean . . . ? What does it imply . . . ?

We will be executed in Baghdad's main square
With a signboard larger than Baghdad on both of our chests
(Understand . . . you may not be executed . . . understand . . .
         you may be spared)
You are forbidden to read . . . to write
To talk . . . to cry . . . even to ask
What Baghdad means
What it means to be human or an animal
To be more than a stone forgotten in Baghdad
You are forbidden to be more than the two legs of a harlot
Or the two hands of a pimp.

Baghdad died of a wound inside us . . . of a wound from within
From a blind silence that paralyzed the tongues of its children
Baghdad was ravaged by the silence
So that we have nothing in it, it has nothing in us . . . except death
And the corpse and the nail.


### Dialogue of the Colours

*for Leopold Senghor*

One evening, oh Senghor
Like all our exiled evenings
In the cold nakedness of our dungeons
Within a short distance
From a blind time that sneaks barefoot
From among
The dust of the road and the edge of my broken window.

The moon, pale as a lie
Yellow as consumption
Sinking in a pond of muddy water
We would ask about the use of a moon
That did not grow even in shadow
What was the use of a time that lies

Like a corpse in a fallow land . . .
In a deserted homeland
Plagued with the one-eyed sultans of history.

I was . . . my son was
And a chat that leads to another chat
About a dawn breaking from between your hands
About your glory . . . what    glory, oh Senghor
About your verse . . . what exquisite verse, oh Senghor
About your home
That opens your eyes on the depths of Senegal
About dark green forests
That spin around a thousand and one questions
About a black beauty
Whose eyes inhabit the sleeplessness of the generations.

I talked to my son
About a sun born in chains
A sun that only shines at night
A sun that wallows in the palms of a child
A sun that creeps under bridges of ants
I talked to my son
About red masks . . . black
Masks that refuse to take on the colour
Of desire in fetters
Or a hurdle
Or a wall
How small is the one who can't tell the secret of any colour
Except that of the bearer of false witness.

I heard my son
Screaming: Father . . . Say no
Spread your two wings as a shadow for us
And a place to pray
For thousands of the slain lie on the road
Pleading for a tear
A candle for the dead
Bleeding in the silence of a woman grieving
For the promise of light
Bursting from the eyes of Mandela
From the eyes of Senghor
Oh Father
Don't extinguish my memory
Don't shortchange my death

Tell the thief who stole my house from my house
My death from my death
Say no . . . We won't allow ourselves
To be slaughtered
We won't allow
The merchants of black skin to make from my skin chains for me
Sandals from my skin
Say no
My death won't become wheat
But salt
Whirling around the wounds of the killer, the thief, and the renegade
And the tyrant and the aggressor
Wound . . . after wound
Say no . . . No, oh my black father
Say no
So I may be born
Say no, oh black god
Oh black slave
Be an eagle so we can worship you.

He remained silent for a long time
I wept for a long time
While I recovered my face from my eye
Son
I know you come
From among the captives of a vanquished time
From among the captives of a time
Hired out to false witnesses
I know you're a bitter Indian fig
A dry chunk of bread
In the cold nakedness of our dungeons
But I
Won't know, my son
In your eyes or my eyes
But in the eyes of Mandela . . . but in the eyes of Senghor
But in a night
That hides all the meanings of light.


## From Behind the Closed Door

The room is dark . . . as you know it
In a captive country
In a forsaken time

As I know it, a closed panel
A memory searching for a closed door
For the lips of a wound closed
In the darkness
The red stain on the slayer's knife
Sometimes
In the blood of the slain
The screen, this captive country
This deserted country
A wonderful dream that consumes
Our steps
Our blood
A thing that was ours . . . a thing that inquires about us . . . within us
But we
Oh my homeland . . . you the slayer . . .
You the slain
From what future shall we glance at our past
From what distance in a closed panel
In a closed door
Shall we seek to know your face in our future?
And you are the slayer . . . the slain is here
And there . . . blood avenging itself on us . . . within us.


### So That We Do Not Forget

*"On the seventeenth of March 1988 the Iraqi regime*
*shelled the Kurdish town of Halabcha in Iraq with*
*chemical weapons causing the death of thousands."*


Even though my memory grew dim
Even though old age extinguished it
Even though the pus and blood dried by my eyes
I still muse about the house that was ours
Which used to hold out its arms to the light at dawn
A vow will bring it . . . or a dream
My house had two small windows
I remember they were smaller than eyes
Too small to let the sun cling to the old wood
Or cause universes to grow larger
The courtyard of my house was no bigger than the palm
Of a child
Wherever I walked I tripped over my shadow
My son taught me
The borders of the world in my house are boundless

He taught me to know myself in a drop of dew
He taught me that my house has a path leading to thousands
        of flower beds
That my house has a door
Trembling through one question and another
Through many nights
And says: come to me
You, coming from any space that was
From any time
He taught me to leave the door of the house wide open
So enter it, you, coming from any space and time
Enter it in safety.


How very small the house was
It was small as a heart
It was large as a heart
Rich with warmth and love
I remember we . . . were
Like the two windows of my house . . . like the door of the house
We sleep, our eyes full of green dreams
Of a mountain in Kurdistan
Yesterday
And while the eyes of all your children . . . Oh, my house
Oh, my country
They were swimming in sunlight
They looked like dew drops from all the narcissus blossoms
And from the flowers
Blew a poisonous wind
And from the eyes of an owl
Which poisoned all your children . . . Oh, my house . . . my country
Among those it killed . . . was my son
Among what it stole . . . was my shadow
The road to my house became a graveyard extending to thousands
        of graveyards
In Kurdistan
Nothing but death and the shadow of death
Not a narcissus dreaming of blooming in a flower bed
The villains didn't leave
Only the dead, the ashes of the dead, and the blackness of smoke
But my future
And the reckoning of the dead
And the blood of the slain will chase the face of Satan
From one mirror to another
From a thousand ages to a thousand ages

The rope will coil around the neck of the hangman
Kurdistan will curse your past
Baghdad will disavow your vice
And to the sweet land will return all the beds
Of narcissus and flowers
And my son will be reborn in all the children.


### Death In Four Voices

*I*

I am haunted . . . every night
By the howling of the wolf crouching inside me
I ask: from where . . . from which desert
Shall I flee from myself . . .?
I flee from an eye taking aim like an arrow
From an ache
Stretching the length of a back bent like a bow.

I am haunted . . . every night
By the howling of the wolf
By the corpse of a man searching in penitence
For the meaning of guilt.


*II*

Once again . . . the ticking of the clock awakens me
I open my window, as I do every morning
I hear the voices of street vendors
Announcing
A history for sale and leaders
Their faces glittering like shining shoes
The slain pleading for a graveyard
And captives
And restless
Sins in al-Hajjaj's sermons and al-Saffah's sword
Here I am
Watching a black sailor spread his sail at sea
I will journey
I will migrate
Here I am
Gathering between two broken teeth
And two black lips
The deception of years, years, years
I spit it out . . . I spit it out . . . I spit it out

But . . .
Who knows . . . the black sailor
The sailor
Is but another vision . . . a deceitful vision.

### III
Exile
A blind memory that wished it had
A homeland in the soil
A homeland, even if its world swelled like a boil
Or a wound
Or a bird that lost its way in the darkness.
A bird that will not find its shadow except in a wilderness
Except
In the dead, exiled beyond the fog-shrouded land.

How great the indignity of exile
How wretched that you don't know yourself as a human
Except
In exile.

### IV
Sleep.
You, a man awake like the whips of torturers
You, accursed man
Hiding behind a tiny fig leaf
You, coming from a thousand questions:
Who are you? Who were you? Where did you come from . . . ?
What doctrines did you learn?
Sleep
All the quarter's dogs are asleep now
And the guard, leaning now on the silence
Of his deaf bullet . . . he sleeps
The pack of mice sleep
Sleep . . .
What is there for you in a dawn that will come without a sun
Or in a sun that will come to you from the eyes of a jailer?
What is there for you in a man born in your wound?
Or in the lender's whip
Sleep . . .
That night I slept . . . when a voice said: wake up
I said: I'm awake
I woke up . . . the courtyard of my house was
Full of my blood . . . Drowning in my blood

I saw my bones swimming in it
And saw the quarter's dogs returning to it
To lick it up
And I saw mice
And the criminal and the lender
And the guard . . .
The guard still sleeping on the silence
Of his deaf bullet, he will not ask what happened
What was.

How miserable I am, a man . . . a house . . . a homeland
That is not born except in death
That does not grow except in oblivion.


### Premature Elegy

Two crutches
And two creeping on the road
Deserted except . . .
Two shadows . . .
And except for these two
And a feeble light rattling in the darkness
 Of two eyes.

She said: the road tired me out and here I am
Sneaking barefoot among the threads of the coffin
And picking up what remains of my days
Of my time . . .
– No . . . no
– Here I am being consumed between the road and myself
My face does not remember anything about my face
My legs dried up
My eyes went cold
My back is bent under the weight of my remains.

– No . . . no
You are still as you were
No, even more beautiful than you were.

She took off her glasses, and turned her eyes
Toward his eyes
She sank into him
Into an eye moistened with death

– And you, as you are
– Even lovelier than you were
It is as if the two of us didn't live
Except outside all the years of the earth
And all the ages
Nor did we grow old . . . neither you
– And neither you, and the warmth of our hands didn't fade
Two palms wrapped around two palms
For the lie is still larger than death.

The road forked
Shall I say: farewell?
How will I return alone . . .?
Stop . . . don't move so far away . . . don't . . . no.

Two walking sticks
A sun sinking in the darkness of a deep red sea
And a woman searching for a shadow
And the remains of the shadow of a woman borne by two crutches.

She wept in silence
The silence was large as death.


### Why Didn't They Apologize...?

I decorated the house
I prepared the flowers' pots and arranged
The red roses next to the white ones
The blue ones next to the red
And said: I will wait
Everything is prepared for a rendezvous . . . so why shouldn't
         I wait . . .?

The night is long
My patience with the night is long
The candle is pregnant with a light that will not fade before dawn
Today I am beyond sixty
By three years
So why shouldn't I wait
I have many companions on the road . . .
Midnight rings in one . . . two . . . three
No one
Four . . . five

No one
Has another rendezvous kept them from mine
Have they all forgotten I'm beyond sixty
By three years . . . ?
That the rendezvous
May not end in a promise?
The candle gathers the remnants of what little time it has left
What remains of a shadow blocking a wall
Of a shadow gathering fire in its wings
And other pale shadows
A question winds around my lip
And sinks deeper into silence
Why didn't they apologize?
Why didn't they apologize?

A deaf table
A head slumped on the deaf table
No one
But the clock strikes past the rendezvous
And the slumped head . . .
And the candle dissolving bereft of hope

He moved his hands closer to his eyes and dozed off
In bitter silence
At a night that may not question the meaning of dawn.

# Ahmed Herdi

Iraqi Kurdish

## Translated by Muhamad Tawfiq Ali

### God's freedom lovers

We Kurds are God's freedom lovers,
We are walls of masonry and steel,
We are the defenders of servile peasants,
We are the flag of unity hoisted high
We are the swords in the hands of the broken
We have risen against tyranny.
Aghas and Begs are feudal lords,
Tormentors of the poor people's soul.
They are blood suckers of this homeland,
They are tools in the hands of foreign powers,
One day we will kick the living hell out of them,
One day we will avenge the people's suffering.
Not even the shackles of a hundred prisons,
Not even the torture tools in the hands of foreign rulers
Not even the gunpowder, lead and steel bullets
Not even the live ammunition of the despised tyrants,
Will affect us an iota or stop us from marching on.
Even if we die on these highways and byways,
We refuse to become lackeys of foreign masters.

# Fereydun Refiq Hilmi

Kurdish

## Translated by Muhamad Tawfiq Ali

### Political Parties [1]

Where are the political parties?
Why aren't they around? What were they up to?
Why are they so behind?
KDP and PUK are just an ass and turkey
Lackeys of Saddam, Islamic Iran and nationalist Turkey.
They wasted six years, just mucking about
They learned no lesson from the past.

My dear Sir, these two whom we followed blindly,
are kings at our expense, living in luxury.
One of them is a regular guest of Saddam,
The other has taken refuge in Tehran.
Seriously, sir, these two are nothing,
To them education and literacy is mere heresy.

What about the helpless and hapless?
What is their bloody excuse?
Why aren't they inclined towards learning?
My dear Sir, today every man is for himself.
Theft and thuggery have replaced struggle
The poor and paupers are about to starve.
How can they think of lessons at a time like this?
An empty stomach can only think of how to survive
Honour and manners have deserted the country
The rich and able have fled the country.
The remaining assets were sold off.
Their families are living on worms and snakes.

The money from European aid has been pocketed,
nothing is left.
The chiefs helped themselves to the lion's share,
they destroyed the Kurds with party politics.

[4-12-1996]

**Notes**

1    KDP = Kurdistan Democratic Party, led by Masoud Barzan
PUK = Patriotic Union of Kurdistan led by Jelal Talebani

# Lamiah Abbas Imara

Translated by Basima Bezirgan and Elizabeth Fernea

### Diogenes

(I carry my lantern at noon
And I search for her)
Colours mix in my head until they are without colour.
All the galaxies of the universe are transfigured into points in infinity.

I lost her
In the commingled blood of two who were slain,
Enemies, now dead,
Who will judge between the two of them?

But even within myself
I ran from her
And she begged me to return.
How will I know her?
Even skin colour changes.

If I wipe away her painted colours
I may erase the original
Who should I believe?
She will be the first to deny me
The first to betray me?
Still, in silence I feel closer to her,
I may touch the outlines of her body,
And time is compressed in this moment of silence
Like the richness of a dream the moment before death.

O, dervish, crouching on the hilltop.
Like a silent devil, you will be covered with snow.
The angels of paradise
Will not rejoice at the sound of music played on a broken string.
So, dervish, don't think of dancing.
Many have come along this path,
Burdened with question marks.
Do you feel wiser keeping silent?
The stone is wiser than you.

Go in silence, dervish, wear the skin of the bear
To remain beloved of God.
Because even your soul has abandoned you
Your own skin rejects you.

I said:
'In Lebanon, I will be guided
By the light of the sun on the mirror of the sea.'

Dust blew, shrouded the sun
And blinded me.
All I could hear was sobbing and weeping
And the neighing of horses.
Was that you tied
Between the two horses?

She said: I saw nothing
So don't ask anything of me.
Go on, carry your lantern
So you can delude yourself
That you are searching for her.

# Muhammad Mahdi al-Jawahiri

## Translated by Terri DeYoung

*This poem was published in the newspaper* Al-Awqat al-Baghdadiyya, *no.* 28
(*28 March* 1951).

### A Lullaby for the Hungry

1) Sleep, hungry folk, sleep
        may the food gods protect you,
2) Sleep, for if you do not eat your fill
        awake, then surely you will in dreamland.
3) Sleep on a frothy pillow of promises
        mingled with honeyed words,
4) Sleep, then the brides of dream
        will visit you in the dark of gloom,
5) And so you will bask on a slice of bread
        shining bright as the fullest moon,
6) And see your spacious cattle pens
        tiled with marble slabs.

\*

7) Sleep, you get healthier! Blessed is the sleep of a man
        during great plights.
8) Sleep upon the lance point,
        sleep upon the sword edge,
9) Sleep until the day of resurrection,
        the day when waking up is allowed,
10) Sleep upon swamps
        where the overflowing depths lift waves,
11) Swelling with the scent of chamomile flowers,
        overspread with the odour of lilacs.
12) Sleep to the humming melodies of mosquitoes
        like cooing of doves.
13) Sleep upon such a nature,
        where Miami cannot be found,
14) Sleep, for Nakedness has wrapped you
        in the garments of passion,
15) Sleep in the dreams of harvesters
        stripped for action.

16) Dancing together as whips strive earnestly,
   whistling with heavy strokes,

17) And flirt the tender ones
   crawling down from your hair.

18) Sleep upon the cradle of injustice and
   pillow yourselves upon dust's cheek,

19) Spread out upon the deaf stones, and
   wrap yourselves in shadows of clouds

20) Sleep, for the one who starves people
   has brought to an end the days of fasting.

21) Sleep, for the God of War has sung
   the Tunes of Peace . . .

   *

22) Sleep, hungry folk, sleep!
   The dawn has announced an ending

23) And the sun has not yet begun
   to torment you with blazing fire.

24) Nor can light blind half-closed eyes
   naturally disposed to darkness.

25) Sleep, as has been your covenant with Slumber
   and its pleasures, since the age of Ham,

26) Sleep, for some future day will quench your thirst
   with wine and honey from a thousand cups,

27) For the pleasures of Afterlife are the wages for the humiliated and
   the alleviation for the hearts thirsting for the heights.

28) Sleep and march forward in your dreams,
   as much as you are able,

29) Sleep upon those estimable sermons
   coming from the Imam,

30) Enjoining you not to seek among
   worldly things the assets of your lord,

31) Enjoining you to leave your joys and
   pleasures for depraved,

32) And substitute for all that
   prostrations and vigils.

33) Sleep upon long sermons
   from noble gentlemen,

34) Sleep so that your promised sustenance
   will be cast down before you in steady streams.

35) Sleep upon those joys
   that do not leave a bowstring for the shooter

36) Leave no tarts! no shortening!
       it would gladden you not to come.
37) They have built houses
       and burst the pathless deserts and poverty.
38) Sleep, for the houris of paradise will hover
       round you with vintage wines
39) Sleep upon leprosy and consumption
       that whitened your blackness.
40) Sleep, for the palm of God will bathe you
       clean of disease's filth,
41) Sleep, for the amulet of the faithful will
       ever protect you,
42) Sleep, for the world is only a Bridge
       raised upon adversity!

    *

43) Sleep, and do not dispute,
       words are not for the slaves
44) Sleep upon that ancient glory,
       resting on a pile of bones,
45) Be amazed at the images of self-made men,
       for you are above them,
46) Raising their crowns from corpses
       where you have spread before them delusions,
47) Ever acquisitive, while yet your blood
       quenches the thirst of the desirous,
48) Sleep, for you slumber is the best
       badge the historian may bear!

    *

49) Sleep, hungry folk, sleep
       you are absolved of fault and blame.
50) Sleep, for precious unity
       demands that you do so.
51) Sleep, hungry folk, sleep
       for sleep is one of the bounties of peace.
52) Factions and parties are made one in it
       and the danger of infighting averted.
53) All sides rest peacefully there
       and hierarchies have no need of division
54) Only foolishness would make you splinter
       the rod of amity by waking up

55) And wildness make you refuse to seek refuge
        from your rulers in being ruled.
56) The soul is like a wild mare
        and the reason there like reins.
57) Sleep, for the reformation of something
        degenerate lies in your doing just that.
58) For the Firm Bond – if you insist on waking –
        will be threatened with dissolution.
59) Sleep, for if you don't, hierarchies will,
        because of you, fall apart,
60) Sleep, for your slumber is a riot that,
        if wakened, will be the worst of sins
61) Where you could do naught but waken
        and renew the strife over and over again?

\*

62) Sleep, hungry folk, sleep
        do not disrupt the work of earning man's daily bread
63) Do not disrupt the work of the merchant,
        the engineer, the lawyer!
64) Sleep to relieve the rulers
        from fears of mêlée and strife.
65) Sleep, so you will free the media of
        charges and accusations
66) So the law may praise in you
        the practice of someone obedient, easily led!
67) Put aside lordliness, for by virtue of your slumber
        the evil of lordly aspiration will be averted.
68) And avoid situations calling for speculation, for when too alert
        one may be accused of wrongdoing.

\*

69) Sleep, for your skin, if you wake, will not
        be able to bear the sting of arrows.
70) Sleep and leave to those awake alone
        to be the archers' target.
71) Sleep and leave the burden to those who would blame
        for there is nothing wrong in your being blamed.
72) Sleep, for the prison walls
        teem with sudden and violent death
73) And you have more need, after the pains of
        capitulation, for a time of rest.

74) Sleep so the Leaders will find in your dreaming
         a respite from an incurable disease.
75) Sleep, for your rights will not suffer,
         you are not heedless, like the beasts of the fields,
76) The Shepherds are watchful,
         they will keep you from being harmed.

                    *


77) Sleep through an injustice, as
         the infant is induced through weaning,
78) And fall upon tribulation, just as
         sword falls edgewise upon sword!
79) Sleep through an army of torments,
         a thronging host,
80) Give the guidance to fate, let him
         rule the reins!
81) And surrender to circumstance
         any apprehensions about the sleepers.
82) For waking – if only you knew – is the
         harbinger of sudden and violent death,
83) And alertness is a sword threatened,
         on the day of battle, with confutation.

                    *


84) Sleep, remnant of purity, sleep,
         pearls among the dross!
85) O seedling sprung from calamity,
         flower flourishing amid injustice!
86) Freeborn, you do not know
         the meaning of malice or vengeance.
87) O torch of light that blinds men's eyes
         without ever being lit,
88) Praise your Lord, what a glorious image you are that
         exults above all beautiful images,
89) For you hide yourself without a care
         or come boldly forth without a veil,
90) For you bear evil patiently
         from mad tyrants.
91) How often you have forborne to censure,
         and scorned mockery!
92) Praise your Lord, you are an image with
         troubles completely in accord.

*

93) Sleep, hungry folk, sleep
        for sleep is the best guard of life and limb,
94) Sleep is the best guarantee for
        finding peace and order at journey's end.
95) Sleep, for in misfortunes
        you will save yourself from the throng.
96) Sleep, hungry folk, do not concern yourself
        with the fallout from my words,
97) Sleep, for the intent of a poem is nothing more than
        a little bead in a necklace . . .
98) Sleep, for how lovely is blindness
        to evil deeds and pretending not to see.
99) Sleep, for how unfortunate are the aspirations
        of those aware of an unbroken sword.
100)  Sleep: to you my greetings, sleepy ones,
        upon you are my felicitations.

101)  Sleep, hungry folk, sleep
        may the food gods protect you!

# Jigerkhwen (Sheikh Mus Hasan Muhamad)

Iraqi Kurdish

## Translated by Muhamad Tawfiq Ali

### I am the Voice

I am the voice of the mountainside
I am the hammer in the labourer's hand
I am the sickle in the peasant's hand
I am the enemy of reactionaries
I am the vanguard of progressives
I am the colleague of the oppressed, whomever or wherever
I am the opponent of the oppressor, whether near or far
I am the comrade of the peshmerge, and of revolution
I am the voice of the workers, whether in London or Paris
I am the sympathiser of the students, whether in Istanbul or Tabriz
I am the hand of the martyr
I am the voice of the Kurdish people
I am a Kurdish revolutionary
I refuse to yield to the likes of Al-Jamail, Shimon and Hitler
I refuse to bow to arms merchants and warmongers
I am a fighter like Che Guevara
I am a comrade of Ho Chi Min
I am a supporter of the Tudeh, whether in Awaz or Tehran
I am a patriot and militiaman, like Salvador Allende
I am a protector of my people like Gandhi and Nehru of India
In the Congo, I am the voice of Lumumba
In Bolivia I am Neruda
I am Castro in Cuba
I am the voice of Kebuchi in Jerusalem
I am the voice of Makarios in Cyprus
I am the voice of Newab and Gorki
I am the voice of Martin Luther King among American Negroes
I am the voice of Jegerkhwen, Mahmoud Darwish, and Lorca

# Jamal Juma'h

Translated by Salaam Yousif (with Emily Howard's poetic emendation)

*from* **Letters To My Brother**

**1**

Thus my brother,
The rainbow swings on the wall.
Thus my brother,
I see you swinging between the tents,
Your hands in your pockets,
And your eyes staring at the void
While thinking of me
As you go to and fro
Exactly as I do here
Next to a swinging rainbow on the wall.

**2**

I see you O prisoner of war
In your khaki trousers
And unpolished shoes
Dragging your feet
Holding your empty bowl
Waiting for the bread ration
Your disheartened eyes gazing
At the shoulders of the one standing in line before you
Waiting for him to move forward.

**3**

Forward O you dispirited
For the war is over
The guns were silenced
The scattered remains buried
And the lost limbs replaced with plastic.
The kings won their crowns

The Americans their oil
The Russians ate meat to their fill
The Chinese got an abundance of neck ties
And the Israelis more land.
You and I, my brother
Are the losers in this war.

**4**

Do you shave your beard every day?
Do you brush your teeth?
Do you dream of the blue sky?
Of sleeping on the terrace?
Of rain waking you just before dawn?
Of your mother's hand as she softly says to you:
"Wake up, Sharif; it's already midday!"
Do you dream of all this
As you cover yourself with your blanket with the cross on it?
Do you dream of all this,
like me
With your eyes wide open under the blanket?


**5**

What time is it now?
Have you slept?
Whispered something?

Read a story?
Why is it that you only gaze
At the desert stars
Recalling my face?
Why is it that I only gaze
At the rainbow
In order to see you?
I see you trembling
In the cold desert night

Raising your collar, which is soiled with powder
While the wind shakes your tent like a sail
And your eyes are fixed on the lantern's wick.

What time is it at your place now?

**6**

Hand by hand
You were lost along with the desert
The scent of water
Was your only compass
(Had the dried bread run out?)
Your hands emptied the last of the bullets
Like raindrops on the sand.

Leaving the gun to roast on the dunes
Farewell O thou death!
Farewell O thou life!
Then the soldiers, their eyebrows covered with dust,
Surrounded you.

### 7

As they threw you on the sand,
Did they handcuff you, O Sharif?
Search your pockets
For the love letters of a young woman who was married lately?
For a blotted out address
Of a brother you have not seen
For eight years?

### 8

I will think of you much
Shielding you with my thoughts
So that the cold won't find you
Nor the heat.

I pray that you forget me
So that I can get a moment's sleep
Without regret.

I will think of you, O brother,
Of your loneliness in the desert,
As your hands sail towards me
Waking me whenever I forget.

### 9

O brother
Mine is a heavy load
My tongue is reeling in the void
What can words do for the dead?
What can poems do with all these limbs?
My eyes have turned inside out
Seeing nothing but darkness
In my brain.
I wish the tears were of black tar
So that no one could see the words.

**10**

Thus, O brother, they disclosed your secret
The bridges were destroyed
The mothers were bereaved
The airplanes flown

The bombs were dropped
The oil wells set on fire
The eyes were put out
And the shaikhs were back
Safely to their base
KUWAIT IS FREE

**11**

Behold the airplane
The wing of the black Phantom
Which lays death bombs
And hatches waste on the sleepy city
Farewell, Jamhuriyya bridge
Farewell, Khillani mosque
Farewell, Suq al-Saray
Farewell, children sheltered in al-Amiriyya
Your parents will come in the morning
To see nothing but your white teeth
Glittering in your roasted bodies
Like diamonds in the coal mine
Of the New World Order.

# Fawzi Karim

## Translated by Saadi A Simawe and Chuck Miller

**What Was My Choice??**

*I*

One has learned to allow a tiny space in the head for contingency.
Yet, losses befall suddenly
– of the river and the date palms that used to balance
of the friends circling your glass like a crescent.

Then you in one moment peel yourself of whom you love
and alone, dim-sighted, grope your way home,
the light of the street lamps heavier than darkness
– the burden of exile than memory.

Tantalizing ourselves with hope,
shielding ourselves against . . . but the question in the middle
       of exiles suddenly attacks:
– What have you chosen?

No longer trusting ourselves
about to desert the self,
annihilated in God's self,
or prefer to watch, like a trap,
the tripwires of another.

*[10 April 2000]*

*II*

When exile took us by surprise,
a surgeon ready-scrubbed
he treated us with scalpels
cleansed us of the dream tumours in our organs,
and pushed us into the last scene of the shadow theatre
in order that we perform for him our secondary roles

Who are we? Fury of a blind man
being led by a thread of loss,
dice thrown on the night's page
without even an echo of their
rolling.

[11 April 2002]


## Robin
### (The bird that was devoured by the cat in the garden of the house)

Nosing about for worms
in the grass, and jumping over the fence
and the cherry branch,
into wet ether in the mysterious horizon.

From the kitchen window I saw you smaller than hand's size
struggling with all your hand's size to hang on
to your limited world.

And I saw you like a thought popped up
in my head; feeling confined, it burst out,
a thought that was stormed by remembrance
of date palms, of the boy enchanted in the shadow of the house
        in al-Karkh,
of the woman
who never weaned me!

How astonished I was,
for you, Robin, have the colour of my wanderlust
in the night of loneliness,
brown-breasted, with gray limbs.
Your call rings in my ears as the sunrays reflected on a knife's edge:
blades/codes no one knows their secrets.
And if my garden was your happiness
it also was your fate.

I prepared the tea, and went on turning the pages
searching for a thought crossed my mind
about a faraway day.
Adding the sugar,
I suddenly saw the cat studying your movements,
the charms of your voice.

Dashed like a thought towards you, Robin,
I startled because remembrance stormed the words
in my head,
murdered them
emptied them of their meanings.

And the cat under the fence went on
searching in the blood-stained feathers.

[28 June 2000]


### Crumbled Paper for Future Poems

I discover in every equation an error
a mental blunder that cannot be heard.
In every tainted sigh I discover hatred
not knowing how to hide it
from my fellow human's eye.

But my sadness has the flavour of a fleeting spring
I find sometimes in the vegetable market
or in my pursuit of a woman
or when I seclude myself in a book!

And often I feel my sadness in two dimensions:
present and past –
the third dimension, the knock on the door
in the middle of the night.

Oh boys of the coast, boys of the coast
I imagine in you between the waves and the ankles
ribbons of gold  flowing from the sunset
turning braids between the waves  and the ankles
while I listen to them
listen.

[2 January 2002]
[SAS and CM]

## Malice

My heart, O God, is void of love
and people's ill feelings crawl
like turtles towards the sea.
Shall I take my refuge?
My mat is the sand, and my cushion is salt
and my home is from what spiders weave!
Or shall I obey a God other than you
in my blood cells, which undress
every dawn to the sun!
But the next dawn will turn them
into manure.

I am void of love, my Lord
and my skin looks like bark
and my taste is bitter that I can hide
and my tomorrow is in a foetus's tissue
which was aborted.

I loved, I loved . . . but . . .

*[14 February 2002]*
*[SAS]*

# Abd al-Karim Kassid

## Translated by Saadi A Simawe and Chuck Miller

**Trilogy of Travel**

### 1 We and Travel

When we sat silent
Travel  was seated in his chair
again beginning  soothingly his talk
you, my lady, and I were fearful.

We were repeating
what Travel said
you and I were waking up Travel
searching for his reassuring  hands

But you and I were strangely asleep.

### 2 You and Travel

You, my woman, did not notice in the noise of Travel
the eerie calm of the people standing on the platforms,
and the foreboding quietness of the trains before departure.
You did not notice in my clam the noise of Travel
and the hubbub of trains;
they convulse as they stop at stations.
You did not glimpse my wary tall stature
when it was waiting in the sudden roar.
You did not notice my stature when it was restlessly stretching this way
            and that
in the jarring waiting rooms.
You  did not know the waiting rooms
and the fatal calm at the moment of leave-taking
and the agitation of departure.
You did not notice this . . .

### 3 A Quiet Decision

As you brought your face closer to mine
I became even closer
and I saw in the star-burst light the face of Travel.
And when hid your shadow in this light
I hid mine too,
And I saw in that ominous light the shadow of absence.

When I saw his face
you did not see mine.
When I saw his shadow
you never saw my shadow again.

[1973]


## What the Shadow Said in the Presence of the Poem

My shadow spoke to me saying:
"You have arrived before me
. . . stay where you are."
And he told me:
"Do not hide your love for you would be exposed,
and do not show it for you would be hidden."

And he said:
"I, if you really want to know, am your eternal fire,"
then he bends over me like a branch
in the presence of water.

My shadow led me to a wilderness
And he said: "Look."
And what I saw awed me.

And he told me:
"No comfort for us
in closeness
nor in separation,"
then disappeared.

Whenever I showed him my hell
He showed me a paradise that has no room for me,

How impossible?
No consolation that I can offer,
and no gift that consoles me.

He said:
"Confession is plight
so is secrecy."
And then he said;
"Do not be like the letter that litters the meaning."

"The bird of your meaning is around your neck."
And he added;
" Desert what you have dwelled in ,
and do not let the letter suffer by  you as you suffer by it,
since you are perplexed."

And my shadow instructed me:
"Two things if you  befriend them you perish:
my friend
and my other friend."

And he said:
"I thought myself a night but I was concealed,
and when I thought myself a day I disappeared.
Therefore I decided not to return in day or in night."


### The Seer

I wanted to stand on the sea,
as I stood on the land,
walking on its whales, its totems, and its dead
but instead I drowned.
Now I crouch
in a sea corner
and over me pass the whales, the totems and the dead.
I do not see ships but only their bottoms;
and of birds,
only their shadows;
and of humans,
only their voices.
In the blue water, I do not see but water.


### Leaves

In my garden, the leaves that float in the air
never stop vibrating
in winter
or summer
when the snow falls
or when the sun rises.
Sometimes
they bend over me

descending from the sky.

In the distant sky
the leaves fly away
green birds.

This sky is crowded with them,
and the tree with stars.

The tree of the word concealed the forest of the poem.

On a leaf my tears flow.

Who stops the vibration of a leaf
and  separates the bird from the branch?

This tree, which is painted with henna,
is my childhood.

In which tree does this haunted bird dwell?

A funeral procession passes
and the leaves follow it.

A bird leans on the air.

Who shook the tree of elegy
at the wedding of my leaves?

A leaf ascends
Mi'araj
a bird plummets.

Oh leaves, bless me.

Leaves listen to the language of birds.

Caravans of leaves drink at the fountain.

From a window in a branch
a nest hangs.

Black shadows shake the tree.

The sky is a huge hill
and the leaves are its birds.

A leaf
spreads its wings
and flies.

In the day of the tree
the night hides.

A bird passes
a leaf bows.

To whom do leaves listen
in the absence of the tree?

The tree is a stature
and the leaf, an eye.

A flower sings
a bird blossoms.
A child is in the Garden.

The tree is my exile.

A cave is the tree
and the leaves are captives.

Under my tree I search for my shadow.

Eternity is a mute tree.

Shadows, endless shadows:
How huge is this kingdom.

Under the shadow of a tree
a candle shines.

If I died
bury me in this shadow.

A tree converses with its leaves.

A bird
or a leaf in the blowing wind?

# Shakir Li'aibi

## Translated by Saadi A Simawe and Ralph Savarese

### My days pass with the beads of the rosary

The nights come
and I watch
for the moon,
which is lost in the dust of the galaxy,
to become full.

One relaxes on mint leaves;
another glows like a nut in its shell;
a third rebels against its own sin
when dawn's face appears in the window.

This night spends its time in a washed-up conch;
that one chases a bygone evening.
While I sleep in the first halo of the moon,
and she sleeps in the saltiness of warm bread,
I also sleep in the sea's saltiness,
inhaling the sourness of the grass,
tasting her acrid body,
eager for the sight of her shameless down.

At daybreak I will run after the dawn as it passes through the fields.
At daybreak everything will split into two isolated beings
amid the darkness's troubling whisper.

### The soul of a pebble on top of the mountain

Remain calm, O Dawn,
and don't keep blinding me with your radiance.
When I would knock at my beloved's door,
I might have been knocking at yours.
You penetrate the soul of a pebble on top of the mountain.
You tempt me to reach for the eternal.
You bring back to me the romantic's mornings.
You are the supreme name in all names
when you illumine my beloved's road.

Stay calm, O Milky Way,
so we don't lose ourselves in your endless alleys.
O Lilies, stay balanced with the line of the horizon.
Such swaying makes giddy the domesticated animal
who picks up the seed and straw in your neighborhood.
How intense is the brightness of the flower!
How intense is the warmth
of the hand on my shoulder!

[20 August 2001]


### A butterfly frozen in stone

My beloved, the breath of the universe
has alighted in the courtyard of the house,
agitating the flowerpot
and bringing to tears the straw that surrenders to the fire.

An angel flutters on your eyelash,
and laurels pulsate on your rib.
A neighbour covets the flapping of your butterfly gown on the laundry line.
I am your lover and brother.

Spring's moan is in your ribs.
The North Wind descends on your body;
the South Wind yawns at your feet.
The Khamsin blows from your sorrow.
The world's winds flood us, you and me, with their wailing beauty.
I will release my last cry in your monsoon,
you, my season's mate . . .

[Geneva, 14 July 2001]


### The stone of the Arabian woman

The night trembles long on the water before you sleep.
The stars ponder the boldness of the bed
where dawn declares itself in your glowing arms.

You are the eyeliner of the Great Eye
that watches my tenuous world.

Sleep, then, in the air blowing on my face from the depths of the unknown.
Sleep in the feather sprouting on the hippo's wing.
I will migrate between your breasts for a little while.


The world is a scented handkerchief,
and Arabian women sing for the past.
Arabian women bite on this handkerchief
while giving birth to the impossible.
Arabian women commit the crime of beauty
in order to conceive of a beautiful man.
Arabian women are enchanted with the eternity of the seven faces;
they sleep on a star at the edge of the galaxy.
Arabian women who have not yet pitched their tents on fertile fields
will not commit to some necessary foolishness
for the sake of keeping fire in their cheeks.
Arabian women, their hair dishevelled, mourn the night of the lover's
          death.
Arabian women who have four pains and three hearts
splinter compassion and jealousy
and multiply in the bark of desert trees.

The slave girl and the princess
converse on the eve of the Ramadan breakfast.
Are Arabian women happy in their dark boudoir?
The beautiful ones erupt with the tears of perplexity.
Their eyebrows lighten in the dark tunnels.
Arabian women have eaten the lips of infinity.
Arabian women avenge themselves on mint leaves
in order to kiss their lovers.
Arabian women assemble in your squared circle.

  *[17 August 2001]*

# Sami Mahdi

## Translated by Ferial J Ghazoul

*from* **Selected Poems** *of Sami Mahdi (written during the Gulf War or just after)*

### War Diaries

#### I. (Feb. 14, 1991)
From gazelles' eyes the pupils dropped
When the bridge was bombed
Lovers' rings shattered
And mothers were bewildered

#### II. (Feb. 16, 1991)
With fire we perform our ablutions every morning
Collecting our remnants
And the debris of our houses
We purge our souls with the blood of our wounds

#### III. (Feb. 24, 1991)
Plenty we have received
What shall we offer you, O land of patient destitutes?
Plenty we have received
So receive us
And pave with us the paths of wayfarers

### Abel's Brothers

The beginning is often splendid
The road
Smooth
The comrade is often
Compliant
Then unawares you
Or both of you are taken
Something concealed in the depth cracks
And floats
Like the corpse of a drowned child.

And you ask for an example?
Then: no answer.
The story is familiar
The rites of suffering
Are repeated in every generation
In every generation there is a slayer and a slain
And a legacy of fear and suspicion.
It is the story of Cain
As he mends his criminal cloak
Fearing punishment.
It is the story of Abel
Searching for his wound
Between nail and tooth.
It is this pervasion of earth's laws
This desolation.

No way for Cain but madness
No way for Abel but resignation
No way for us for seven thousand years
Except this.

# Nazik al-Mala'ika

Translated by Basima Bezirgan, Elizabeth Fernea, Ferial J Ghazoul, Ibtisam S Barakat, Saleh Alyafai and Jenna Abdul

### Jamilah and us

Jamilah! Beyond the horizon, far beyond the borders of nations, you weep.
Your hair loose, your tears soak the pillow.
Are you really crying? Does Jamilah cry?
Don't they give you music and song
Didn't they make offerings, of words and more words to you?
So why the tears, Jamilah?

The details of your torture were on every tongue,
And that hurt us, it was hard for our sensitive ears to bear.
You were the one imprisoned and shackled
And when you were dying for a sip of water
We marshalled all our songs
And said, 'We'll sing to you, Jamilah, through the long nights.'
All of us said: They gave you blood and fire to drink.
All of us said: They put you on the cross.
But what did we do? We sang, we praised your heroism, your glory
We said: 'We'll save her (Yes, we will)!'
We made promises, false promises, drunken promises
And we shouted 'Long live Jamilah! Long live Jamilah!'

We fell in love with Jamilah's smile.
We adored her round cheeks.
The beauty that prison had gnawed revived our love.
We were infatuated with her dimples, with the braids of her hair.
Did we not use her suffering to give meaning to our poetry?
Was that a time for songs? Songs, be ashamed.
Be silent before this noble suffering.

Their intent was evil. They cut her with sharp blades.
We gave her smiles, good intentions.
They hurt her with knives.
We, with the best of intentions, hurt her with ignorant, uncouth words.

The teeth of France tore her flesh.
She was one of us, our kin
And the wounds we inflicted are more painful to bear,
Shame on us for all the suffering of Jamilah!

[BB and EF]

**Note:** Jamilah Buhrayd was a young Algerian girl who, as a teenager, fought against the French occupation of her country. She was imprisoned and tortured by the French, and became known throughout the Arab world as a hero of the Algerian revolution. Algeria gained its independence in 1962, Jamilah was released and still lives in Algeria with her family.


### To Poetry

From the temples' incense of bygone Babylon
From the clamour of waterwheels in southern deserts
From the nocturnal cries of a turtledove
And the echo of harvesters chanting the sunset tune
That voice, your voice, will return
To my life, to the years' audition,
Haggard with the scent of a sad evening,
Ears of grain weighting it with raving fragrance.
It will return with a strange lyrical echo:
Frog croaks in sleepy dusk
Filling night and streams
With languid monotonous sounds.

That voice will return
To my life, to the audition of the evening.
It will return and I will hear the chanting,
Moon-fresh echoing nights of rain,
The repose of twigs
As they sip drunkenly heaven's nectar,
Perfumed by clouds,
By visions, by greetings of the stars.

I will roam Existence
I will gather the particles of your voice from cool springs
From the mountains of the north
Where even lilies whisper songs
Where pines tell nomadic Time
Tales throbbing

With musk, tales of the shades' passion
For the brooks, of the wolves' chants
For spring water in the forest shades,
Of the dignity of pastures and the philosophy of a running stream,
Of a ram in deep depression
Spending the day
Chewing grass and thoughts
Drowned in the mist of abyssal existence.

I will gather the particles of your voice from Heaven's joys
On an ancient evening
By the Tigris, heaving with yearning,
The cheer of night revellers
Sipping water ripples
Dashing against the shore,
Summer moonlight  fills the evening with images
And the breeze passes, like lips touching,
From other lands:
A Scheherazadean night
In its tender darkness
All feel and dream, even silence,
All enamoured by light.

I will hear your voice when I am
Amidst Nature's commotion, in moments of madness
When echoes of thunder evoke
A thousand legends of History's youths
Of perished epochs and of nations no more
Of tales told by the boys of Aad
To the girls of Thamoud
And stories chanted by Scheherazade
To that mad king
On winter nights.
I will hear your voice every evening
When light dozes off
And worries take refuge in dreams,
When desires and passions slumber, when ambition sleeps
When Life sleeps, and Time remains
Awake, sleepless
Like your voice.
In the drowsy dusk resounds your wakeful voice,
In my deep yearning
Your eternal voice that never sleeps
Remains awake with me.

I feel its painted echo filling the path
With fragrance, with colours' dew.
Your unknown voice
I have grasped, oh joy, its honey-laced secret
I grasped – only I and the silence of the Time.


### Myths

*Dedicated by the poet to Daisy Al-Amir*
*in commemoration of an evening at which the two*
*poets "philosophized even the chairs, tables, and curtains."*

Life, they said
Is the eye colour of the dead
The footsteps of a vigilant killer.
Its wrinkled days
Knit a coat of poison
That ceases not from killing.
Its dreams are the smiles
Of an ogress's numbed eyes
Behind which, death stares.

Hope, they said
Is the bitterness of the thirsty
Seeing on a wall
A glass in a drawing.
It's the frowning colour
In the eyes of a bird that cried
When it found its nest sundered.
Awake with hope,
It awaited the morning
To come with a miracle
And mend the ruins.

Bliss, they said
And I searched for it in all caring eyes
In the stories of misery
Written on some people's faces.
In time, as it is slowly devoured by the years.
In a flower, as the ghost of withering
Stalks its fragrance.
In a brilliant star
That would shine no more.
They spoke of bliss but I found no trace of it.
Has it been here but long passed?

Silence, they said
Is only a myth
Invented by an inhuman being
Whose ears can listen
While its soul in ashes lies buried.
It has not heard the screams
Streaming from the fence
Or from the paper shreds in ruins
Or the dust, or the seats in ancient places,
Or the glass dressed in cobwebs,
And a coat hung on the wall.

Youth, they said
And I inquired.
They replied there will come a time
When fog disappears.
They spoke of heaven beyond the mirage
And an oasis for the weary.

Then when I arrived at youth I found
The dreams of tomorrow
At the closed gate, crucified.

Immortality, they said
And I found it a shadow
That emerges from the shrivelling of life
And flings itself in a leisurely way
On the graveyards.
I found it a word
That lingered on the lips of those
Who mourned their past
As they denied it.
They sang for immortality
As they passed. Alas!
They spoke of immortality
And I found all that is
Would not last.

Hearts, they said
And I found them no more than doors
That lead to graveyards
Where the feelings are buried
And the imagination is dead.

Their damp walls
Swallow all beauty
And beat with unbearable ugliness.
Thinking of hearts, pale, I fled.
And I shall not return.
What disappointment!

Eyes, they said
But I found eyelids
With no sight.
And I'd known lashes
That are tied to stones.
And heard of cellar eyes
That are hidden
Inside doubt curtains
Eyes that are called eyes
But to all save evil
They are blind.
And I'd known thousands of those
Whose eyes are sheets of glass
Blue as the sky
But behind the blueness bellowing darkness.

They said and said
Their chewed up words with the wind flap
In a world of ephemeral sounds.

Those who are weary with no respite
Those who are forever lost
They spoke and I spoke
But all speaking comes to an end.

What myth! What imaginative irony!

[FJG]


## The Lover River

Like the unbridled wind he winds after us.
Where shall we turn?

Unconcerned
He runs through wheat land

His arms spread
In the glitter of the morning
His hands drunken
They shall meet us and take us in
And drown all our terror
No matter where we turn.

Wordlessly
He runs and runs
And conquers our towns
His brown waters
Not yielding to dams.

He is chasing us yearning
To hold our youth
In his affectionate folds.

He is still chasing us
With a kind smile on his face
His feet are wet
Leaving red footprints everywhere
He has roamed East and West
Always with tenderness.

Where shall we run?
And he has slowly, firmly, and quietly
Embraced the shoulders of our town.

From his lips, mud kisses
Have covered our sad pastures.

This ancient lover we have known well
Slides endlessly toward our hills.

This familiar guest
We have built our villages as lodgings for him.
And every year he remembers
To come down the valley to meet us.

Now that he has come in the midst of night
We have vacated our huts and are departing
Knowing that he will follow us once we are under way.

For this lover we pray

And into his hands
We empty our boredom
And all our complaints.

He is a god today.
Has not our city washed its feet in his waters?
He rises and pours treasures into her hands.
He bestows upon us the mud
And death that eludes our eyes.
Have we anyone but this lover god?

[ISB]
*[Mala'ika wrote this poem after the dreadful flood of the*
*Tigris River in Baghdad, 1954]*


## The Hijrah [Migration] to God

I knew you in the passion of my prayers at night,
and in my piles of carnations.
I knew you in the greening of the myrtle.
I knew you in the certainty of death and the grave.
I knew you in a farmer sowing seeds on the ground,
and his axe in his hand blossoms.
I knew you in a child with black eyes,
and in a old man with withered cheeks.
I knew you in a sufi, rich in heart and feeling.
I knew you in the devotion of a monk celebrating mass.
I knew you in the fullness of the sea waves running barefoot,
and in the lashes of blue eyes, and the lips' preoccupation.
I knew you in the echo of the bells.
I knew you full of night raining on the world
and in threads of dreams, and the perfume of drowsiness.
And you throw in my way heaps upon heaps of roses,
and you give me water in a most precious cup.

I found you standing in the essence of a song,
and in the sadness of the gloom of autumn.
I found you in the wound of a thirsty flower,
I found you in the nighttime recitations of the Quran.
And you built a nest under the veil of darkness
for a frightened lark and a homeless turtledove,
their bones folded in sadness,
for a refugee woman whose bones are folded on sadness,

for an emigrating caravan, expelled from their homes.
I found you sending the rain
to fall on an unwatered land,
and giving it water in celestial cups.
And you hang a moon in the sky of our being,
and you give it to the misty night of sorrows,
and you give it to a thirsty grove,
its plantings forgotten by the rain.

I found you inspiring the determination which fills the arms of men.
I saw you holding back the earthquake
from the village, and the young, and the mosque.
I saw you as sugar in the lisping of children,
and I saw you giving a wondrous song,
even though the singer did not ask.
And you come to us at no appointed time,
and you open the locks that are closed.
My king, you are the taste of summer in my life,
and you are the radiance of the moons.
Your love is planets and seas.
The yearning of the high tide is for you,
and you are the secret of the low tide's desire.
And you are the abundance of poetry,
and you are the freshness of my desert oases,
and you are the shining of secrets,
and you are my flowing,
you are the outpouring of light and perfume.
You scattered lushness and pearls across my green shores,
and into my soul you poured fire.

For you I scatter roses and prayers.
For the sake of your eyes, o my king, I break my rubies,
and in your hands I scatter my leaves and my years.
I come, and my breathless lute is seized by perfume,
and the tight string sings praise and devotion,
and whispers your name like a poem.
Perhaps you will shower me with roses;
perhaps my sight will be filled with fragrance,
so that its oceans flood with shells and corals,
and its blood-red rubies and its marble bow in rapture.
You guide the boats of my present in the stream of memory,
and you shower my days with the scent of your clear light.
You make my springs pour forth, and you purify my depths,
and from you streams the sweetness of my celestial poems.

It suffices that my royal love mentions my devoted songs,
and the touch of God, the touch of God, colours and perfumes them;
he dilutes his secrets in them, and scatters them
across the continents, above the forests and all kinds of water,
a scent of right guidance and touch of prayer.

O my king, the journey has lengthened, lengthened,
and ages have passed,
and between locked worlds I have sailed, asking at doors.
I carried with me the wounds of fedayeen,
and the taste of death in September, and of mud.
I carried with me the sorrows of Jerusalem, o my king,
and the wound of Jenin,
and a night of high walls that cannot be scaled.
So where is the door? Where is the door?
My sacrifices are heaped at the altar,
my Quran is hidden in the mist,
and the agony of my Al Aqsa mosque
cuts me like a knife.

And there is no Mu'atassum whom I can call,
and there is no Salaheddin among us.
We sleep at night, and wake at dawn wounded,
stabbed, killed.
And you grew angry, o king, o praise your angry face.
And how do we make peace with tyranny?
How do we shake hands with Satan?
Did you not enrich our cities with the perfume of roses and the Quran?
How can we spend the night in captivity?
And how can we sleep, expelled from our homes?
Garlands of flowers, all wilted, but for the lily of sorrows –
our homes lie at the mouth of a volcano.
And you stay with the slain, o my king, and with the wounded,
you stay at your post, vigilant.
And here we have lost the religion, and fought our beloved fedayeen.
We spilled blood in Beirut,
we poured blood in Amman,
and with our hands, we made our land a guillotine for our people.

*[SA and JAR]*
*[Kuwait, 28 Jumada al Akhira 1393 AH/ 29 June 1973 CE]*

# Dunya Mikhail

## Translated by Salaam Yousif and Liz Winslow

### The Jewel

It no longer overlooks the river
No longer is in the city
No longer on the map
The bridge that was
The bridge that we used to cross every day
The bridge
The war tossed it into the river
Just as that lady aboard the Titanic
Tossed her blue diamond

### Santa Claus

With his beard long like war
and suit red like history
Santa Claus came smiling
He asked me to take something
You are a good girl, he said
so you deserve a game
He gave me something like poetry
As I hesitated, he encouraged me
– Don't be afraid, baby
I am Santa Claus
I distribute beauty to children
Haven't you seen me before ?
– But Santa Claus whom I know
comes in military uniform
and every year distributes to us
some red swords
toys for orphans
artificial legs
and photos of absentees
to be hung on the walls.

[SY]

## Christmas

### 1

Somebody is knocking at the door
How sad
It is Christmas and not you

### 2

I don't know how to add your absence to my life
I don't know how I subtract myself from it
I don't know how to divide it
in the communicating vessels.

### 3

The time stopped
at twelve o'clock
The watchmaker got confused
Nothing wrong with the watch
The whole matter is
that the hands remained in an embrace
and forgot the world.

## Snow Storm

*To Lori*

What sweet children!
They rush to awaken us
we, the snow-women
just born now
from a yawn or nostalgia.
Accumulated outside
to let the spoiled storm
pass through our bits.
Sometimes it covers us
like an earnest god
with leaves from heaven.
Ball-shaped under the hands
of the sweet children
we grow and smile.
Once they fix our eyes
we look grateful.
We never cry.
We look to rush them.

We can't wait
to have our feet.
We want to go there.
The celebration will start soon.
We will point our fingers
which they are making now.
We will soon point
to the balloon
which is rising up to our voices.
Look!
We can't wait
to move
into our things there.
It is taking too long
to put our feet
that we – how sad
walk in a sunny day.

### The Prisoner

She doesn't understand
what it means to be "guilty"
She waits at the prison's door
until she sees him
to tell him "Take care"
as she used to remind him
when he was going to school
when he was going to work
when he was coming on vacation
She doesn't understand
what they are uttering now
those who are behind the bar
with their uniform
as they decided that
he should be put there
with strangers of gloomy days
It never came to her mind
when she was saying lullabies
upon his bed
during those faraway nights
that he would be put
in this cold place
without moons or windows

She doesn't understand
The mother of the prisoner doesn't understand
why should she leave him
just because "the visit has finished"!

## America

please don't ask me, America
I don't remember
on which street
with whom
or under which star
Don't ask me
I don't remember
the colours of the people
or their signatures
I don't remember if they had
our faces
and our dreams
if they were singing
or not
writing from the left or right
or not writing at all
sleeping in houses
on sidewalks
or in airports
making love or not making love
Please don't ask me, America
I don't remember their names
or their birthplaces
People are grass
They are born everywhere, America
Don't ask me . . .
I don't remember
what time it was
or what kind of weather
language
or flag
Don't ask me . . .
I don't remember
how long they walked under the sun
or how many died
I don't remember

the shapes of the boats
or the number of ports
. . . how many suitcases they carried
or left behind
if they came complaining
or without complaint
Stop your questioning, America
and offer your hand
to the tired
on the other shore
Offer it without questions
or waiting lists
What good is it to gain the whole world
if you lose the Soul, America?
Who said that the sky
would lose all of its stars
if night passed without answers?
America, leave your questionnaires to the river
and leave me to my lover
It has been a long time
we are two distant, rippling shores
and the river wriggles between us
"like a well-cooked fish"
It has been a long time, America
(longer than the stories of my grandmother in the evening)
and we are waiting for the signal
to throw our shell in the river
We know that the river is full
of shells; this last one
wouldn't matter
yet it matters to the shell
Why do you ask all these questions?
You want our fingerprints
in all languages
and I have become old
older than my father
He used to tell me in the evenings
when no trains ran:
One day, we will go to America
One day, we will go
and sing a song
translated or not translated
at the Statue of Liberty
And now, America, now

I came to you, without my father
The dead ripen faster
than the Indian figs
but they never grow older, America
They come in shifts of shadow and light
in our dreams
and as shooting stars
or curve in rainbows
over the houses
we left
behind
They sometimes get angry
if we keep them waiting a while . . .
What time is it now?
I am afraid I will receive
your registered mail, America
in this hour
which has no usefulness
so I would toy with the freedom
like a domesticated cat
I wouldn't know what else
to do with it
in this hour
which has no usefulness . . .
and my sweetheart
there, on the opposite shore
of the river
carries a flower for me
And I – as you know –
dislike faded flowers
I do like my sweetheart's handwriting
shining each day in the mail
I salvage it from among ad fliers
and special offers
Buy one Get One Free
and an urgent promotional announcement:
You will win a million dollars
if you subscribe to this magazine!
bills to be paid
in monthly instalments
I like my sweetheart's handwriting
though it gets shakier every day
We have a single picture
just one picture, America

I want it
I want that moment
forever out of reach
in the picture which I know
from every angle:
the circular moment of sky
Imagine, America:
if one of us drops out of the picture
and leaves the album full
of loneliness
or if life becomes
a camera
without film
Imagine, America!
Without a frame
the night will take us
tomorrow
darling
tomorrow
the night
will take us
without a frame
we will shake the museums
forever from their sleep
fix our broken clocks
so we'll tick in the public squares
whenever the train
passes us by
tomorrow
darling
tomorrow
we will bloom:
two leaves of a tree
we will try not to be
graceful in the greenness
and in time
we will tumble down like dancers
taken by the wind
to the places whose names
we'll have forgotten
we will be glad for the sake of the turtles
because they persist along their way
Tomorrow
darling

tomorrow
I'll look at your eyes
to see in your new wrinkles
the lines of our future dreams
As you will braid my gray hair
under rain
or sun
or moon
every hair will know
that nothing happens
twice
every kiss a country
with a history
a geography
and a language
with joy and sadness
with war
and ruins
and holidays
and ticking clocks . . .
And when the pain in your neck returns, darling
you will not have time to complain
and won't be concerned
if it remains inside us
coy as snow
that won't melt
Tomorrow, darling
tomorrow
from the wooden box will come
the jingling sound of
two rings:
they have been shining for a long time
on two trembling hands,
entangled
by the absence.
Tomorrow
the whiteness will expose
all its colours
as we welcome back what was lost
or concealed
in the whiteness
How should I know, America
which of the colours
was the most joyful

tumultuous
alienated
or assimilated
of them all?
How would I know, America?

[LW]

# Murad Mikha'il

## Translated by Sadok Masliyah and Christina Coyle

### Don't Despair

*For my daughter, Naurait.*

Don't despair my dear daughter!
Dawn is breaking the horizon
The hopes and dreams of paradise will lead our caravan
And life's thorns will no longer hinder our way
Don't give up my sweet little daughter!
O my sweet daughter, don't despair!

### Talk

Life says, "If I never knew pleasure, man would live like a beast."
Death says, "If I were Satan, I'd resurrect my victims from their graves."
Earth says, "If I were barren, living beings would devour each other."
And God says, "And had I not fulfilled my promise, I'd have
          destroyed everything."

### Three Flags

Humanity raised three flags atop three mountains.
Wove the first flag from hope, and dyed it with blood.
Knit the second from deception, and wet it with regret.
Made the third from flesh, and tore this flag with its fangs and claws.
Humanity then burned these flags and mourned the ashes.

This is the nature of humanity:
Destroying all it establishes
Establishing all it destroys
Until the day it repents.

### The Beggar

In the temple of my soul, demons pray
In the court of my conscience, evil-doers quarrel
And from my cherished illusion, I beg to be released

My path is covered with thorns
My freedom is buried under gold
My pride is hidden by ignorance

My sky is a space of hope
My earth is a field of greed
My death is proof of my self

Who will grant me love to live on?
Who will uncover the treasures of Time?
And, before morning, who will make me rich so I need not beg?


## The Voice of Conscience

I am a night mute as my sorrow.
There is no limit to the sky of my imagination,
Or a shore to hold my sea of meditations.
In my serenity, I welcome the glory of death.
Within my being, I worship the morning and consecrate the dawn.
In the depth of my soul, I plant winged flowers of light which glow
            with affection.
I create magical pictures to express my soul.

Hatred clouds my peace,
Noise muddies my drink,
Desolation lifts the curtains of the unknown.

I am a flower unwithered by autumn's desert winds.
I am a branch unbroken by winter's storms.
I am a dream that does not end by waking.
I am weak, but the strong cannot devour me.
I find strength in my weakness.

From beyond society and from the depths of Hades,
I hear the wailing and despair of your soul,
I touch the bleeding wounds of your heart.
I listen to what you say, reflecting on it,
I read the pain and distress between the lines of your letters,
And I see the shadows of ghosts settling in the gloomy cave of my hope.

You mixed your wine with mine,
And here I am, mixing my wine with yours.

Your spiritual desires were reflected in the mirror of my soul,
And here I am, my desires reflected in the mirror of your soul.
You hear me weep in the midst of rejoicing,
You watch me dance in the midst of grief.


## Crazy Satan

Tyrants created my pleasurable madness
From this pleasure flows the blood of greed and the tears of hope.
While I walk, under my feet nations are destroyed, crowns are
       shattered, hearts are crushed.
From my dust, worlds are formed as dark as my desire.

My shadow forms a night where my dreams are like fluttering
       curtains covering the mountains.
From the mass of my emotions, I carve suns that pour forth
       illuminated tears to enlighten dim hearts.
From my gaze that burns the veils of conscience
       flow rivers of disappointment and seas of remorse.

*

The stars are eyes glancing at me
And the dark is a light opening within me.
While wise people, like rocks, resist my temptations
I am a wave that ebbs away from them but their foolishness
       brings me back.
This is why you hear me moan under their feet
And witness my defeat in the face of the blind power of madness,
       O God of Satans!

I whisper in the hearts of living beings,
So they ignore my deeds.
I wrap the intellectuals in the winding sheets of lethargy,
So they worship my insanity, admire my evil, and stare at every
       stage of my madness.
I see what I do not feel and feel what I do not see,
But I feel the fingers of the unknown treating my deep wounds
And the breath of life in my soul,
So I consider myself a Satan among angels.

*

Oh God of insane people and Satans!
When will these fears disperse and these clouds scatter?
When will truth control violent storms, demolish old thoughts,
Crush the rigid intellectuals, plant mercy and compassion in
        cruel hearts,
And give power to the weak in order to combat the adversities of life?
When will my screams echo back as heartwarming hymns?
When will lost souls be resurrected into madmen?
When will I fly beneath heaven and hover day and night over hell?
The night is nothing but a feather from my wing and the day but a
        spark from my flame.

O God of madmen and Satans!
When will your madness drown me and your errors guide me?
When will your blood quench my thirst?
When will your pains heal me?
When will your hymns make me cry and your moaning give
        me pleasure?
Why do I cry so that you laugh? Why do I die so that you live?
Why am I so defiled and you so consecrated?
Why am I cursed and you so blessed?
And why do I ascend to the abyss, while you descend to the heights?
I am a microcosm of you, and you are an enlarged essence of me.
Had it not been for both of us, madmen and Satans would never be known.


### The Imprisoned God

My heart overflows with love, so what is this wine for?
My soul moans with pain, so what are these winds for?
My hope is like a star above the evening's gown, so why these moons?
My flowers are daughters of winter, so what is this dew?
My imagination is the product of darkness, so why this light?
My freedom is my conscience, so what are these shackles for?
My paradise is my cave, so what is this palace?
You have no pearls in my ocean, you have only shells.
You have no waves in my sea, you have only drops.
You have no breeze in my sky, you have only wailing.
You have no scent in my flowers, you have only petals.
If you banish me for taking what is yours, why do you beg at the
        doors of my prison?
If you set me free because of your gluttony, don't you know I am full
        of angry lions and hungry lepers?

If you scream like spoiled children when dividing my spiritual treasures,
Don't you know your vaults will never hold them?
You say, "Let's destroy all graves and shatter the skulls of the dead."
Did you inherit my dead dreams in your schools and temples?
Did you touch the tears I shed on the palaces of your empire?
If you free me from this prison's darkness, I'll welcome death on a
        wooden cross.
Haven't you sacrificed your souls at Christ's feet?
Didn't you use incense to purify yourselves at Socrates' tomb?
Do you intend to grieve when I leave?
Didn't my voice, that penetrates the cloak of my oppression and
        tyranny, cause you misery?
Didn't my moans melt your frozen hearts?
And if you say, "Let's admit our weaknesses,"
Won't you fear my sharp fangs and claws?
And if you pray to God in order to rid yourselves of my evil,
Don't you know that God only heeds the prayers of restless souls and
        deprived hearts?
And if you stand motionless at the bars of my prison,
Don't you know that immobility means non-existence?
You disavow me saying, "He's a crazy God, descended from hell
        to sow seeds of evil."
But didn't you say, "If evil did not exist we would not know good?"
And didn't you say, "If there was not darkness, we would never
        enjoy the morning?"
I'm a prisoner of your repressive ways.
I'm a victim of your Ash'abian* greed.
Is there one person among you who will free me and avenge my blood?
I see you walking with broken wings to the corners of my palaces.
While in my cave, I'm like an eagle undaunted by storms or heavy rains.
I see you following in the shoes of your ancestors,
Wearing their ragged shrouds, being led by their aged thoughts
        in order to die again.
I walk as a stranger among you,
Leaving footprints on the face of the sky,
Covering myself with darkness,
Led by my lost freedom,
To convene with the ghosts of darkness
And meet with the tyrants of the night.

---

\*    Al Ash'abia: Nicknamed "The Greedy," was a mythological trickster figure
who used deception in order to promote his own self-interest.

## You Have Your Calamity And I Have Mine

### 1

You have your calamity, with its shower of evils.
And I have my calamity, with its concealed powers.
You have your calamity, with its breath that poisons the air.
I have my calamity, with its tears and blood that water the earth.
You have your calamity, with its epidemics that pass from generation
        to generation.
And I have my calamity, which dies in my heart then revives a
        longing in my spirit.
You have your calamity, with its sparks from the oppressor's fire.
And I have my own calamity, as it inspires courage from weak heroes.
You have your calamity, so be content with it!
And I have mine, but am still searching.
You worship your calamity as if it were an idol.
I have my own calamity, freeing it as if it were a caged bird.
You have your calamity and I have mine.

### 2

Your calamity clouds the bright sun of Truth.
My calamity is a moon crowned by light and surrounded by mist.
Your calamity is a hell which devours innocent hearts and naïve minds.
Mine is a self-consuming fire.
Your calamity is slaves who die thinking they're free.
And my calamity is free men who die thinking they are slaves.
Your calamity tries to possess hearts and chain souls.
And my calamity flies in a narrow sky on unseen wings.
But your calamity is a realized hope, a preferred principle,
        a homeland in which you belong.
My calamity is disappointment with a ray of hope, blasphemy based
        on sound ideas, a world full of promises.
Your calamity destroys with cannons what civilization has built,
Replacing it with pillars of greed and evil deeds.
And my calamity is suffocated yearning, a flowing of tears,
Convulsive moaning.
Your calamity is a deluded person wearing garments made of
        righteousness.
My calamity is a preacher who stands among graves guiding the dead.
Your calamity is a curse from the lips of life.
My calamity is a blessing from the lips of death.
You have your calamity which is covered with moss.
I have my own calamity which is in perpetual flux.
You have your calamity and I have mine.

### 3

Your calamity uses blindness as a net to trap people, building prison
   walls from darkness.
You eternalize the hero as god, create prophets from illusion, create
   religion from deceit.
And on the day of resurrection, you disgrace worshippers behind a
   curtain of darkness.
But I sow truth from imagination.
Unafraid of light, I open my heart to the morning.
Under the gown of light I burn my passion and as if it were incense,
   offer my heart as a sacrifice.
I walk with one million prayers, while at the altar of my soul are one
   million prophets.
Then as dawn appears, your calamity increases while my calamity fades.
You have your calamity and I have mine.

### 4

I say to you: Darkness will not hide your repugnant deeds.
The eyes of the night stare at you, its ears listening.
I say to you: You live and die only for the sake of your own body.
I say to you: Your calamity is like unripe fruit, a cup of bitterness,
   a bottomless well of tears.
I say to you: Every night your calamity is a raven calling from the hill.
I say to you: Your calamity is an eagle devouring owls and falcons.
But you say to me: Your calamity is a scorpion's sting, a dog's bite,
   a snake's poison.
Your calamity is a donkey's bray, a frog's croak, a monkey's dance.
Your calamity is a fox's trickery, a jackal's death, a lion's prey.
Your calamity is that you harvest heads by following orders, burn
   bodies in the name of duty, and oppress souls in order
   to obtain a piece of land.
And I say to you: Your calamity comes from me, and from you
   my calamity comes.
You have your calamity and I have mine.

### 5

Leave me alone with my calamity which does not accept tears as comfort.
Leave me alone with my calamity which does not seek loneliness as solace.
Leave me alone with my calamity which feeds on my liver and
   drinks my blood.
Leave me alone with my calamity which time will never age
   and centuries cannot bury and hope not resurrect.
Leave me alone with my calamity which tempts me with its lightning
   and shakes my existence with its promises.

Leave me alone with the ghosts of my calamity with its eulogies of
	sadness and misfortune.
My calamity is in you, and in you is my calamity.
You have your calamity and I have mine.

### 6

Your calamity consecrates sorrow, then lives within it.
My calamity has power, but fears it.
Your calamity stammers, but is mute.
My calamity is mute, but speaks in a thunderous voice.
My calamity comes from you and from you comes my calamity.
My calamity is you and in you is my calamity.
You have your calamity and I have mine.

# Sajidah al-Musawi

Translated by Basima Bezirgan and Elizabeth Fernea

## Four beats of the heart

### 1

Wind
In the house of the heart
The wind howled.
It whipped the curtains
So all the heart's secrets were bared.

### 2

Confession
The words were all arranged . . .
The lines, the letters
Even the sentences . . .
And I was about to speak
I was about to say
What filled my heart.
But something stayed my lips
What stopped me
Was shyness.

### 3

Thanks
'Thanks' stood, bewildered.
Should it come forward or go back?
'Thanks', shy, must go back
What you gave,
The promises you've kept
Remain more splendid
How can 'Thanks' ever pay splendour back its due?

### 4

Violets
She fell
Into the violets
And the dew caressed her.
His eyes shone at her fragrance
She lay in the heart of the violets.
And in her he smelled his own perfume
And his love . . .

The wind came
She was frightened
The violets closed their petals around her.
When the wind departed
Her soul sparkled again
Among the violets.

# Awad Nasir

Translated by Saadi A Simawe with Daniel Weissbort
and Ralph Savarese

**Three Poems**

### 1 Parade

The show square is filled with all manner of people –
soldiers, police, obligatory supporters –
for today is the big parade.
They took my son from his school
and emptied our house of me and you.
We watch from our hiding place what the General's shadow
is eradicating bit by bit.
You lie in a cloud
that at any moment could be your coffin
as I find in the painted curves of your eyelids a bow
to defend the domes of your breasts
or the fragrant tranquillity of a woman sitting for tea.
Then, suddenly, the thunder of the police invades your eyelashes.

*[London, 29 March 2000]*

### 2 A Poem Looking in a Mirror

You know you are old when you are fifty lines long
and heavy with rhyme.
Who has declined first, you or I?
You helped me to come to terms with myself.
You said:
"Stop wasting your time; for only you can make wrinkles disappear.
Push upward till you see beyond them."
And so, I shall remove poetic cosmetics
and renounce the drone of traditional rhythms,
which burden the golden tune.
Come, let's erase what words do not need
and go together.

*[London, 30 March 2000]*

### 3 A Moment of Love

There you are, my love, in front of me,
at the edge of my death

and near my madness.
An apple blossom in your hair,
silver shimmering on your neck,
your waist a dash of olive green in the field of my yearning.
In your black skirt you are a gypsy night and an Arabian moon
as the figs melt
and butterflies, your butterflies, alight on my heart.
I was a child again, naked on the grass,
as the guards of the orchards
tightened the noose around us.
At that moment we had nothing but ourselves
and love exploded like African drums.

*[London, 2 February 2002]*
*[SAS and RS]*

### Trilogy of the Man in Black

*The War*
The sidewalk of days was innocent,
even the siesta was no more than shade and an arm as a pillow.
The bar used to slide from a cool corner to replace the bus
and under my shirt I carry five boxes.
At our threshold my mother collapsed when war broke out east of the
        two rivers.
The waiter studies the shape of the last ray of sun on the table,
someone knocked at the door,
my sister opened.
Birds, poems, and liquor leapt from the five boxes under my shirt
I stared
and saw that our life has been turned upside down:
all of the dead stood up
and I was the only dead one left.

*Love in 2000*
A rooster stood on a rubbish heap
preening,
in the hope of reaching
a dreamed-of sun.

*Death*
Man lives his life
suspended like a piece of rope
as the rope gradually unravels

*[London, 22 March 2000]*

## A Poet's Fate

My country does not belong to me
nor I to it.
For five millennia my country has been no more than imminent exile.

It is my destiny to steal away like a thief
and enter like a thief
I am the one who steals fire from the creator.

But it's my destiny,
that of an ear of wheat,
which when it grows tall
is threatened by the one who wields a sickle.

*[London, 9 May 2001]*
*[SAS and DW]*

# Muzaffar al-Nawwab

## Transcribed and translated by Carol Bardenstein

**Note:** *Like most of Nawwab's poetry, this poem exists and circulates as a performance, either live, or listened to by its audience on cassette tape. I have tried, to the extent possible, to keep some of the performative features in view for the reading audience of this transcribed translation, including Nawwab's repetition of certain segments for effect or in response to the audience reaction, and providing occasional "auditory" footnotes about the recorded performance. This translation is based on my transcription of one particular performance of this poem that has circulated widely in cassette form. Other performances and recordings of this poem will necessarily vary to some degree. Poor and distorted sound quality comes with the territory of poetry circulating on multiply-copied samizdat cassette tapes. Although every effort was made to correctly transcribe the entire hour-long performance, at times this was impossible due to the poor sound quality. I take responsibility for any errors that have resulted.*

*I would like to express my profound appreciation and gratitude to Saadi Simawe for the many hours he spent and intensive, painstaking work he did with me in going closely over both the transcript of the poem and its translation. He went above and beyond the traditional role of editor in the most generous of ways, and his suggestions, feedback and input were invaluable. [CB]*

### Bridge of Old Wonders
*Jisr al-Mabahij al-Qadima (1976-77)*

#### Side One of Cassette
Nawwab: "The poem I shall recite now is long. Perhaps I will try to skip over or leave out certain sections. It is my most recent poem. It is difficult to talk about what is going on, not just a matter of politics, but also fundamentally a matter of culture and civilization. For this reason, talking about what is happening in Lebanon, in Palestine, is not easy. In this poem, the symbols of the self, revolution, woman, and trees, are all blended together. This is because for me, a truly political point of view touches upon all aspects of life."

King of depth –
I visit the stars of the sea,
and couple them with the stars of the night
I prolong my visits
at the site of the secrets of creation
[*Applause*]

King of depth,
I visit the stars of the sea,
and couple them with the stars of the night
I prolong my visitations
at the site of the secrets of creation.
Full of musk, my heart unfurled in the water
When my hand reached to touch the lush, haunted plants
With a rosy lust clinging to the drops of night-dew upon them
A language ripened into being.

The virile stag breathed within me
with such shameless lust and pleasure
coupling with four she-gazelles
stripping from them the coats of two spring seasons
It has worn me out, exhausted me, I am so tired,
My heart is spent from the exquisite pleasure
of so many escapades.

The letter
*nun* of the word *niswa* (women)[1]
has placed its dot in your night as a lantern.
How brightly you shine!
Give the women back their dot.
I have been shining so radiantly for this moment,
While the letters of passion on my lower lip lay sleeping.
The wave has transported me out of the cloak of my irreverence
It has washed away the pomegranate blossom
and left it sad in the cold water
The child plunged into the water without his sandals
Run , wave! Run!
Run, wave, run!
Somewhere between sadness and the sea-coral,
we have entered the phase of many doors.

My foot tripped up against the ivory door, so I knocked.
"Who is that knocking?"
You have no answer.
You dissolve into your voice.
You knock upon another door of wood
worn smooth in a pattern beyond your understanding
"Who *are* you?  Come back when you have learned how to knock.
Find out who you are."
A letter whose power I do not know yawned,
and impregnated the she-camels of the night

while the rhyming "r's" of Abu Sakhr al-Hudhali's sad love poem
lay sleeping . . . [2]
The very best door sent me away,
not realizing that my heart cannot be easily bought.

"Who are you? And what is the story of your soul?
What of the known world and its days have you lost?
And who have you come to visit?"

I was overcome by a sweet stammering,
My heart is like a tender shoot trembling in front of the scythe
The fear in my soul is profound
I can never let my feet cease their long sad journeying
with the party of the castrated ones chasing after me[3]
[Applause]
I can never let my feet cease their long sad journeying
with the party of the castrated ones chasing after me
Oh, seeker, you had better search for another door
Oh, seeker, you had better search for another door
My curiosity flourishes in the face of rejection

The gods guarding the doors have closed them tight
They have put something behind the doors as well
I extended my hands to touch the lush, haunted vegetation
When a rosy lust happened to touch the night-dew upon it
Beware! Be careful, for you are so inexperienced!
Knocking just gives rise to many more mysterious doors
Your keys are made of a language that locks whatever you open
You turn away, as a woman on the shore does,
from those who do not enter between the letters of her delights
We consider you to be a person of keen intuition
so do not spell out the body of the beloved, but read it all at once.

This violet hue, like a night orchid
Its femininity melts into the one whose hands reach out
and who knows what true depth is
He will purify the letter *hamza* by waving the incense thrice[4]
until he drives away the spell, and unties its knot.
Between his fingers, both morning and the cumin of passion grow
The morning breeze exposes her thighs . . . oh . . .
Pressing down the sweet basil of your soul
Oh , . . . oh . . . such wonderful pain!
Oh, wafting breeze, so profoundly pure and chaste
How could you push the door open on the lover?

The ship's helm sleeps
The lover has become drunk with rash defeatist thoughts
The breeze asks to be let in, after two parts of the night have passed
But the mariner-lover did not consent
Then the breeze came bearing fruit.
The diligent mariner said:
I have tasted nothing but the tip of the breast ,
I have abstained from the other desired delights,
slowly sipping the amber from the breast of passion
I held her rosy nipple in the night, reprimanding it
My palms filled with pistachio nectar
My baby finger caught fire,
Between the rose and the flesh, and the flesh and the rose
It was consumed by fire!
It gave off a light, a distinctly Arab light.
At night, there is no trusting my middle finger –
for on this finger I spin the treacherous rulers, one and all![5]

I will tell you in the third section about the rules of the *hamza*,
and in the fourth section, about these treacherous rulers.
As for now:
The taverns of the world are dull and listless,
With the passing days, boredom has settled in my heart,
like the boredom of a whore waiting for business, chomping mindlessly
Oh Ibn Dharih,[6] this tavern is cold!
Kindle your voice, that some of the evil might depart
Oh, Ibn Dharih give us a tune
Give us some of the pleasures of the seventh key[7]
Sing a sparrow-melody,
Do the chant of a woman's navel
A chant of knocking on a mysterious door.
"Who are you?
We've told you to listen to these familiar sounds."
Gods of the unknown, I have brought the latest kinds of grief,
My soul is a downcast colour,
which I wrapped in the sash of a nubile woman.

"Who is that knocking again?! We warned you!
What do you want? You have gambled on a raft
That cannot even cross a narrow canal!"
It has been said that you ridicule all crosses and all idols,
to which you have made blasphemous toasts
But the wind carries you,
and you raise your wine-flask as a sail, in rough times.

"How did you dare to knock on our door at night??"
The pleasures are sleeping behind the door without their clothes on!
Your mouth is watering . . .
How can pleasures be naked?
You start to become delirious, and begin uttering unintelligible sounds,
You try to get away from your body's stuttering
The walls of your grief are sweating profusely
There are even beads of sweat on your thumb-nail
You kindle the twig of sumac at a woman's thighs
By the goodness of God
the fertilization was consummated
and it gave rise to a precious creation.

You lit the fire, and the insects became crazed,
You lit the fire, and the insects became crazed,
The wave surged, the putrid foam rose, and the rotting egg grew agitated.
"You, on this tired raft,
which you call a 'ship of passion'
When you light it, this putrid egg will hatch vilifying filth!
Do you have any lanterns with you?
Pure kerosene no hands have touched?
And a soul capable of seeing even in these rotten times?"

The mariner of mariners lit the lamps of his boat,
He left them at a low flicker,
The mariner of mariners strung the pearls and lights and sounds
of the sea together on a string  for his beloved,
and left them at a low flicker.
His beloved has the most beautiful of *hamza's*,
She has the most beautiful
*mim* I have ever seen[8]
And she has a body that the gods of wondrous mixtures
have created by combining all of the perfumed essences of creation
He practised self-love, endowing her with such perfect beauty
that it embarrassed her.

I know the mariner of mariners, the one whose story I will tell you
He used to take great pleasure in fighting the delightful filth
His eyes shone like embers, from the fever
He sent the fever wrapped in leaves of passion to the house of his beloved
The house of his beloved is in al-Sham,[9] they say,

The house of his beloved is in al-Sham,  they say,
They say it's near the wooden bridge, and the house of Ali Ibn Jahm,[10]

In Ramallah, they say.
It has been said that it is at Bab al-Khalq,
And even in Targhuna.[11]

"Who are you?
How do you dare to pay visits in these suspicious times?"
The mariner of mariners was silent,
keeping his story hidden inside a living sea-shell
Because in a police state, termites can even hatch their eggs
between a man and his wife in their bed-clothes.
They even assign the sex of the newborn,
and determine precisely where on his buttocks to put the sultan's seal.[12]
And if he believes in the ruling party,
then paradise is his lot![13]
[Applause] [Repeats][14]
And woe to the unbeliever![15]
All the Arab regimes without exception
hang him in the public square
Leaving him out there for hours.
Even in our public squares, there is secret coordination behind the scenes.

Have any of you noticed that the silence is spreading
And the rats multiplying?!
With police cars pregnant in the streets, doing their dirty work?[16]
This is such a despicable ritual
That is why he hid his story inside a living sea-shell
and held fast at the helm of his ship.

His eyes, from the fever and the sadness, glowed like two melancholy stars,
He sent that fever wrapped in leaves of sadness to the home of his beloved.
She sat down to wash herself, preparing to receive the fever[17]
She braided her hair with roses and cold oil and mint
The neighbours heard them crying from the fever
on the first night of the month of Shaaban,
They said, "let us close this window and be done with this heartache."
He has infatuated all the girls of the neighbourhood,
and fashioned blind moths made of teardrops
The girls awoke from sleep, and closed the window
The women's *nun* had not slept at all[18]
The dot of the women's *nun* was erased by all the flowing tears
The *nun* arrived as a crescent-moon above the ship's helm
There was a strong, devastating wind,
The forecast from the helm is that a storm will soon rage
He was ill at the helm on that night of Shaaban

Fighting off dreams so intensely bright and radiant
and winds so strong that he had to close his eyes
"Where is the land?" he wondered.
He thrust his wild frame into the night's stars,
The tattoo-marks on his wrists completed the string of stars,
    extending even beyond it.


"Where do you want to go?
Your neck stretches farther than God has apportioned!"
He said: "That's how it was created."
"This is sufi logic.
How did you come to sufism, having a body oozing with such verdant
pleasures? How did you swell and expand so wondrously, being made
of such raw clay?"
You love the break of day,
but take no delight in a night without a body by your side
from which you take leave in the morning,
with tree-branches mourning over it,
giving off the light of opposites.


You say, "I have come into the state of light!
In the first year, it was the usual kind of light."
"And then? and then?"[19]
"In the third year, it was a concealed kind of light."
"And then what?"
"Then came a darkness which extinguished all of my lamps,
even those I had inherited."
Then I had to grope and feel my way
My feet tripped over the one who had taught me,
he became a stumbling block.
I have wasted so many years of my life trying in vain to revive him.
The corpse was rotting. How could I hope to prop it up?
"You mean you tripped right over the one who taught you the . . . "
"Yes, I am sorry to say."
"How could this have happened?"
"Just like that," he said, "it just did.
It is in the nature of things,
that the rhythm gets thrown off by strange piercing sounds."


How I long for the old familiar lane!
My heart has grown heavy, a chimney
drenched in a downpour of rain
that shows no signs of abating.

My spirit has sunk, except for one knot of passion
Just when the ship was about to embark on its journey,
a letter shot out like lightning from beneath the door, confident
             and dignified
A head peered out from the ship's helm,
all kinds of Kufic grammatical inflections were etched around its eyes
No other script has this kind of beauty, neither the Thuluth,
nor the Kufic nor the Ruq'a
I saw the garments of aroused passion tightening on my body,
So I cleansed myself with the water of creation, in preparation
I took hold of this lyre, and tuned four decades on it
I tightened the pain of the fifth and seventh keys
The Basran grammar opposed me, and so did the Kufic grammar.[20]
Someone I do not know was seated, someone who knows a Syrian grammar.


Let the wind gently rock you,
Your offering was a plentiful one of red wax and myrtle
All of your candles have passed under the bridge
And you have gone so far out at sea!
"So where is Basra?"[21]
"Indeed, where is Basra?"
"Basra is in the heart's intentions."
"My intentions are pure, made of such innocent, blind faith
Where is Basra?  Where is Basra, I miss it so!
My compass indicates several Basras.
For months now my heart can rejoice only among the palm-trees."
"Do you navigate with a compass?"
"When it is advantageous to do so."
"Haven't you gotten dizzy?"
"Only when I have lost hope."
"Oh, you on that exhausted raft
You call it a ship, no harm in that.
Be as optimistic as you want, call it whatever you want
But lackeys have been conspiring a deal on the oil of Basra
While al-Mutawakkil[22] the leader has been preoccupied with a mole
             on his testicles
Let the wind gently rock this boat
Relax, take it easy, it's not the end of the world.
Stretch your arms
The sun will soothe your exhausted body,
let it flow into your body and you will become as strong as a palm frond.


The poor, made of tattered rags of the night,
and of the fear of Mutawakkil,

have thronged together at the gates of Basra
wth palm fronds and disease
as their weapons.
The coldness of the night has extinguished their zealous lamps,
al-Sayyab was with the children, shaking his palm frond.[23]

They have been waiting for you for so long!
Show them the strength of the palm frond!
Show them the strength of the palm frond!
Go ahead, take a gulp of wine to invigorate and sharpen your senses
Behold! Your lanterns are trembling
the delightful shivers of intoxication
"What can you tell us?"
"I dance before it starts –
Let me show you my joy, here I am dancing, laughing[24]
Look at me, look at me! –
Until the dance attains a sober, dignified air."
I have resisted and fought against all of the sharks
with this palm frond
which only sharpened its stalk.
I hoisted the flag up onto it, do you hear?
Right there in the midst of the castrated ships,
bearing two giant roasting skewers.
The descendants of Basra infuse you with the forces of light
How wondrous it is, and oh, my lord, how beautiful are these eyes.

"You have been at sea for two oppressive decades,
Hasn't the salt of grief eaten away at your sides?"
"I just held fast to this palm-frond.
Whoever has a palm frond in the night will be saved
So hold on to your fronds tightly, all of you."[25]
"And what about the loneliness, oh captain?
Answer us – how could you stand the loneliness?"

You lower your eyes a bit,
"I used it to kindle people's passion, which cured my gloom."
"Oh, lord of the stormy sea, did you also manage to find love?"
"More than there is on earth and on a
calm, peaceful day.
She has the most beautiful of *hamza's*
and the most beautiful *mim* I have ever known."
The abandoned children of squalor listened to you
for you teach like a prophet
If you come to Basra, Hassan of Basra[26]
will

refuse to acknowledge you
Oh, how this Hassan of Basra fluctuates and waffles,
Oh, how they bared your thighs,
which rejoiced like a bull just set free to copulate
with the ruling party.
At which people gasped, and averted their eyes from the sight
They said: "Heaven help us, he cannot be human!"
He has flaunted the lowest, most degraded acts imaginable
right in the face of the authorities
for all to see.
He has incited even the most lowly.
"Your Excellency, what he teaches is very different
from the teachings of our high priests
And he has ridiculed all of our temples.
Your Highness, we have a suspicion that he
loves the wooden bridge of Karkh,
and not the Bridge of the Danube."[27]


Gasps and groans of disapproval arose from all sides of the gathering

"He's committing international blasphemy!
He's impaling the conventions of the notable classes
Raising up bull's testicles
Jeering and ridiculing right in front of the palaces
of the ladies and gentlemen of the republic!
He's reviling our way of thinking!"
They said "He should be killed. Exiled!
To kill him is not enough!
He must be mutilated after being killed three times."


"Oh!" cried the rat-ministers, "he is stepping on the tail of the Minister
    of Oil!"
[Applause]
They say that the Minister of Oil has a tail that he keeps hidden
[Laughter] [28]
"Oh! cried the rat-ministers, "he is stepping on the tail of the Minister
    of Oil!"
They say that the Minister of Oil has a tail that he keeps hidden
    in an American pocket!
[Laughter, strong applause]
"Oh!" cried the rat-ministers, "he is stepping on the tail of the Minister
    of Oil!"
They say that the Minister of Oil has a tail that he keeps hidden
    in an American pocket,

with which he casts his vote against terrorism.
Your Excellency, he claims that the sheikhs
of Abu Dhabi, Bahrain and Ras al-Khayma
are concealing tails thinner than a rat's tail,
and when they bend over, bowing down to worship the shah,
it sticks out a little from beneath their robes.
[Strong applause]
Your Excellency, he claims that the sheikhs
of Abu Dhabi, Bahrain and Ras al-Khayma
are concealing tails thinner than a rat's tail,
and when they bend over, bowing down to worship the shah,
it sticks out a little from beneath their robes,
an auspicious sign of the impaling stick to come!
[Applause]
And  when they bend over, bowing down to worship the shah,
it sticks out a little from beneath their robes,
an auspicious sign of the impaling stick to come!
I'm going to shove it up your asses!
[Applause]

You worms, I am going to impale you![29]
Did you hear what I said, ruler of Basra?
I'm going to shove it right up your ass!
Those who were dying of hunger cried out,
"The victorious impaling stick has risen, impale! impale!"
Bring on the Syphilis King!
This king delights in getting the rod up his ass! Impale him!
Those who were dying of hunger cried out,
"The victorious impaling stick has risen, impale, impale, impale him!"
Bring on the Syphilis King!
This king delights in getting the rod up his ass!
Behold, here is a party that chooses to get impaled of its own free will,
"there is no coercion" or any such crap![30]

Oh, master, carry your palm-frond now, like a prophet
Shake them out of their scorpion nests  by force
"Oh esteemed ruler," cried the sanctimonious ones,
"in his poetry, he embellishes holy sentences
with words that embarrass the dictionary!"
What can I do if so many of the vilest of insults
glisten so copiously on your beards?

Another rotten, despicable one of them
who was croaking among the people added:

"You used to drain our revolutionary charge!
"You son of negative charges!"[31]
[*Laughter, applause*]
"What can I do if your party's battery is empty?"
Another one had the look on his face of someone surprised
at unexpectedly getting a menstrual period, saying
"You have made some arrangement with the authorities,
insulting them, while getting us into trouble!"

Beware of listening to what they say, be strong!
Whatever they may say, the fact is that you teach like a prophet.
The mariner of mariners has truly given you the key,
and he has given you the palm-frond.
He has given you the stars of the Milky Way,
and has given you the gift of being able to be a child
when it is time for play
and a sword when things get serious.
"So what things did you see?
And what things do you see?"
"I see nothing but the helm."
"That's just sea-foolishness!
Your knowledge is becoming very mysterious and cryptic now,
the veil of language has blinded you."

"But master, where is Basra?
And what do I care about the sea if it cannot take me to Basra?"[32]
"The sea will not take you to Basra."
"Yes it will!"
"The sea will not take you to Basra!"
"Yes, the sea
*will* take me to Basra!!"
"No, we tell you, the sea will not take you to Basra!"
"Then I will carry the entire sea and take myself there
Or Basra will come to me, God willing, by the law of desire,
and I will carry her back!"
"And if you are delayed by bad weather, then what?"

Oh, birds of promise, come here!
Your cries, mixed with the dawn,
presage the arrival of the mariner of mariners,
and whatever the storm of the ebbing tide did to him in the night,
did his devoted heart start wavering with misgivings?
Did he have what he needed in the way of provisions, sea-knowledge,
and lost paradise anguish to see him through?
The storm of lies wreaked havoc with the glories of his youth.

I know him, I know this mariner of mariners
He would never leave the bosom of his battle-ship!
The bad times have sprinkled him with salt,
his fingers have grown grease-stained from his diligence at the helm.
The ships of dwarfs claimed they would accompany him
but then capsized when they saw him on the wave
celebrating the cosmic wrath, receiving lightning bolts from God,
and the signs of earthquakes and thunder.
He would gather up the most loyal sailors of those days
and those at the ebbing tides, far and near,
and they would try to decipher how many years it would take
for the tide to come in.

The mariner of mariners is infinite and limitless.
Boats for hire, however, have their limits.
With a drop of ink between his eyebrows that was wise about
the weather and the ways of the sea, he said:
"The book of the sea is a book of many changes, oh beloved ship-mates.
The truly expert sailor is the one who can predict change before it happens.
If such a sailor errs,
it is only because the North Star has changed its position.
This unshakable wisdom has been passed down by sailors
from generation to generation.

One of the waves hit the rudder,
and the ship lost its balance for a moment.
He stared, between dreaminess and wakefulness.
This is a fateful night.
The ship's timeworn wood sharpened the waves' fangs.
"Cast the anchor . . . I think I see fire!"
He pointed his thick finger towards the faint light
at the end of the horizon
as if there was a port concealed behind the cosmos.
On the boat there was an icy-cold wind
that blinded the sailors' faces
except for those who had faith.

"Captain!" said the one standing at the lookout,
with white rain cleansing his prophecy with pureness
"Captain! Hold onto your lamp with the tenacity of ten lives,
for the way to the port is frightening,
and in the middle of the night,
the route to the shipyard for repairs is a most perilous one,
with many dangerous lairs."

And there was one well-known sailor,
the sea had dwelt within him for a long time,
and the traces of torture had been growing upon his thighs
since the time of apostasy.
Take your knife, we are not safe along this coast.
Behold the spreading trees of blood of the two brothers,[33]
that bespeak horrible events . . .
The darkness is monstrous indeed,
and the night may be overturned against our will.
Judas is hidden among some people,
in spite of all appearances of goodness.
We pray for God to protect you, oh master of our ship.
The merchants dealing in morals are many, so make haste!

The master came down,
and disappeared behind some of the more suspicious pathways
in search of a way to repair the ship,
this was of utmost importance!
Just at that moment everything began to break out and gush forth,
the blood of the two brothers flowed, and it stained the clothes
of the one who was forced to traverse the precarious byways
Someone will be killed on this night
Someone will be killed on this night
or bribed.
Or maybe something unforeseen will happen.
We considered every possibility
except that the port itself would be the killer
except that the port itself would rise up to the boat,
tempting some of the sailors to cast the anchor once and for all.
We considered every possibility
except that some of the sailors we trusted
would turn out to be collaborators.

The lantern of experience was extinguished
Neither star nor familiar moon shone
The lowly assemblage of troops gathered together,
then began dividing up,
charging and attacking, tearing at your clothes
Your heart felt the coldness of their dagger
This adventure was destined to happen.
The captain whispered under his breath:
"It was a false, deceptive fire,
the book of the sea is a book of many changes,
oh you lovers of our ship."

He took out faded pages that time had eaten away
and examined two ancient maps, and lost himself in them
The god of the night said: "Your fears are unfounded.
The ships of the revolution will be repaired,
and will again set sail,
and even if they stop, the port will stretch out to reach them."
The mariner answered: "Oh lord! The water!
The water has seeped into our ship!"
"The ships of those who are loyal are not sunk by water,"
the lord responded.
"Except for when the heart begins to doubt its strength,
and when the spirit grows tired."

The mariner of mariners sent his keen intuition out to test the sea
He leafed through the pages of God's Quran,
God's Gospel and Marx's Capital for a long time
There he saw the white bear and the fair-haired bear and the apes,
and some sailors who conspired to toy with his beard[34]
He vowed, in the name of the people and all the days of hardship
To fight against them until the boat reached its destination again,
or to die trying, but victorious.

He stood the test well in the night
struggling in desolation for over two decades
and felt dizzy and seasick for months, the life draining out of him,
but still he managed to advance the ship, to keep sailing
Everything got mixed and blurred together:
dry land and sea, clouds and stars, weariness and the night.

The conspirers arrested his power[35]
He was lowered into the darkness of a vault
in which a scorpion cannot trust its mate.
They revived him with musk, saying
"We don't want to harm you, we only wish you well –
why should you feel unsafe?
Take whatever you want from the port.[36]
Lend us the boat and the crystal compass
and we will dispatch the fortunes of Abu Abbas al-Saffah.[37]
For the emir of Basra is waiting, and the Arab League is waiting."
"God forbid, I shall not betray even a piece of straw on this ship."

How beautiful, master, you have such sumptuous wisdom,
How magnificent, how wondrous, how beautiful you were
when you stood your ground, unflinching, firm.

How beautiful you were
when you spat on the "deal" being offered.
You took delight in your firmness, you stood firm, may God affirm you
Some foamed in a rage, others trembled and shook
The powers fantasized that you would comply
A cross was brought in at night, and you were hoisted up onto it
How beautiful you were, adding another light along the road.
I know when you are alone you cry,
"Where is Basra?"
"Oh lord," you cried, "hasn't it arrived yet?"
You heard a foul, tumultuous noise,
Throughout the night you were enduring death,
while they celebrated, having looted the boat,
stolen the crystal compass,
and arrested the sailors.

They came to you again in the morning
offering you the same "deal"
Again, while being tortured, you spat on them
They went on tormenting you for a long time,
and prevented you from seeing the wooden bridge of Karkh.

How trivial and worthless they are!
They silenced your voice.
How ridiculous and worthless they are!
They claimed you were insane, a sufi lunatic, and a communist –
how could you be of all of these?!
How worthless, how trivial, how insignificant they are!
They carried away the port, the treasury, your red flag,
and even the bushel of eggplant!
How all of these?
The bald one who dyed his white hair said:
"To conceal the deal, your body
will be left for the owls and ravens to eat,
and we will sail on without you.
So accept our deal before you miss your chance
Participate in the "peaceful solution" just a little bit."
You sons of bitches, how can you participate "just a little bit?"[38]
[Applause]
They carried away the port, the treasury, your red flag,
and even the bushel of eggplant!
How all of these?
The bald one who dyed his white hair said:
"To conceal the deal, your body

will be left for the owls and ravens to eat,
and we will sail on without you.
So accept our deal before you miss your chance
Participate in the "peaceful solution" just a little bit."
You sons of bitches, how can you participate "just a little bit?"
You mean getting half-sodomized?
[Applause]

Your spirit grew disgusted
You were like someone forced to swallow a rat
The sea grew agitated, and the horrors glowered
A powerful wind almost overturned all principles of the sea
The ship's wheel began spinning around them
Nearly knocking over the one who held onto it protectively
They got all confused and bewildered,
deception and trickery surrounded them
Secretly they conspired: Cast the anchor!
We will negotiate with this loathsome fate again
My master, they did not know the ways of the sea,
As for the crystal compass, it laughed as it was extinguished
They stood in front of you, and the dripping sweat soiled them,
They preached unity,
but they added a tribal tail to their divisive regionalism.
You saw the white foam drying on their backs
It was hard for you to see this,
for you longed to stand alone at the helm
Only you,
only at the touch of your strong, determined hands
does the helm respond and rise
You alone sail through the night, and have no cross and no idol
Your flag is the palm-frond, and the waves kiss your courage.

They reached for your legs, and cried out, overcome by the wind:
"Mariner of mariners!
You will get one third of the ship if you deliver our cargo,
its owner will say "I am indebted to you,
and any of the sailors that you want will be eternally at your service!"
You glowered at them:
Lying sons of bitches,
they're selling you one third of a ship in exchange for your life?
then granting you the favour of serving their master?
I spit again, for here is exactly the right place for spitting, and so I spit!
You weep in anger
You curse all of the whore-houses of Basra
in this flowering age of the republic.

They have prevented you from seeing the wooden bridge of Karkh
And these nine years[39] have made you melt with sadness
They said that your voice violates the values of the republic
By god, your mere existence scandalizes them.
"Take part in the peaceful solution just a little bit!"
You have been visited by a Baghdad childhood,
and Sitt Nafisa[40]
and the wooden bridge.

We have seen him courting and singing such heartfelt praise
of this wooden bridge.
Who could love an old bridge?
He used to kiss the lantern of the bridge
and write verses of passion.
He travelled all over the civilized world,
he saw the bridge of the Danube, but he did not like it.
He sailed on a small raft that could not even cross a narrow canal,
On that night, oh . . .
Oh, what a night!
You became sick, at people, at all the wildflowers
reading even the asterisks that separate between the Quranic verses.
You order the wave to be calm
and all paths to paradise have been cut off
There is nothing, except for a mountain
forming a circle around your throat,
and from behind the sea-fog,
your heart smokes all the night
as a sign of love and presence.

If the longing becomes too strong and overwhelms it,
then the heart will catch fire
and the perfumed essence of the Absolute
will become one with the mariner
When incomprehension overwhelms all
and the paths become confused and entangled
When despair has reached its limit,
and the blaze of fever shakes the dust off your soul and off the wind
and the boat has rocked from one abyss to the next, oh master,
Then unfurl your soul into the timid wood
And the balance of the world and the cosmos will be restored.

This land is called "The daughter of the morning"
This land is called "The daughter of the morning"
The wandering Arabs left her behind,
gathering pomegranate blossoms
at the Mediterranean.
They journeyed across two deserts,
and when they noticed they'd forgotten her,
they found all the filth of the world in her
and they recited an elegy.

This land is called "The daughter of the morning"
This land is called "The daughter of the morning"
The wandering Arabs left her behind,
gathering pomegranate blossoms
at the Mediterranean.
They journeyed across two deserts,
and when they noticed they'd forgotten her,
they found all the filth of the world in her
and they recited an elegy.

Do the dead care how their graves are decorated?
Does the ewe care about the shape of the slaughtering knife?
What consummate dissonance!
A breast on the ground,
lying next to two small hands
the size of  grapeleaves
A child grows up among the burnt corpses
Oh betraying Arabs, recite your elegy![41]

Do the dead care how their graves are decorated?
Does the goat think about its pastures
as it is being readied for slaughter?
What are the merchants of al-Sham cooking on hell's fire?
The plague is imminent
when a troubled star full of holes appears
it emits a deadly light
that illuminates the eye-sockets of a skull
the wind flickers and plays inside it
at Tal Zaatar.[42]

All the dust of the world
cannot close the eyes of a skull

searching for a homeland.
The capital of the poor has fallen, just a little while ago[43]
And in response?
Impotent castanets are clicking and jangling all the way to the White House
The testicles of the Arab leaders trembled with pride.

Over here, you sons of bitches
shouted the light-haired fatso
He gunned down a child
pulled the pacifier, all bloodied, out of its mouth
and decorated himself with it as a medal.
Here, you sons of bitches, right over here!
The children froze, and despair wiped the features off their faces
God stood with the dirty children,
The capital of the poor has fallen!
[Applause][44]

A child tried to cover the corpse of his grandmother
For it is shameful for a grandmother's thighs to be exposed
They gunned him down, and he fell, right on top of her thighs . . .
There, there, my son, it's alright, this way
her thighs will be covered.
Does a woman in a tent give birth to an army?
You sons of filth, sons of Palestine
You will return to the land of Palestine, alright
but as corpses.
The children looked to the Arab nation for help:
the testicles of the Arab leaders trembled with pride.
Naft ibn Kaaba announced . . . that a meeting would be called.[45]
Now is not the time for commentary.

The time will come for that, that too will come, that too will come,
The wild card in this game has become known
[Applause]
The children looked to the Arab nation for help:
the testicles of the Arab leaders trembled with pride.
Naft ibn Kaaba announced . . . that a meeting would be called.
Now is not the time for commentary.
The time for that will come too, it will come,
The wild card in this game has become known
As has the one who gets cut swallowing razor-blades against his will.

How can you not see the rottenness?
Oh wise ones, the capital of the poor has fallen

because of the rottenness!
As they say, in ancient times a rat destroyed the Great Dam of Ma'rab[46]
and it has fallen!
Lined up, women raise their arms in the air,
and walk, one by one.
The pregnant woman walks around with the
site of her womanhood exposed
He shoved the pregnant woman down to the ground
They pulled out a womb
in which a *fedayee*[47] was being formed in the night.

Have you heard, oh Arabs of silence?[48]
Have you heard, accursed Arabs?
The hatred has reached the wombs!
Have you heard, accursed Arabs?
Palestine is being erased from the womb!
The adherents of the American religion in Mecca
and the market are at their peak!
It's a public auction, oh noble ones!
Thirty killed in an hour, oh noble ones
Eighty for the merchants of al-Sham
Eighty-eight for the Kuweiti cancellation of the constitution
Ninety for the Petrol King
Look here, you filthy bastards
Anyone who slows down is shot by a machine-gun.
Silence, silence, silence . . .
What is this silence called in Arabic?

The rivers of joy sank quickly in the night.
The dead children twitched as one body,
The dust of the earth has made the savagery known
Hatred is not enough any more.
We have heard your cry again,
God rose up from the earth
holding the entrails of children in his pleading hands
He wept in embarrassment and shame in the night.[49]
He begged the people to return to Tel Zaatar
God too is from the capital of the poor
He has gotten used to these neighbours
He has gotten used to the clothes strung between the tents
He would even gather up their clothes from the line sometimes.

Don't come near! Don't come near! Don't come near!!
Let the children's flesh play its last game

of hide-and-seek
No one shall ever interrupt this game.
The testicles of treachery have swelled and grown.
Have you heard? Have you heard?
I hear the voice of the angry people in my flesh
Don't take revenge, don't take revenge, don't take revenge!
What is the price of one child?
What is the price of a dimple?
What is the price of two eyes laughing in the morning?
What is the price of a healthy pregnancy in the corner of a tent,
with the betrayers at the door?
What is the price of lips nursing and gurgling?
No! No! No!!!
Do not come near!
The flesh of the children will play a final game of hide-and-seek
The killer must have something besides killing
The killing here seems so meagre to him!

Twenty for the beard of Qaboos[50]
A public auction
Seventy for the lion on the Iranian flag
A public auction, gentlemen, let's go
Ninety for the summit conference
The fig-leaf has fallen.[51]

The noble ones came down from the summit
with their genitals exposed
Among them was Mr Silent by God[52] trying to cover up his genitals
The most embarrassed of all was the old hairy mammoth
[Applause]
The noble ones came down from the summit
with their genitals exposed
Among them was Mr Silent by God trying to cover up his genitals
The most embarrassed of all was the old hairy mammoth
The silent masses averted their eyes.
This is truly shameful!

Don't come any closer!!
The circle is closing in on the massacre
The corpses of the children are joyless,
I detect the smell of nursing babes
and their green talismanic beads
sprouting in the burnt flesh
Were they really children such a short time ago?

Don't allow any child to pass through this alley
The burnt flesh will smile at him, for him
The Church of Mar Sharbal burns children![53]
This flesh gives off a rosy smoke
making even the cheek of religion blush red
Go away, go away, get out of here, get out, go away!
Step further away!

Keep the lights away, and let Tel Zaatar get used to the darkness.
It's not time yet
The capital of the poor has fallen
I will not cry over these glorious fighters
I will not cry at all
I only pity and cry for the one who is seeking his state[54]
at a summit meeting
[Applause]
I will not cry at all
I will not cry over these glorious fighters

The noble ones came down from the summit
With the traces of rubbing their heads together
showing on their foreheads
The most embarrassed of all was the old hairy mammoth
Have you ever seen someone carrying around an extinct tusk?
Arrest him!
For he is the king of all of the whole lot of those pimps
He sank into the mud of betrayal, except for the tip of the tusk
which could still be seen
He spread mud and dirt on all of the cloven-hoofed creatures
He made the betrayal total
He united the flags of treachery
The trumpet-blowers chewed their cud
The darkness is deadly.

This is an Arab night.
The massacre was conveniently extinguished before the summit meeting
I accuse the mammoth of Nejd[55] and his disciple,[56]
The pimp of Syria and his side-kick
The judge of Baghdad and his testicle
The King of Syphilis[57] . . . little Hassan the Second[58]
The blotted rat of filth in the Sudan[59]
And the one sitting beneath the square root sign on the sand[60]
of Dubai, all wrapped up in his robe
And the one in Tunis too, all bow-legged from calf to neck.

*[Applause]*
I accuse the mammoth of Nejd and his disciple,
The pimp of Syria and his side-kick
The judge of Baghdad and his testicle
The King of Syphilis . . . little Hassan the Second
The blotted rat of filth in the Sudan
And the one sitting beneath the square root sign on the sand
of Dubai, all wrapped up in his robe
And the one in Tunis too, all bow-legged from calf to neck.

Alright, alright, I'll make an exception, for the poor wretch
in Ras al-Khayma
*[Laughter and applause]*
And the one in Tunis too, all bow-legged from calf to neck.
Okay, I'll make an exception for the poor wretch in Ras al-Khayma.
He was day-dreaming during the crisis
With his lower lip drooping like a camel's
I'll make an exception for the poor wretch in Ras al-Khayma
He was day-dreaming during the crisis,
With his lower lip drooping like a camel's
And his nose was like a howdah atop a hump.

Don't come near!
Be the night![61]
Be fate itself!
and dark ambiguous entities,
with no lanterns.
Don't come near!
Be fate itself!
and dark ambiguous entities,
with no lanterns.
With no oriental shrieking to spoil this butchery
which needs to be nursed.

Proceed in silence, be the night!
Chanting in blood
Whoever got mutilated,
Or died a slow death,
Will march at the front of the funeral procession
And the gouged-out eye, and the severed hand
The severed thigh, the burnt corpses
Will be hoisted up in clear view

The sea-captain says:
No oriental wailing
and very slowly.
Slower, slower, slower . . .
Leave the bodies just as they are
Slower now, slow down.
This kind of slow, measured pace is dignified.
Now they've placed the slaughter
at their Excellencies' religious bank account.
The account of the financial religion
The slaughter account.
Honourable fathers of the West:
Greetings!
Now they've placed the slaughter
at their Excellencies' religious bank account.
The account of the financial religion
The slaughter account.
Greetings, honourable fathers of the West,
and salutations
We're oriental filth
We've come to extend this thanks to you.

You who love our ship, whispered the captain,
No wailing, no oriental shrieking
Proceed in rows, for the West loves order
It has no interest in backward displays of emotion
welling up from the miserable East.
Who are those people, anyway?
Garbage, oriental filth
They're far beneath your rank, oh lords of capital
We are oriental filth
The most worthless kind of dust
We present our corpse as a down-payment for your friendship

Slower, slower . . .
Article Three will watch from the window
Article Three of the treaty ratified
between the Soviet Union and the United States[62] in Glasgow
Just who are those people, anyway?
Garbage, oriental filth
They're far beneath your rank, oh lords of capital
The most worthless kind of dust
We present our corpse as a down-payment for your friendship
Slower, slower, slower . . .

Article Three will watch from the window
And will bless this peaceful settlement of slaughter
Praise Article Three!
Glory be to Glasgow!
Bless the agreement of the two bears!
The priests made us fear nuclear bombs
But they've slaughtered many times more people than that
This logic has holes in it, and delivers death,
and squadrons, and oil treaties
So slow down, slower, slower . . .
Why hurry?
The forces of deterrence have arrived
The honchos of the summit meeting,
in spite of their differences of opinion,
have all joined together.
The deterrent forces are here
The miracle of the twentieth century has happened!
[Applause]
The deterrent forces are here
The miracle of the twentieth century has happened!
With oil we have destroyed Lebanon,
And with oil we will build Lebanon
Oh God, enough of this shame!
Oh Lord, enough of these bulls!
Oh Lord, enough!
Here is my roasting skewer,
I will heat it to red-hot with the hatred
boxed inside my heart,
a prisoner of the slaughter-house,
fire burns within.
Lord, we extend your righteous path all the way
to the victims of Tel Zaatar
and Damur.


Let's bring on the apes!
You apes! You animals!
I challenge any of you to raise your eyes as high
as the shoes of a
*fedayee,* you apes!
[Applause]
I challenge any of you to raise your eyes as high
as the shoes of a
*fedayee,* you apes!
The hell-fire here is no laughing matter, you apes

The enraged people have come
I hear intestines churning with the pain of hunger
and rage
They're all coming bearing two skewers, one in each hand
Oh lord, enough of this shame
Oh lord, enough worthless leaders who are full of holes!
[Applause]
Oh lord, enough of this shame
Oh lord, enough worthless leaders who are full of holes!
Now is the time for hell-fire!

Toss the first of the treacherous dwarfs into the fire
Bring that other one too!
"Who are you?"
"I am Yatruq . . ."
"You son of a . . .

Toss him in too!
Bring the pot-bellied one!
Have the masses of Bahrain bring him here!"
"I swear, by God, I am Sheikh so-and-so the son of Sheikh so-and-so,
grandson of the Sheikh . . . "
"Enough of this filthy tribe!"
[Applause]
"And who are you?
Throw him in too!
Bring the pot-bellied one!
Have the masses of Bahrain bring him here!"
"I swear, by God, I am Sheikh so-and-so the son of Sheikh so-and-so,
grandson of the Sheikh . . . "
"Enough of this filthy tribe!"
The fire of God will roast you, head-coil, fattened belly and all!
Here is my skewer, oh lord,
I'm heating it up.
We will have no mercy on them.
Lower them slowly into the fire
For centuries they've been enjoying themselves at our expense
For centuries they've been roasting the people on the fire of their spits

Slower . . . slower . . . slower . . . slower . . .
We'll recite the graves of children
and sit in front of the Church of Rome[63]
We'll display all of our goods
Gentlemen, oh gentlemen!

Tourists from the civilized world!
You with the fancy perfume!
This is Tel Zaatar!
Here is the frail collar-bone of Fatima the daughter of so-and-so
And here is so-and-so, some anonymous filth,
who died on the bridge of return
Here are some top-quality skulls,
you can make Christmas lanterns out of them
The most beautiful icons and relics imaginable!
These blackened vertebrae belong to
two orphaned children from the slaughter-house
who burned alive clinging to each other
[Applause]
These blackened vertebrae belong to
two orphaned children from the slaughter-house
who burned alive embracing each other.

Go ahead, touch them, touch them
Have no fear
This oriental filth is cheap
Oh, you sir, from the Land of Freedom
These gouged-out eyeballs are the latest models
Produced by the Statue of Liberty
These aren't made of porcelain!
These gouged-out eye sockets, not of clay.
It's genuine, from a body that used to shine like a candle!
Then the sons of Chamoun roasted it to get rid of
the revolutionary thoughts.[64]
That's all we are . . . bones, a skull, dung, orphans
But we will take history by storm
That's all we are . . . bones, a skull, dung, orphans
But we will take history by storm
And we will fill your world with the suspicious poor
We will strike at your comfort, house by house,
We will choke you by day and by night
God forbid feelings of mercy be aroused in any one of you
It would be easier to get mercy from a stone.
I invite you to a spectacle of oriental splendour
For your pleasure, I swear, just for your pleasure

Naft ibn Kaaba declared . . .
What did Naft ibn Ka'ba declare?
The whole world is preoccupied
The calculator has gone haywire!

There is no power and no strength save in God
Naft ibn Kaaba doesn't know what Naft ibn Kaaba declared!
[Applause]
I swear, this is just for your pleasure
Naft ibn Ka'ba declared . . .
What did Naft ibn Ka'ba declare?
The whole world is preoccupied
The calculator has gone haywire
There is no power and no strength save in God
Naft ibn Kaaba doesn't know what Naft ibn Kaaba declared.
Naft ibn Kaaba is so surreal!
My god, enough of these cows!
Oh lord, enough of these rulers who are full of holes
Every poor person shall carry two angry skewers
Come join together all you wretched of the earth
We'll tear the masks off the whoring classes
A cat could eat what feeds a whole family for a year in Aden
The big companies rob us,
then issue instructions
The terrorist Arab thieves
roam the airports of the world
In the airports of the sons of pigs and perfume,
we are searched thoroughly
We are searched right down to our vertebrae
The police dog is trained to detect the smell of an Arab
And to distinguish refugee from non-refugee
These police dogs are definitely
in cahoots with the Arab authorities,
and the American ones,
and the apes.
[Applause]
Apes! You apes!
Gentlemen, tourists of the civilized world!
In the East we have apes for leaders!
I'm sitting in front of the Church of Rome
Displaying all of our goods
Here is the overwhelming Arab hunger that owns all the oil,
Here is half of a Gulf
Here is an accord that will deliver the coast of Basra
Here is Rakhyut[65]
And here gentlemen, all of the tears must be shed
I weep lava.
Has anyone heard of Rakhyut?
Has anyone heard of Rakhyut and Hawfa[66]

No, they are not constellations, or great discoveries
but they are parts of the Arab nation:
a kingdom of hunger, pestilence and vomit
and of revolution as well.
[Applause]
I witnessed it, I saw it with my own eyes:
a pregnant woman eating the vomit of her feverish child
and feeding the other child with the same black vomit
What wonders Arab oil has done for us!
We belch to the point of indigestion from hunger
While the Oil King is afraid of rats getting at his cash
And the West, in all its wondrous nuclear superiority and perfection,
gathers us for oil, and slaughters all of us for oil.
Long live oil!
Long live gas!
Long live the King of Farts![67]
[Applause]
Long live oil, long live gas, long live the King of Farts!
Long live Ras al-Khayma
Long live, long live, the beard of Qaboos ibn Said[68]
Long live, long live, long live oil!
Long live, long live, long live gas!
Long live the King of Farts!
Long live Ras al-Khayma
Long live the beard of Qaboos ibn Said.[69]
Does anyone know the taste of salty vomit?[70]
And does anyone know how the fig-tree,
the precious source of goodness,
was taken away from her hands?
She kept looking around until it dried up
and almost died.
Just then a root extended and lengthened
and sipped the water of paradise from the hand of God
For the fig-tree in the Arab land will never die.
This fig-tree could not be beaten by Khartit![71]
It debilitated the Allies
and exhausted the Shah
In your name, in your name, in your name[72]
I declare out loud
I call upon the people
Upon everyone to bear two giant skewers
Covered with nails
Now, now, and not tomorrow![73]
The doors of the Arab nation will be closed to the ruling apes!

Apes, apes, apes!
Ape-regimes!
Ape-parties!
Ape-institutions!
No, no! Even the droppings of apes are more respectable than you!
They fought amongst themselves: the swords of Sunna and Shi'a
And the Allawites and even the old extinct fossils[74]
Rams clashing horns
Bulls mounting each other
Fates playing music that forces the rats to dance.
Then they all gathered underneath his robe
and sealed the deal with a kiss.
And Naft ibn Kaaba announced . . .
What did Naft ibn Kaaba announce?
Naft ibn Kaaba calls a meeting . . .
and the prices go up.
Naft ibn Kaaba goes to relieve himself . . .
and the prices hold steady.
How wondrous is this community of apes!
And the bone, oh Naft ibn Kaaba!
You choke with the bone of Fatima the daughter of so-and-so
and that so-and-so died on the bridge of return,
we didn't have time to bury him.
This bone from Fatima the daughter of so-and-so
These burnt vertebrae could be used as rosary beads
For the religious clergymen
This excellent brown vomit from Rakhyut
Does anyone here know about Rakhyut?
This is the declaration of the armies of betrayal
This is Tel Zaatar
This is Damur
And Sinai, and Antakiah, and Greater Tunub
and Lesser Tunub, and Abu Musa, and all the rest.[75]
But gentlemen
No one will dine on the Arab East on a golden platter.

Naft ibn Kaaba announced
That a meeting would be convened
It's coincidence, I swear, sheer coincidence
That there were six members
And that the corners of the star are six in total
Oh, star of David, rejoice
Oh, Masonic Lodge, go wild with delight
Oh, finger of Kissinger . . .
For the royal asshole is hexagonal!

## Notes

1   The name of the letter in Arabic is *"nun"* (pronounced like "noon"); it has a "dot" placed near the middle and above the other written part of the letter (loosely comparable to the "dot" of the English letter "i"), and its sound value is comparable to that of the English letter "n". *"Niswa"* means "women" in Arabic.

2   This is a reference to a famous love poem by Abdulla Abu Sakhr al-Hudhali (d. 700 AD), the "r's" referring to the monorhyming endings of its verses with the letter *raa* in Arabic, the rough phonetic equivalent of the letter "r" in English.

3   Reference presumably to the Baath party.

4   *Hamza* is another letter of the Arabic alphabet, having the sound value of a "glottal stop" in English, as in the glottal stop of words beginning with vowels, such as "and" or "often," although it is considered a consonant in Arabic.

5   He uses the expression *"hukkam al-ridda"* here – an allusion to those "rulers of apostasty" who betrayed Abu Bakr in early Islamic times – to refer to contemporary Arab leaders.

6   A reference to the pre-Islamlic poet Qais ibn Dharih, who is well known for his love poetry dedicated to his beloved Lubna, from whom he was forced by his parents to separate.

7   The seventh key of the musical scale.

8   References here are again to the letter *hamza* of the Arabic alphabet mentioned above, and the letter *mim* which corresponds phonetically to the letter "m" in English.

9   Traditional (i.e. pre post-colonial demarcation into 'nation-states') way of referring to the area of "Greater Syria", spanning much of what today is Syria, Lebanon and Palestine.

10   Ali Ibn Jahm (born c. 804 AD), a Baghdad-based court poet under the reign of al-Mutawakkil (847-61 AD) who ultimately fell from favour, and was imprisoned and punished for unbridled expression. (These threads of his life-story have clear parallels with that of Muzaffar al-Nawwab).

11   Ramallah, Bab al-Khalq, Targhuna are locations in various parts of the Arab world.

12   Here Nawwab is alluding to a *hadith* that relates an exchange between Muhammad, Gabriel and God, which makes reference to God's determination of the gender of an unborn child.

13   Here the poet adapts a traditional Islamic reference, to give a new, irreverent meaning. His formulation in Arabic *(idha aamana bi-al-hizb al-haakim, fa-al-jannat(u) ma'waahu* – meaning, 'if he believes in the ruling party, the paradise is his lot / place') echoes and resonates with the Quranic reference *(idha aamana bi-allah fa-al-jannat(u) ma'waahu* – 'if he believes in Allah, then paradise is his lot').

14   He repeats the segment immediately preceding the applause, starting from "the mariner of mariners was silent" to "then paradise is his lot." This seems to be a pattern in his performance: if he receives enthusiastic applause for a particular segment or line, he goes back and repeats that segment.

15   The same wording used here by Nawwab, *"waylun lil-maariqi,"* is found in traditional Islamic sources.

**16**  The implication here is that the police cars are fully loaded up with prisoners they are rounding up in the streets.

**17**  Possibly an allusion to the feverish state of Muhammad, at the time of his prophecy.

**18**  Here again, the reference is to the Arabic letter *nun*, in the Arabic word for women, *niswa*.

**19**  In this section, the poem is composed (and declaimed / performed) in the manner of a dialogue, with one voice asking the other to continue the story, saying "and then?", "and then what happened?" Both to avoid awkwardness, and because in some instances the distinction between dialogue and non-dialogue sections is not altogether clear or unambiguous, I have not placed quotation marks around all such segments.

**20**  Here the poet refers to the renowned schools of grammar that were based in the cities of Basra and Kufa, using them simultaneously to allude to the more contemporary association of Basra with more conservative, right-wing political forces, and of Kufa with those on the left.

**21**  In the coming section the poem is pronouncedly composed and performed as a dialogue between two voices. I have delineated the two voices to the extent that they are clearly distinguished in the poem, by opening and closing quotation marks for utterances by each respective voice.

**22**  Reference here is made to the historical caliph al-Mutawakkil, and two slaves, Wasif and Bagha, who conspired against him.

**23**  A reference to the Iraqi poet Badr Shakir al-Sayyab (1926-1964).

**24**  The sense here conveyed strongly through the tone of his voice, which is in a roused and rousing tone of ecstasy and elation; the text alone does not suffice to convey this.

**25**  The language used here, in Arabic, *("wi'tasimu bi-il-sa'fa jami'an")* echoes and resonates with the Quranic reference *"wi'tasimu bi-habl(i) llaah jami'an"* – ("hold on tightly to God's rope").

**26**  Abu Sa'id al-Hassan al-Basri (632-728 AD) was the leader of a sufi *tariqa* or movement. This segment appears to be alluding to internal conflicts the poet had with the communist party in Iraq.

**27**  Here "Karkh," a major quarter of Baghdad, can be understood to be loosely referring to Baghdad, Iraq, the "east" in a broader sense, and "Danube" to connote Europe, or the "west" at large.

**28**  As evidenced before, an aspect of Nawwab's performance technique is illustrated here: he recites a line, which receives enthusiastic applause, after which he repeats that line or segment before going on to add another line, or "deliver another punch-line." He thereby creates an internal rhythm of performance that builds to a series of "crescendos," both in terms of the intensity and variation of his voice, and in audience response. The performance of his poetry is shaped by a dialogic quality or relationship (between poet and immediate audience) that is only partially evident in a textual transcription / translation. Nawwab's "second-tier" audience, those who listen to taped recordings of his dialogic performance of poetry (and who constitute the vast majority of his listening public), experience the added effect of looking on or listening in to the interaction between the poet and his primary audience, which is crucial to their experience of his poetry.

29   These threats of impaling are uttered in a fierce and loud roar.

30   The language used here *"la ikrah(a) wa-la batikh"* – "there is no coercion or any crap" [the last word is literally "watermelon"] is an irreverent allusion to the traditional Islamic formulation "There is no coercion in religion" *"la ikrah(a) fi al-Deen."* The political party mentioned here may be an allusion to the Communist Party, which has been accused of forming an "unholy alliance" with Saddam Hussein and the Baath party in 1973, conveying here that "no one forced you to do it."

31   Here Nawwab brings up associations with "positive and negative charges" common in Communist Party discourse, as well as the connotation of someone who is a "negative charge" being the one penetrated in homosexual terms.

32   This section of the poem is an internal dialogue in which the narrator speaks to himself in two voices, made distinct in performance by a combination of pauses, and variations in tone of voice.

33   Cain and Abel.

34   To mock his dignity, manipulate him.

35   This is a pun in Arabic, difficult to convey in translation. The expression he uses here (*"alqa al-qabd 'ala qabdatihi"*) combines two idiomatic uses of the word *"qabd;"* *"Alqa al-qabd 'alayhi"* is the common way of saying "they arrested him." Instead, the poet combines *"alqa al-qabd 'ala"* [they arrested s.o.], with *"qabdatihi"* [his grasp, his power], as the object of the verb "arrest."

36   He is being offered a pay-off in exchange for giving up his struggle.

37   The founder of the Abbassid Empire.

38   Here again we see Nawwab's performance technique of repeating a segment after there has been hearty applause, after which he delivers a "punch-line."

39   Of exile.

40   The poet's nanny.

41   The term used here again is *'arab al-ridda.* See n. 5 from translation of Side One of cassette.

42   The Palestinian refugee camp in Lebanon, which suffered a notorious siege and massacre in 1977. This section of the poem focuses on Tal Zaatar, and because of this section, the poem is often informally referred to as the "Tal Zaatar" poem.

43   Beirut.

44   In performing the poem, Nawwab repeats here the section beginning "the plague is imminent" through "the capital of the poor has fallen."

45   A mock-name of an Arab leader of one of the oil-rich states, literally meaning "Oil son of the Kaaba" (the Muslim holy shrine in Mecca).

46   Sed Ma'arab (Dam Ma'arab) is a legendary dam in ancient Yemen. The legend speaks of a rat that kept chipping at the great dam until it collapsed.

47   Guerrilla fighter.

48   He shouts and shrieks this and succeeding lines.

49   This section is read/performed very dramatically by Nawwab on the tape, he does not merely recite, but weeps and shouts the verses.

50 Ruler of the United Arab Emirates, Qaboos ibn Sa'id.

51 In the Arabic original, a mulberry leaf is referred to, but in the sense of the English connotation of a metaphorical fig-leaf (as covering something up, or as dropping off to reveal what lies underneath), so I used the latter in translation.

52 In Arabic it is *al-Samit billah*.

53 A church in Beirut.

54 A reference to the Palestinian leader Yasir Arafat, who has been perceived by the Arab Left as a desperate leader who compromises principles to gain recognition from Arab rulers as leader of a state.

55 Reference to the Saudi ruler.

56 Possibly referring to any of the other "like-minded" Gulf states.

57 Probably referring to King Hussein of Jordan.

58 King Hassan of Morocco, in a diminutive, thus mocking form of his name.

59 Reference to Jaafar Numeiri, then leader of Sudan.

60 Referring to one of the small Emirates.

61 He is addressing a plural subject here, in the Arabic *kunu layl(an)*.

62 SALT (Strategic Arms Limitations Treaty) between the US and the USSR.

63 The Vatican.

64 Reference to the Chamoun family of Lebanon, and the very pro-western Maronite Christian president and politician Camille Chamoun.

65 A town in Iraq.

66 Towns in Iraq.

67 Here the poet puns using the word *"ghaz"* which means gas, or gasoline in the first instance, followed by *"ghazaat"* – the plural form which means bodily gases, intended here to have the humorous and lowly inflection of the word "farts," which it can also have in Arabic.

68 Sultan Qaboos ibn Said, ruler of Oman. Calling explicit attention to the beard in this manner is a common way of mocking someone's dignity, ridiculing them.

69 The performance of this is done in a rousing, boisterous, rhythmic manner, with the crowd (the audience) joining in and clapping to the rhythm. This ends abruptly and dramatically with the final words of this line ("Qaboos ibn Said") before turning joltingly to the sober and graphic tone and image of the next line.

70 Calling back the image of the preceding section, with the pregnant woman eating her child's vomit.

71 A mythical monster.

72 The "your" here is plural in the Arabic, so can be taken to refer to being in the name of the people.

73 This wording, *"al-an, al-an wa-laysa ghadan"* calls to mind the lyrics of the song *al-Quds* by Fairuz.

74 References here are to divisions along religious sectarian lines.

75 Names of towns and locations in various parts of the Arab world.

# Salah Niazi

Translated by Saadi A Simawe and Melissa Brown

## The Thinker Between The Bronze Shield And The Human Flesh

I still live somewhat behind
The locked gates of my hell.
Here I am being held on the walls of the lit halls
And the eyes of people encircling me:
Oh my God, how torturous is the public eye.
The secret guards
And the khaki police
Have mined all my roads and the gardens of my space
Until I have become my own prison and my own fences.
My life insurance cannot understand the nature of my existence.
Such a policy does not know that I am sculpted in a monument:
From no sleep I wake up – the same statue,
The same pose
Without sleep I dream:
If I turned into another person
And saw in my mirror something
That moves like a toy . . .
If I were . . .
But I do not see what I dream of in the mirror.
The footsteps surround me
and eyes stare at me.
Oh, invisibility hat (I wish I owned you) . . .
In my head there are numerous valleys, mysterious labyrinths.
How can I escape, how can I extricate myself?
Can I escape my flesh-metal, can I liberate myself from my moulded blood,
Can I pull out of my steel pedestal
And my theological missions?
The locks have rusted on my lips
And my history, geography, and my school playgrounds
Have become desertified.
My cities are polluted and suffocating
And my villages fight with stones of my steles
My metal muscles cannot gather my body parts.

A few moments and the hall will sink into darkness.
Then where shall I go or how hide from
My grave machine-like face?

How can I escape my philosophy
That forces me to be absolutist?
How can I liberate myself from my own prison
As I believe that my closed fence is nobler than any freedom?
And my redemptive mission
Lies in the fact that I have lived,
Died in my world of oblivion.

The thread that is loose in the wind
Is stronger than a taut one
In my desert there is no Zamzam[1]
Nor is there an anchor in my river.
I closed the wind,
Forcing it to sink into my windowsill.

In the seed of what philosophy has the practice of violence arisen?
Like the semen in the father's loin,
Violence is our great legacy.
Even our children's drawings
From the very beginning
Look like wild jungles
Where battles are fierce, hot and red . . .
From the flame that is painted on the darkness of a blackboard,
The picture grows
And the myth goes on:
Dark "saints"
And black hoods
Passed from here, no ascension was heard
And many candles panted in our hands
And gradually the lights disappeared
And the saints and the hooded men
Departed into a secret dungeon,
And the doors were locked
And the whispers became louder.
The movements of robes were heard.
(The plot is planned and buried in fangs.)
And the fangs clanged
"Hallelujah" . . . Becket returns.[2]
The doors are lit
And the public squares and bars were decorated
And a window sang
And voices uncoiled
Fireworks exploded into an amber rainbow
With khaki music

And the national flags flew high.
Here . . . here children jumped
– Jungles clashed –
Children climbed shoulders
And faces turned pale yellow with fear,
Street vendors danced, holding adorned pictures:
Heroes glow
And heroes are torn to pieces
Like smashed toys,
Only body parts
And broken necks.
Many a nation fell,
And generations come and go
Except for the dark priests
Who smelled blood in the triumphal arch,
For the cathedral
Was an entombment.
O Miriam,
They already knew
The wrong, like the right, had to run its course;
No exit out of the fatal course.
As always,
The hired vassals, the dark priests
Were in the cellar of the cathedral.
Lightning . . . thunder . . . bleeding . . . maggots
And a "horse" abandoned in the historical zoo,
Unaware of what was going on around him,
Unaware of what was going on the government's halls,
Pulling the waterwheel
Gyrating in a coffin.
The conspiracy was hatched again, and again,
And the declaration was announced.
A horse was hanged on the wall, in the horse colours neigh.
Between the throne and the waterwheel there were miles of weeping.

The Chorus was out of tune with the nation:
"We do not want anything to happen,
Seven years we have lived quietly,
Succeeding in avoiding notice,
Living and partly living."[3] . . . etc.
The hired dark priests,
Lightning . . . thunder . . . bleeding . . . maggots
The footsteps encircled me, and staring eyes approaching
Yet I am here: eternally the same, not bigger, not smaller,

In my steel cast.
Scientific terminology
Frightens me like a coffin
Tailored exactly for the corpse.
So where do I turn? Where to escape to, how break loose?
Oh, you, all the birds of the world help and be my dwelling.
Oh, you, all the trees of the world be my cities.
Oh the map of the world be my unknown neighbour.

How much is the noise of the news, running around the clock
About tormented capitals.
Children's drawings accumulate in the news
Like wild jungles,
Clashing hot and bloody.
And from the flame painted on the darkness of the blackboard
The murdered are scattered
And the captives' addresses
And the wives' pictures give birth on the other side.
From which trap should I slip away?
The psychiatric labs,
The scientific interpretations,
The bombings, the political movements, the secret organizations,
The tattered cease-fires
And the news agencies, the newspaper columns
And a recanting of an activist
(Who wishes no one would read it).
There must be a stand
Against the dark followers
And people's eyes surround me, clinking to me:
How frightened, restive the public eye – the leech – makes me?

Oh , invisibility hat!
My head is full of valleys and magical labyrinths,
Between sleep and waking and the hardship of travel,
Train schedules, currency exchanges in another capital.
And we never thought we would go to the next.
And the square is lit, and forests of lights clash
In the billboards:
A plastic girl tells a forbidden love story
About an epileptic woman who convulses like an arch
And about salons pained with the flame of lust
About the rhythm of the drum
The hiss of the flute
And the Arab desert.

Darkness becomes spotted in my eyes
And the sunray gets lost in my thick jungle.
Oh how terrible, the most terrible thing in prison is the windows.
This is my history no time can accept.
My geography is in ruins.
I must run away: for how long must I remain my own prison?
Which direction is my way?
The names of things have intermingled.
The negative is not different from the positive and both are equal to
          nothingness.
What philosophy generated the seed of bloody violence?
The threads of blood
Are dripping in the hats of the dark followers
– My refusal is an attitude, the refusal of my refusal is another attitude,
Is another refusal, is a frame of mind
About a man wandering like a loose thread
Among the worshippers of the past
Who are the slaves of the future.
The present does not appear except at the nightclub
In the wax waists of women.
Where do I begin my history, my geography?
My books kill each other with invisible hands.
The picture,
How does the jungle move in the picture,
And the flame of the painting sizzles in the darkness of the blackboard?
My borders are defeated.
Nothing remains but my illusionary walls.
All kinds of thoughts have penetrated them
So my walls are a sieve.
Light blinds my eyes with bright spots
And empty circles.
I can see neither the light nor the darkness.
Again I am nailed to my steel base,
The public eye – the leech – clinging to me
Through the locked doors of my hell.

How far is the silver disc of the sun from me,
How desolate this grave is, how brutal.

[London, 1971]

**Notes**

[1]  Zamzam: sacred well in Mecca, also called the well of Ismail. The pre-Islamic legend tells that the Zamzam was opened by an angel to save Hagar and her son Ismail, who were dying from thirst in the desert. The water from the well is considered to have healing powers, and Muslim pilgrims still collect it in bottles to bring back to their home countries.

[2]  A reference to both the Archbishop of Canterbury St Thomas Becket's famous murder in Canterbury Cathedral in 1170, and TS Eliot's play about the event, *Murder in the Cathedral*.

[3]  These lines are from TS Eliot's play, *Murder in the Cathedral* in *The Complete Poems and Plays , 1909-1950* ( New York: Harcourt Brace & Company, 1980: 180.)

# Abdula Peshew

Iraqi Kurdish

## Translated by Muhamad Tawfiq Ali

### Fratricide

In this damned country, what haven't you apportioned like
      your own farms?
What used to make us proud was the memory of our martyrs you
have turned into bridges for yourselves.
I dare not carry a pen, I dare not wear a shirt
as you have apportioned even the colours, damn you![1]
Is it student or pupil? Is it woman or lady?[2]
You have divided even the words in the dictionary, damn you!

You divided even the twin shores of the greats Khani and Haji Qadir.[3]
You divided even the natural elements of earth, water and fire.
What have you done? Whom have you spared?
You have apportioned even prostitutes, thieves and robbers.

You have divided one homeland into two.
Roaming town by town, village by village,
you have divided the hearth of each home into two.

Other people have one common history, we have two.
Other people are lumbered with one leadership, we are lumbered
      with two.

Is there anybody who has not heard of Ba'th?
Is there anybody who does not know Ba'th?
Until recently, he was a ruthless thug, a bloodthirsty murderer.
Now, thanks to you, he is back with a vengeance,
incognito like a secret agent, invisible like death.
He has turned into TNT explosive.
He is disguised among the wads of Dinar notes.
He has infiltrated our dining table,
clinging to us by the feet, he follows us everywhere.

In the headlines of your newspapers, I see Ba'th.
In the cabinet posts of your leaders, I see Ba'th.
In the 50/50 power sharing, I see Ba'th.

In the killing of prisoners and extractions of confessions, I see Ba'th.
In the ringing of the bell and the knock on the door at midnight,
        I see Ba'th.

Thanks to you, one of my eyes is dancing with joy
because the other eye is unsightly.
Thanks to you, one of my arteries is hysterical with laughter
at the severance of its fraternal artery.

In my occupied hometown, I see the turban on the head of partisans
which for years looked like a crown.
Now, thanks to you, it almost resembles the helmet of a soldier.

Two dead bodies lie there, brothers they were.
They shared the same dream, but they differed in colour.
The distance between them is bridged by
the burning sighs of a mother and father.
As for their leaders, they are enjoying themselves
in merriment and mirth.
The gap between them is bridged by
the enemy's dining tables with glasses of wine.

**Notes**

1   Yellow and green are the colour codes of the KDP and PUK, respectively.

2   Both KDP and PUK have their own student and women's organisations with differing titles.

3   Ahmedi Khani (1651-1706) and Haji Qadiri Koyi (1817-1897) – poets and early apostles of Kurdish nationalism, in the northern Kurmanji and southern Kurmanji (Sorani) dialects, respectively.

# Abd al-Rahim Salih al-Rahim

Translated by Saadi A Simawe, with Ralph
Savarese, and with Daniel Weissbort

### Everyday

The stubborn donkey
rises up with the rooster at daybreak
to follow exactly the same route.

At nightfall, the stubborn donkey
returns with his heavy load,
exhausted, saturated with sorrows.

The stubborn donkey,
after the usual vicissitudes of life,
stretches his limbs in the dark
and caresses his thoughts
and jumps among the stars
like a distant dream,
ethereal and alone.

[SAS and RS]

### Poisonous Illusions

The stars above
that have always fascinated us
carrying us off into the labyrinth of the imagination
are probably spying on us.
Have they deceived us all these years?
Perhaps it is the stars
in their awesome beauty
that are snatching away our souls.

[27 April 2001]

## The Road

We have lost our way back home
a sudden dread seized us
we may never find our way back
because we are getting further and further away.
We sat on a mound in the wilderness
staring at each other
while the evening bled cold into the sky
and a hollow weeping echoed through our souls:
Why have we lost our way home?
Why have we lost the way?

[14 April 2001]


## Wailing

At midnight
An owl flies from my breast
hooting harshly
the wind snatches up the call
and carries it over highway, track, roof
At once there's an answering call
tearing the night's mute robe
moaning in pain.
At once the two cries join up
wailing in unison
at the soul's gates

[4 March 1993]

## My Heart

Sparrows
hop about casually
waking the morning with their song
rubbing the tops of their heads together
and flying off into space with a cry
So why doesn't my heart also take wing?

Glittering fountains
leap
and prattle among the pebbles and rocks

reaching like light into the new grass
laughingly winking at the flowers.
So why doesn't my heart also laugh?
Clouds
eagerly soar
fragrantly bathing the face of morning
silvering the new leaves
and then galloping off on the backs of wind-horses.
So why doesn't my heart too gallop off?

*[21 July 1996]*
*[SAS and DW]*


## A Shadow

Like a spooky shadow
under a disc of moon,
a cat crouches on a wall.
Then he sneaks with terrifying silence into a distant hiding place,
leaving behind him
in the darkness
an uncanny moan.

Nobody knows
his secrets
nor the intention of his steps.
He alone understands that darkness is the way into what he wants.

*[SAS and RS]*


## Who Are You?

He walked beside me smiling
teasing
winking at me
and joking endlessly.

He told me our journey was over
and the appointed hour for return had come.

I asked: who are you?
He answered: Death.

My blood ran cold
and my sight clouded over.

Trying to reassure me, he said:
"If you are rash enough
to want to stay on in this vale of tears,
be my guest!"
With that he vanished.

*[10 May 2001]*


## Who?

Who wants to claw my heart
so the tears flow?
My trees have withered in this trackless wilderness
and my stars lost their way.
Who claws my heart?
In the valley of the soul I scream: Wake!
But I am even more hopelessly lost
I search for the pure fountain that once glittered there.
My mirror is smashed
And I see only a monstrous desert that gnaws my trees.
Who claws at my heart?
Water is my element
but desert surrounds me
The sky of the sand is covered with a litter of foliage.
Who in the trackless wilderness can see
the pure fountain that once glittered there?
Who?

*[24 February 1996]*
*[SAS and DW]*

# Yousif al-Sa'igh

Translated by Saadi A Simawe, Ralph Savarese and Chuck Miller

### An Iraqi Evening

Clips from the battlefield
in an Iraqi evening:
a peaceable home
two boys
preparing their homework
a little girl
absentmindedly drawing on scrap paper
funny pictures.
– breaking news coming shortly.
The entire house becomes ears
ten Iraqi eyes glued to the screen in frightened silence.
Smells mingle:
the smell of war
and the smell of just baked bread.
The mother raises her eyes to a photo on the wall
whispering
– May God protect you
and she begins preparing supper
quietly
and in her mind
clips float past of the battlefield
carefully selected for hope.

[18 February 1986]

### Habitude

Every day when I returned home
I used to ring this bell,
now mute.
Although I know there is no one at home
still I ring it just because
for many years nobody has rung it, this poor miserable bell.

### Intermittent

Tonight
the nightmare was  very condensed:
A dining table
A bottle of wine
Three glasses
And three headless  men.

[SAS and CM]


### Supper

Every evening when I come home
my sadness comes out of his room
wearing his winter overcoat
and walks behind me.
I walk, he walks with me,
I sit, he sits next to me,
I cry, he cries  for my cry,
until midnight
when we get tired.
At that point
I see my sadness go into the kitchen
open the refrigerator ,
take a black piece of meat
and prepare my supper.

[SAS]


### The Final Question

Love begins with a question
It ends and the question remains (without an answer)
We keep searching among words,
between fingers and memories
and between queries in our  conscience
and other quandaries  that share our beds.
Our suffering keeps growing
until the final question.

[SAS and CM]

## The Tune

A car stopped by my house
Two men got off
They rang the doorbell.
I came out.
As they saw me
They began playing a tune;
The first rapped a tambourine
The second blew a pipe . . .
Immediately I understood
and followed them
dancing
while my tears flowed copiously.

[SAS]


## Thread

A thread of white maggots
Creeps between my bed and the door.
I wake up
And crush the slithering thread with my feet.
Then I go back to sleep,
wake again
only to find the thread
has become longer.


## Turtle

A turtle entered our house.
We were very disturbed.
My wife said:
– Throw it out.
Our neighbour said:
– Kill it.
The maid said . . .
The Imam said . . .
All the neighbours gathered
and every one suggested a solution
while the turtle was listening

while the turtle was weeping upon herself
and us.

[SAS and CM]


## Wake Up, Yousif

Once, I was martyred
and kept watching myself,
for a few seconds intoxicated,
whispering: O God, how delicious is this death;
you just go to war in a dream and get martyred!
But then a small sparrow startled me,
and I tripped.
I felt as if I were falling from a mountain.
The grass gently received me,
the grass became my bed
and put me to sleep.
I thought: have I been dreaming?
And then the grass whispered:
"Try to get up
so that I might straighten myself out."
And the sparrow said:
"I will leave some of my feathers in your wound as a witness."
I said to myself:
"How on earth can I be sure that I am a martyr now?
If only I could touch my collarbone
where the bullet is melting like a sliver of ice
and flowing onto my heart.
Oh, if I could only get up
or scream."
I tried, but to no avail.
And I wondered:
What is a person in my situation to do,
for I have not been a martyr before,
and I am so afraid of embarrassing myself in my martyrdom
and having the poets shame me.
Am I dreaming?
What torture is this?
To die as a martyr
and to remain after your death,
lying on the grass?
A cloud passes you,

and a sparrow lands on your wound
and the wind . . .
You feel it is about to rain.
Then, I said to myself:
"I have to be patient,
for this is the chance of a lifetime.
It is cloudy
and the wind is blowing."
It began to rain,
and the grass was wet,
and the sparrow was wet.
And I thought that a scent had entered the depths of my soul,
the scent of a woman who just gave birth to me.
It wouldn't be long before she dropped her placenta on the ground.
No,
this is not a dream, I thought.
In the middle of the night the woman gave birth to me;
to this hour, I remember
the warmth of her womb
and the smell of the umbilical cord.
And I laugh
as I remember
that at the moment of my birth
I kissed the midwife's fingers
and she, deeply moved, embraced me and cried.
O, you who gave me my birth certificate in the middle of the night,
who has the power to give me the certificate of my martyrdom,
to allow me at the moment of my death to feel the warmth of a placenta
and the aroma of my homeland?
Am I still dreaming?
My eyes seemed wide open.
The rain had stopped,
the grass had dried,
and I was still saying, "I'll become a martyr."
What torment was this?
Dreaming with my eyes wide open?
There was no one to close my eyes,
no one to whisper:
"O, Yousif . . . you are dreaming,
so wake up."
But I loved the dream so much,
I didn't want to wake up,
and I begged for a few more seconds.
What's wrong with that?

For I have not died as a martyr before,
and I am ignorant of what a martyr should do.
The grass said:
"Lie down like a cross,
stretching your arms along your sides,
and when the poets come to you,
don't worry,
just close your eyes
and let them cry upon you
until your crown of thorns is completed
and your hair has turned gray around your temples."
My soul was inflamed,
the crown of thorns complete,
the world entirely dark.
And I was still lying on the grass,
aware of my shame
and watching some maggots come out of my mouth
and eat my poetry.
Wake up, Yousif.
Wake up.
Wake . . .

[1 June 1986]
[SAS and RS]

# Aziz al-Samawi

## Translated by Alex Bellem

### Iraqi Sorrows

To you I brought sun and fire . . . as bows
To you swords prayed from joy, kissable
It is your nature to straighten thoughts . . . in my head
Wound me all over . . . joy . . . it doesn't matter
My sorrows burst open like a rose and I raise my head . . .
Even though your palm . . . is silk . . . and frightened of touch
Look touch the blossom . . . the myrtle will colour
I feel my wound
    like embers . . .
        kissable in your palms
The thread of blood . . .
        streams away . . .
        along down the Euphrates . . .
            far away
Anger gleams in my head . . . and echoes:
    Our hands resist like a halo, uncrushable
    and your eyes are a neighing that blossoms into a tangible dream
    It's a disgrace for people to walk . . . in people's degradation
To you songs are green . . . and overflow like rivers
And to you the deep secret which embraces secrets
Shook my height . . . a spear . . . waiting to avenge you
I worship you . . . a wind when it plays havoc with fire
If time turns against you . . . in death we'll turn back to you
The blood has overflowed . . .
      in your hands . . .
        my wounds . . . ideas
I don't know whether times have changed . . . I don't know whether
people have changed
I sent two suns as my vow to Abbas[1]
Moonlight: the sound when joy rises in my head
Strikes this conscience . . . with that one
And makes the blood . . . strengthen the people . . . for the people
Grief is a star which falls . . . from the rim of the eye
My mother cried for you . . . twice upon my chest
Your grey hair laughed in my hands Mother, and the years lit up
Like a halo . . . whose moon was trodden into the mud
I see you in my dream . . . orchards laughing

The secret slaughtered me for you . . . and my blood ran both ways
Crucified upon your door
                    Who is it . . . where are you from . . . ?


When rifles gleam . . .
                    the people's palms sweat
The yearning to see you trembled in my hand, a goblet
But look how the yearning fled and doubts arose
Let the blood . . . strengthen the people . . . for the people
I place my blood on your palm to light up as a *mawwal*[2]
My soul is like horses when long swords neigh
My eyes flying with joy like a myriad of doves
The pulse goes along with you . . . a torch in the hand of a horseman
My blood is in your notebook . . . a rose and children's drawings
    If the poet weeps blood and anger . . . it's deadly
His height cries out:
    Ascending as a song . . . and descending
                            as a moon
                            in the wind
He prays for the wound and the horses light up . . .
                        and cry out
And he prays this time . . . against the wind
                        No . . . I won't fall
The wound wakes before dawn . . . it really wants to shout out:
When rifles gleam . . .
                    the people's palms fill with tears
Oh woe, how many sensitive rivers ripple in my hands
And he wept before leaving
The talk became charred in his heart . . .
                    and the pulse of the people was choked
        What torch . . . will bring the people . . . to the people . . . ?


[Skikda, Algeria, June 1980]


### Mountain of Dreams

    I prayed for Halabcha[3] and my palms were lit by fiery sweat
Sad, the mountain breathes in the poisoned winds of shame
        Each sob of a child
                the voice
                of perfidious
                slaughter

The screams of the people . . . in the darkness
                              like stars . . .
                              of anger and fire
"Mustard" ignites death, flame and stone in the breast
Terrified eyes . . . fall
              a neigh of bleeding
                              darkness
                    and time come round.
Never . . . will the winds die . . .
        the conscience of the rocks trembles and shouts
The city is full of corpses which scream in the bleeding and collapse
That moon smoked
              darkened
              and fell
              in the winds . . .
Where are you, oh Iraq of the people?
Oh night of the goblet-holding lover
Oh tear of a friend on my cheek, kissable as a morning star
I know you hold your head high.
A neigh of the first civilizations, a head held high
Sumer . . . Babylon . . . Assyria
              Horses of flame
              among the books . . . kissable.
My palms moonlight to you:
              That is you, the sad one
                    your rivers
                    sing
                    and roam
              Oh woe is you
                    woe is you
              a friend who lights the darkness
                    songs
                    of candle . . . and myrtle[4]
    Your yearning is a blue time . . . an untouchable moon
    I can just make out
    the homeland –
    a tear
    of grief
    in the goblet
Remember, oh Iraq of the people
Gilgamesh: songs of fire.
      A neigh of the most distant yearning and the awe of remembrance
The homeland roams my palms, a dove of ember and fire
Go tell the rebels for me

the torches ignite . . . awe . . . for anger and revolt
Death turns to moonlight
   joyful ululations blossomed our mountain: fighters
      I worship you, oh mountain, when fighters are yours
The wound is a bloody rose . . . smouldering
The wound . . . is the dove's breast and its beating wings
The wound . . . roams the length of you and takes my hands as a
dreaming river
The wound . . . ahh . . . the wound
   if the shirt flutters . . . colours
I roam crazy in your palms, a little moon, and I return mourning
                          from joy
the mountain is darkness and neighing which takes the rebels' hands
      blazing anger . . . fires
   the mountain would tremble for a child who went to sleep hungry
The mountain is green in sleep
The mountain is an ember lighting the homeland's night;
                    moonlight, darkness
You are an awe and a neigh which takes my wounds as doves.
      You are a wind which flares up my words
         You . . . a dream before sleep.
A shirt which lights my fingers as blazing songs . . . dreams
The mountain is fear and silk
The mountain is a captive's tear
The mountain is an awakening of conscience
The mountain is the ship that takes the darkness: daylight
   The mountain will wander my conscience to the end of the
struggle.

   *[London, April 1991]*


### Neighing of the Fingers

My fear is a filly . . .
   that sets me alight
      in your hands . . . as a neighing
The stature roams, moonlike, songs and night
The woe from travelling, oh my soul, all the woe
Darkness and your shirt is a morning
Every step is exile and slaughter
The night takes all my madness
My secrets roam . . .
   they take me

and roam off again
They take me . . . as winds of anger and horses
Poetry gleams in my fingers, as a voice and *mawwal*s
   Your stature . . .
      takes my eyes
     as nights which set nights alight
        with joy . . . moonlight and neighing
Horses illuminating on a long dark path are awesome
The colour of the fingers . . . light up . . . like a rose of shyness at night
   which takes my yearning . . . there
      the yearning is moonlit . . . there
         you are there
Darkness . . . without a homeland . . . just tell me where to find you
I release my hands . . . in exile . . . a dove of joy . . . to go there
Your memory . . . a star . . . without morning
   Where can I find you . . .?
   Where are you . . . where can I find you
You fall in the tears . . . I don't know where to find you
I walk. On embers . . . hoping that you'll come . . . and I'll find you
                                        Where can I find you?
Alone the bleeding cries out:
   There is no homeland for the wind . . .
      it could all fall upon us
         but the hands of refusal won't fall
It takes my shirt unexpectedly . . . the wind is by nature mad
A torch ignites in the pulse . . . with your passion it'll never fall
You are the woe
You are a wind . . . which will light the darkness . . . as storms of horses
You are a river with a terrified spring and stream
It is you who'll take my palms as songs . . . and night
   Suns of joy and cardamom flash past my lip
You are a secret which lights the long night
Your night . . .
   embers which ignite embers
   and sleeplessness is the exile of the genuine
You are that sword when it gleams like a neighing
You snatch dreams of joy
   a forelock
which inclines . . . upon me
Joy takes my eyes . . .
   you are joy . . .
   sight and guide
   that's you . . . that light
   that's you . . . a cure for my eyes

That's you . . .
   of what morning . . .
   all my wounds gasp together
If it were up to me I would bring life like a torch and light in your hand
That's you . . . where are you going . . .?
    My whole height burst into flame . . . with a boom
This is you who departed . . .
 And this is me, a lifetime in your hands, all my life I cried dead
The nights burned in my soul . . .
   I died an ember . . .
       and was not extinguished.
I go crazy for you, burning in both meeting and absence
Don't you know that conscience is a book
And don't you know that time . . .
increases estrangement
   and fills the cup of love with earth
My soul is mad for you, wanting the sword as a cure and cautery
                                             for my wounds
I worship you . . . all of me . . . you take me . . .
   as nights which light up
       on your hands . . . a neighing
My eyes fall . . . in the moonlight . . .
Bleeding
flows
down
the shirt
Take me, all of me, between your hands and wipe off the wounds of
the murdered
Each time the pulse awakens
   it flashes . . . past the eyelid
           startled . . . like the star of Canopus
I roam like a mad wind . . .
   that lights up the night of departure
           moonlight and *mawwals*
My dreams fall in my tears as nights of bleeding and horses
The horses illuminating on a long dark path are awesome
You tremble, meanings and books
   bend over in grief
       stand up . . . and bend over again
You are the night
You are the fear . . .
Oh Mother, the morning sun is the colour of shyness in your palms
This yearning which takes my eyes is tears and dreams
You are the candle . . . in the sad river . . . you roam

You would be the sight
   if the cowards extinguished my eyesight
Ouf . . .
My fear made me sick for you
My fear . . . not of you . . . for you
My fear is our walking in the evening
My fear is like paper on the embers
My fear . . . where . . . far away, intoxication in your eyes
My fear is a stature that flicks its forelock like a foal
My fear is joy that takes me as a halo of grief between your hands
My fear is this greyness when it gleams as a blue day in your hands
My fear is all the people imploring me for you
My fear is a poet between your hands
And the soul prays
   in your hands
      a yearning of grief and worry
I am dazed . . . and I want to learn this time
All the madness . . . goes round in my eyes and I don't understand
Oh rose of sorrow . . .
Oh night-time embers and the smell of blood . . .
You burst open . . . ANGER
   you shine
      and close up again
   I've never seen . . . a moon extinguished
   and I've never seen . . . an exiled river
No . . . and I've never
            seen . . . a homeland covered in blood
   Where are you taking me . . .
Where are you going..?
   Kufa[5] is moonlight in your eyes, an anthem
Basra[6] prays for the departer on a dark street as a martyr
The snow is sad for the dazed man who stands alone
The torches roar in my pulse, I don't know where they're going
My dreams roam . . . moon-like . . .
   nostalgic in their joy . . .
         they shine and yearn more . . .
You are an anthem in my hands
The stature roams . . . and takes all my yearning . . . away
The foal is awesome when it lights the wind in the heart of the high
                                    flames, like an echo
A neighing wakes in my fingers a madness for the heart, like an echo
The wind is stubborn . . .!
   and the foal of departure is really stubborn
SILK . . . my hands breathe and I say far away

The sparkle of joy in your eyes . . . a new Iraq
My fingers sweated . . .
    and all the songs wept . . . and they didn't know
    am I, or are you, the martyr . . .!
In poetry my voice gleams . . . horses and anthems
The orphans' clothes rejoice and the tears of the "slaves" laugh
All the cold couldn't extinguish my heart – if it wanted to leave – it
                                   knows what it wants

Cold didn't gather my soul
No . . . and neither . . .
    did the grave of snow extinguish the vein
I want . . . and I don't want.
The night takes all my yearning.
I cannot feel the morning
No . . . and neither . . .
    does the sun of dreams flash by me at night
Whenever the wound wakes . . . dead, and I say more
The woe, all the woe:
If the wolf of betrayal stopped on the road as a flag and a guide
If the furthest dream passed by on one leg, limping
And if the neighing . . . stumbled upon the voice of this homeland
And the woe, all the woe . . .
    My hands light up in the darkness . . .
        and they scream . . .
            the woe
the woe, all the woe . . .
Never in my life have I seen a murderer praying over the murdered
               My fear is the rose of impossibility! . . .

*[Skikda, Algeria, December 1989]*


### Suns in the Night of the Massacre

I awoke, all of me embers, there's no homeland in my home
I forgot my name and the light of my eyes and I don't know in which
                                 dream
    I stayed
Every time I extinguish the wound . . . the wound wearies . . . I weary
    darkness . . . and my hands become dazed
           a blue moon . . .
                  I yearned for you
I roam all of me in the moonlight, songs of grief and secrets
my grey hair flies to you before the wind . . . secrets

the shirt's roses roam crazy in my hands, embers and secrets.
Aah . . . you, the Euphrates that ignites my suspicions as songs and fire
your horses a startled wind that lights grief's night, moonlight
                                                and daylight
Awe and neighing . . . your days are horses
A flag ignites the wind . . . and charges
                    At your arrival
                        I sent
                        two wounds as tall as me:
                    one took me to you,
                and one I lit to the homeland as a bleeding torch
 A homeland flashes past the eyelid, a filly, and disappears for years
The moon is clear in the river . . . memory, nostalgia and scent
Oh, who would send the wound . . . a torch of reeds . . . in welcome
    Remember well . . .
            the despicable: is a despicable dagger
            and the scent: is moonlight and scent
The yearning fluttered in a broken rib
    my hand is a dove and through the years keeps circling
Take me, you are joy and I headed for your home
        my hands are the fire of refusal
                darkness
        but to you . . . I prayed
I wanted you: a neighing to take my hands as songs and blood
I wanted you: Sayyab's Basra[7] . . . let me understand . . . I want to
                                            understand
There are torches wanting to talk in the houses
A filly roams my hands infatuated, a dreaming moon
Men are veiled by starvation
The fear collapses, is destroyed
Blood moves,
a revolution lights death's darkness
                moonlike . . .
                on a dark day
You're sad but your rivers dawn joyful
Your hand is the yearning of all those in love with you, wounded for you
Your heart dreamily infatuated embraces . . .
                    the wounds of the martyr . . .
                    whose bleeding length
                            swims . . .
Your conscience would be Abbas's[8] filly
        if a horseman
        fell . . .
        slaughtered by it

I wept for your swords, a dark day
The yearning lights up from grief, an ember
       but no . . .
       not once
       did my soul bow . . .
            and I wasn't humbled
I remember when he used to come veiled, crossing the reeds and marshes at night
A neigh and moonlight in your eyes . . . to straighten my broken spirit
Between the *faleh*[9] and the *faleh* . . . a martyr . . . hanged and slaughtered
You are Iraq and from where shall I bring you
Take my hands as your two shores
This is me, a dark sad river with two cold shores
Take my soul as a blue flame of two beating wings in your palms
   I implore your hands
      and I worship your rivers
      take me with you as your two wings
The darkness roams your earth and I remained songs of grief
   my mother wails . . . for you
      and your rivers grieve . . .
         nights without morning
            aah . . . how many sad dawns
               I prayed . . . without a homeland
Every revolution starts in the morning . . . aah . . . from where do you start
Don't you know the reed shack . . . is darkness and a dream with two suns
Your sword is long and gleams in the night of departure . . .
                to where . . . ?
Your stature rejoiced . . . at walking
Your stallion is sad and shines in your eyes, weeping
I wanted you yearning . . . to inflame me . . .
  a moon
    in your hands . . .
       I sang . . . until morning
  You are a friend
  compassionate
sad . . .
  and you turn like moonlight . . .
   The stature's neighing
 takes all my fingers
     I burst into flame . . . a mania of joy
The Upper Euphrates rose carrying the worries of the people
Covered the corpses with tears . . . amongst the roses and myrtle
Smokes tobacco until morning . . . the sun an ember in the cup
Sad, the river receives the corpses at night

Sad and afraid are its shores in darkness and woe
                              sad . . .
              death is in your eyes but you haven't made a will
          I know your conscience
                  as a moon . . .
          a tide which carries you. A yearning
            that takes my palms
                  as sails of the first ship
                      I lit up . . . from joy
My mother's grey hair dawned on you like sadness and a blue Euphrates
Mother, your palms are nights and embers . . . by moonlight . . .
                                              the river sweats
She would flare up, a horse on the shores, if she saw a moon . . . drowning
I wanted you to be a friend and a homeland in the soul . . .
I wanted you to be a ship and a moon, I don't know where we'd go
My wounds roam . . .
                  in the darkness
                      flags of flame . . . I lit up
          I cry out aloud, you hear me and don't reply
Your grey hair shaken by the wind . . .
                  startled . . .
                      and upon your shoulders . . .
              a day of madness . . . roams . . .
                              and falls
Let go the prayer-beads and fortune-telling . . .
                  you won't find luck among the rosary's beads
                      your foal, neighing and tears . . .
                          your sword, sad and radiant . . .
And you are far . . .
      your conscience is not cloudy
              no . . .
                      and you showed not a tear of grief
You stayed alone all your life, sad on the snow
Oh the bewilderment of the people
Oh the bier of the martyr and the smell of the myrtle
Oh river of grief – why not luck – for the people
          I sent you candles in the hands of orphans
              I sent you this myrtle washed in my mother's tears
      upon its shores
Oh river, your water is sad
Oh river, those roses are afraid and sad
Oh river, the homeland became a wretched child's tear
Oh river, my mother's grey hair is a wind gleaming in the night
                              of grief . . . to where . . .?

She cries out aloud, you hear her and don't reply
She keeps crying out
    to you . . .
         Oh Defeated, look
          I've cut off my sidelocks
I fall on your shores, a voice, humbled to you
a sinking moon lit up by grief for you
Aaah . . .
Corpses choke in you and you are choked by corpses

*[London, May 1991]*

### Notes

1    Abbas was the half-brother of Imam Husayn ibn Ali bin Abi Talib, who was the Prophet Mohammed's grandson. They were both killed in the Kerbala uprising of October 680 and are revered by Shi'ites. Abbas is believed by the masses to have the power to grant their wishes and they therefore offer him pledges. They believe that he has the ability to inflict severe punishment on wrong-doers and those who infringe upon others' rights (see the *Encyclopaedia of Islam*, pp. 607-615).

2    A *mawwal* is a non-classical Arabic verse form, usually sung, consisting of seven lines which are broken down into two triplets and a final line rhyming with the first triplet. The rhyme often employs words which sound the same but have a different meaning, e.g. *limm-eh* (gather it) *l'imm-eh* (for his mother) *lemma* (when). As a traditional folksong, usually accompanied by the haunting tones of the reedpipe (*nay*), to those in exile the *mawwal* is evocative and nostalgic.

3    Halabcha: a Kurdish mountain village attacked by Saddam's (Ba'athist) forces in 1988 with chemical weapons. The lethal mixture of sarin and mustard gas killed an estimated 6000 predominantly women and children in that one attack.

4    Candles and myrtle hint at the paradox of joy and sadness. In the first instance, they are an expression of rituals of supplication and prayer, performed for someone who is absent. However, one would also light a candle and bring myrtle as an expression of joy and good luck, for example, for someone getting married.

5    Kufa: A city in the heartland of Iraq. During the Abbasid era it was known as a centre of learning and culture.

6    Basra: An ancient port in the south of Iraq, on the Gulf. During the Abbasid caliphate it was the other major seat of learning.

7    Badr Shakir al-Sayyab was the Iraqi poet considered to be one of the pioneers of free verse. He was born in Jaikur, a village on the outskirts of Basra.

8    See note 1.

9    *Faleh*: a large five- or six-pronged fork used to catch fish in the marshes.

# Shakir al-Samawi

## Translated by Saadi A Simawe and Chuck Miller

### Quartets of Inner Whispering

*Wake*
Midnight sleepless heart
no companion or thought to still the loneliness
no dream to redeem the soul
the perplexed eye sees complete desolation.

*Meditation*
A cloud of light floats
in my blood it rains moonlight
washes away grievance in its secret wine.
woke up from my awakening heart utterly confused
it saw the soul in fate's hand ember in an ember.

*Half Dreaming*
My heart sees earth as a mirror       my shadow disappears in its
listens to a sound of a lyre                          mercury
My heart converses with a mute child the hand of its player in a
uttering inconceivable sounds                        wolf's mouth
                                        the world  contracts in labour,
                                        not knowing what will be born

*Dreaming*
A red shadow in moonlight           moving at  the willow's edges
I saw eyelids speak with eyelids     to faces without lips
a man on a cloud                      growing invisible rice
a shepherd driving a star          a madman  counsels a soothsayer

[28 March 1968]

### The Dream of a Snow Flower

In the night that lasted a lifetime,
a flower was haloed by snow flakes
in this storm
that blooms over its snow a forest of stars
it remained a pale bloom
that had merely heard a distant rumour of warmth

The salt in its sap
told the flower about:
a plant that oozes with warmth
a branch that shines a glow
a springtime that incandesces like paradise
when warmth washes its soil.

(The flower then coloured all its thoughts with this imagined warmth).

One day the cloud passed
painting its rains on its shadow:
one drop like the eye of the sun
another drop a pulse in every touch
a third drop like a tremulous wedding hallelujah
the fourth drop awaits this earth-warmth.

(The flower began dreaming of the coming of this warmth).

The wind passed singing, and left its echo
telling the flower:
"Once the world was happier
when the dawn rose from the  warmth
and from the sky glowed sunny noon
and the air sparkled scent
and the sun had mercy in the heat of the afternoon.

(The flower began consecrating offerings for the coming of the warmth).

The sun saw the flower's dream
and bowed to wash over it with benevolence.

(Quickly the snow flower melted to its roots
and so gave its being to the soil).

   *[27 July 1972]*


### A Solo for the Lone Intuition

Oh my heart, you must remain alone
O warm heart you melt into my blood
You are a tune that plays prayers on my soul
songs of the cross and the nails.
O conscience, pray for my wounds that heal as they multiply.

My life that seeks your time in the nights
That deliver or abort.
Heart, stay a stranger
(– for your strangeness is your paradise that accompanies you
and in this paradise all the nightingale's songs chant).

Remain a stranger
without stanzas or rhymes
remain alone with the memories that dawn,
insight enough to sustain profound sense.
Stay with the kiss
that becomes lips
through which all the rapture of your veins flows.
Remain as resilient intuitions that won't disappoint you
whenever your hopes fail.
Remain alone.
(– For what do you need a shadow which will darken your roads,
you will stumble when it disappears).

Stay alone
then you need not reconcile nor offend
nor your songs ebb away
and your sorrow crest.
Stop with grieving, stop seeking
happiness
finish screaming, no longer seek silence
don't be shocked by the grotesque,
keep aloof
(– trust your own rhythm
it is your only companion).

Keep to yourself
like a river with no origin or mouth.
No sun, no eye, no anger
no dream, no blinding sight, no sorrow, no cause.
No flowers to wither
no guilt to creep into your hands
and no regret that brings grief.
Keep back
(– the sweetest thing is this isolation
wherein no storm
nor clouds).

[Baghdad, 5 July 1972]

# Sadiq al-Saygh

Translated by Saadi A Simawe, Salaam Yousif, Emily Howard and Ralph Savarese

### White Sleep

White sleep
Led me to a white dream
To something mysterious, white

I thought I touched gossamer
Or a bone
A coffin, or a white cloud

When I woke up
I found my hand
Had touched your face,
Oh death.
Who appears now
Distant
Nebulous
And cannot be recalled.

[SAS]

### Schwartzkopf's Copters

Schwartzkopf's copters
Stick to the skin
Like glowing insects
You call out to them
They ignore your call
You drive them away
They return
To gnaw and gnaw and gnaw
Although I am dead
With half a face
And without a specific form

[London, 1994]
[SY]

### Sanctions

On the street today, I sold
A bag heavy with gods
Out of sheer hunger.

*1998*
*[SY and EH]*


### Mysterious

In the public square
you keep squatting.
The breeze fondles you
like the jet
of a white fountain.
Birds talk with you
in Solomon's tongue.

In the sound of the spray,
you hear a quiet music
saturated with perfume
and Spring's piercing smells.

Suddenly,
you get up, dropping
whatever you are carrying on the ground,
and point to the air with your finger,
shaking your fists in the faces of the passers-by.


### Dread

Layla,
promise that you will be my salvation
You have put your hands on my heart
and I have released you

Layla,
my lips tremble
and my hands are cold

Layla,
I am in a well
staring at the bottom
while you depart
like rings on the water

Layla,
I am frightened of you
Your heart is a devouring machine
crushing time
mocking my blindness

Layla,
you are the scent of death
sprayed into merciful eyes.

*[SAS and RS]*

# Badr Shakir al-Sayyab

Translated by Ibtisam S Barakat, Mustapha Kamal
and Ralph Savarese

### The Singer Has Aged

It was only yesterday
When I used to write my verse
And my blood would run with joy in my veins
And I would set out and aimlessly hum
Amidst the brooks, flowers, and palms.
I would sing, and savour the taste:

Food for my soul
Starting with the chirping of dawn
Until nightfall
Food . . . but my soul
Feels the hunger and shuns the nourishment
Of its hopes.

Now it is the echo of my soul
As it struggles to last longer
That I turn into verse
And gain from it nothing
But the bitter ridicule
That rises on a reader's face.

The singer has grown old
Illness turned him into ruins
And shook his songs.

Yesterday, when he used to sing
Night had to restrain its drunken stars from falling.

And today, a thousand lines from him
Cannot stir a palm leaf's attention
Or the evening's local wedding
In the eyes of Aram and Dufla
Or the drums that shake the air.

The singer has grown old
But in spite of this, listen to him
That you may bring him the joy of an illusion
That his tunes forever remain young
When he speaks of love
In either tears or breaths.

The singer is dying
Would you hold back from him
The broken branches and blossoms?

Listen to the singer
That you may hear his tunes
As he sings a farewell to his youth:

"If you ever pass by me, with your eyes, wish me peace."

The singer has come and sung his farewell.
Believe him!

He has grown old. Have mercy on him.

[ISB]


## Love Me

I never deny my past,
but all those I loved before you
never loved me back;
nor did they ever have pity on me:
sometimes I loved seven women at the same time –
their hair fluttered over me
and the fragrance of their breasts
carried me instantly like a ship to China.
I dived into a sea full of fancy and ecstasy,
collecting seashells,
searching in vain for pearls
only to find a palm tree's long braids
shading me.
I rummaged among numberless shells, hoping
to chance upon a pearl that shone like a morning star.
But then, as I lost my nails
and my hands bled,

only water and clay oozed out of the shells:
a smile dripped on my lips,
like tears suddenly sprung from the depths of my heart,
because all those I loved before you
never loved me back.

I see these women sitting in the balcony of my fancy,
my pain rushes to uncover the silhouettes of their faces:
the first one betrayed me for a fool
because her new lover had means;
then one day he woke up and walked out on her.

And because the second one was older
(or was it because
her beauty and youth told her I was not prince charming?),
she dropped me.
For a long time, whenever
I saw leaves drink the morning dew
and buds bloom,
I dreamed of her and smelt her fragrance.
Yesterday, I saw her standing at the bus stop,
and I hurried away.
Curse the old witch.
Did you think that your beauty
would prevail over Time when even the Tower of Babel
collapsed under its blows,
and the phoenix herself
never rose from her ashes?

That other woman
the early dawn opens
jasmine and lablab shrubs in her dimples.
She left me
for a castle and a car.
But with one blow, her husband lost everything
and now, impoverished and disgraced,
he sits and reads the newspaper on his doorstep.
Whenever he evokes the past for her,
and boredom devours his heart.

That other woman and her husband were beholden
to appearances.
Now she spends the night drinking and gambling,

and when sleep overcomes her,
she misses the sun, the morning dew,
and the river giggling to the passing sail.

And that other one?
She was my poet and my world.
I drank poetry from her eyes,
and I used to drowse in the shadow of her verse:
all her past and youth were like rendezvous for me
on a shore where only the moon treads.
There, birds slept; and when rainbows sprinkled their dreams,
they woke up and took off spreading their shrill cries
light came out of their upper feathers,
and shades of the night throbbed
under their nether ones.
(Where are our summer sunsets in Jaykur?
On the mirror-like water,
a murmuring boat carried us.
As I recited verses to her,
the hills and palm-trees rustled,
while grapes dreamed on their vines.)
But we travelled different paths;
now a prison cell has buried her,
and only a candle keeps her company:
she still remembers me and sobs.
But I don't cry over her.
I lost faith in the Arabs,
in Mecca, in its prophets,
its caves and its valleys.

And the last one?
O my wife, my destiny!
Did infirmity have to cripple me so that
without her
I would look like a drunken dead man?

And here I am; everyone I loved before you
never loved me back.
Why you? Pity may have moved you.
I will not forgive God
if mercy, not love, let Him
pour me heavenly cups.
O, give me love,
quench my thirst,

rest on my chest,
and let me sleep on your breasts. O
the scars that enveloped my heart
and clogged my veins!
O, do love me,
because all those I loved before you
never loved me back.

    *[Paris 19/3/63]*
    *[MK and RS]*

# Sheikh Selman
Iraqi Kurdish

## Translated by Muhamad Tawfiq Ali

### Community School

We welcomed him home, the headmaster
With a doctorate from Europe.
Listen carefully to the headmaster,
Reciting the school's roll call:
Mr Hypocrisy? Present, Sir!
Where is Mr Fairness? He went to hell, Sir!
Mr Righteousness?  Mr Honesty?
Sir, they were brothers who, last year,
Were sentenced to two years each.
Where is Mr Patriot? Why isn't he around?
What is his excuse, the year has ended?
Mr Dear Sir, don't be misguided.
His name was somehow misspelled.
Actually, his real name is "naughty"*
He is actually the son of a gun.
While recording in the school register,
You were so depressed,
Instead of "naughty", you wrote "patriot".

**Notes**

The poet uses the English word "naughty", which sounds something like "weteni" which is the Arabic word for "patriot". Like English, Kurdish is amenable to puns. But this is the first time I have met such a cross-cultural pun in Kurdish poetry.

Although this poem is explicitly critical of the situation in Kurdistan it is implicitly critical of the Kurdish leaders.  Nonetheless, it is very moving.  So much so, that it inspired another poet, Fereydun Refiq Hilmi, to compliment the former by complementing the original with many more verses of his own.  The latter is an explicit indictment of the two main Kurdish political parties which were hell-bent on fratricide at the time.

# Hashim Shafiq

Translated by Saadi A Simawe with Ralph Savarese,
Ellen Doré Watson and Melissa L Brown

### The Mountain

I have washed the mountain,
I have washed the stones and the snow,
and I have washed the sand.
I have washed the pebbles
and the wind that clings to the trees.
I have washed the mountain,
I have lit the paths
and the back ways around the mountain.
I have lit the caves and the stairs
and the hideouts in the folds of the mountain.
I have washed the summit
and every crevice of the mountain
so that my loved ones might pass
in the forenoon of the mountain day.


\*


I will kiss my beloved's tears
and her other gestures.
I will kiss my beloved's drowsiness
as she teeters on the edge of sleep.
I will kiss my beloved's insides.
I will kiss the air that sleeps in her lungs.
I will kiss the fluttering of her eyelids.
I will kiss the sway of her flowing dress.
I will kiss her deep wound covered with roses.
I will kiss her laughter before it issues from her lips.
I will kiss her thoughts before they form.
I will kiss her evanescent scent.
I will kiss her breath before it alights on the pillow.
I will kiss every inch of my love.
I will kiss her voice,
her cool shadow,
the colour of her discontent,
the shape of her delight.

I will kiss her intuition,
her fiery mind.
I will kiss her dreams
while she is deep in sleep.
I will kiss her stirred imagination.
I will kiss the gentleness in the edges of her clothes,
the elegance of her steps,
her dalliance with the wind.
I will kiss her desperate panting
and her lust coagulated in silk.
I will kiss her reflection in the fountains,
her appearance in mirrors.
I will kiss her flanks and her curves
and the space underneath her nails.
I will kiss the sunset as it glows on my beloved's cheek.
I will kiss my beloved's heartbeats
and her apprehensions.
I will kiss her feelings as I sleep,
intoxicated beneath her sky.

*[21 September 1999]*
*[SAS and RS]*


## Destinies

My daughter works each night
to make my knee her pillow.
I tell her tale after tale
until she falls asleep.
I tell her about the silk of the moon.
I tell her about coloured waters,
walking playgrounds,
the buried fortunes in her hair.
I tell her about scattered stars
drifting down through the sky like feathers.
I tell her about a blue orange
and a mountain circling the city all night
and a pure white elephant.
I tell her about everything.
But when she asks for my story, I slip
around this corner and that
until she drowses on my knee and falls asleep.

*[18 November 1996]*
*[SAS and EDW]*

## Picture of a Tyrant

O Tyrant,
Tell me, how did you manage to build all these dungeons in your heart?
How did you stretch all the desert on your tongue
and devour all the stars that once crowded our roofs?
You have annihilated the air we breathe and smothered our sunshine
until all suns have decayed.

Tell me, Tyrant, how did you carry the homeland on your shoulders
        one morning
and take it into the wilderness and dismember it?
Why did you drag the joy of our breaths into the suffocating depths?
Why have the landscapes of imagination that used to fly with our
        kites disappeared?
Tell me, how did you consume even the space,
and how did you spy on our souls with those huge telescopic lenses?
Where did you get all your metal eyes and your heart shielded in wood?

Tyrant,
O, Tyrant,
How did Time become your brother and Fate your companion?
Who gave you permission to build all these fences around our mouths
and these dungeons in our depths?
O Tyrant, you who measured my life by the number of nails in my flesh,
who threw your stone bread to the masses.
What has happened to my molars?  I want to gnaw on these fences.
What has happened to my claws? I want to crumble this fortress.

Tell me, who made me suckle my milk mixed with humiliation
when I was still playing with the moon?
Who poisoned my toys? Who drank my river to the last dregs?
Who shot holes into my shadow and stored it in jail?
Who dried up light and made darkness flow?
Who filled the valleys with salt swamp and turned plants into stone?
Who, Tyrant, turned mirrors into deserts and shattered the rainbow?
Who, Tyrant, chewed up my entire homeland
and  gave the children dust to swallow
and stole the innocent teasing from their eyebrows?
Who took away the beauty from our women and gave them
emptiness and loss?
Who widowed femininity and voided childhood?
Who prohibited life and sanctioned killing?
Who, Tyrant, led you to my guitar, to the cottage of my stars?

How did you creep into well-being and bankrupt it?
What bad omen helped you find my cradle of wildflowers?
Who dulled my father's flute?
Who trampled on his only cloud?
Who turned my mother's anklets into chains
and tore to pieces her gold ornament?

What a Tyrant you are, when you make the wind spy for you.
Where are my words that the wind has carried to you?
Why do you always search my poems for weapons?
Why do you always mutilate the feathers of my four-winged bird?
What a Tyrant is this who annihilates clouds and the vastness of space,
and tightens borders with a noose?
What Tyrant are you, and from what desolation have you come
with all these bloody badges
and this iron welded around your neck and your shoulders?
What Tyrant are you and from what cave did you conjure all this terror?
You are always pregnant with dark labyrinths and ever-changing masks,
and always ripe with torture and treachery.
What womb spewed you out on the sands?
Tell me, you Tyrant, how did you manage to build such a great wall
between your skin and your heart?

Tell me, whose flesh is this on the rubble?
And to whom do these birthmarks behind the bars belong?
And whose is this shrouded scream buried in the grave?
I am no longer able to discern things.
Oh, Tyrant, is this a flower, or cement?
Is this a plate or a drum?
Is this nectar or sludge?
Is this a homeland or a guillotine?
I don't know what has blurred my perception of things
So that now, the cub mews and the rat roars.

Oh, Tyrant, enlighten me about the essence and principles of the universe,
about the disease of lineage,
about the heavens where you were born,
about the meteor that carries your name,
about your manliness that is inscribed on swords,
about your shields that are left on Mars,
about your arrows and your spears that have hit the stars.
Instruct me on the history of the hired poets,
and of your glory that is engraved on their tongues.
Tell me about the rhymes showered on your diamond chairs

and of immortality woven into your military coat.
Tell me of your henchmen who are experts in tanning live human skin,
in making art from human bones.
Tell me about your guards and watchmen
and the secret armies of your spies that invade our throats
and watch our lips and our hearing.
Tell me about your mastery in inflicting pain,
about your cunning and your shrewdness in polluting women.

Tell me, Oh Tyrant, before you vanish forever.

*[SAS amd MLB]*

## Mirage

Nobody told me when I was born
that my life would be harder than my father's and son's lives.
Nobody told me when I was a child
that life was full of pits and tunnels and trackless labyrinths.
Nobody told me when I was a youth
that my homeland was not a homeland
and that my enemy and friend are aligned against me
and my lover would be as fickle as a chameleon.
Nobody, except Brecht, told me when I was a young man
that exiles are shoes,
and only Sartre told me
that political parties are religions,
and only Abu al-Atahiah[1] told me that mankind is a curse.
And when I became an adult,
I did not tell myself: Beware of tomorrow.

*[29 October 1997]*
*[SAS and RS]*

**Note:**
1    Ismail ibn al-Qasim Abu al-Atahia (AD 748-826), a major ascetic poet,
was born in Kufa, Iraq, and died in Baghdad.

# Ronny Someck
**Hebrew**

## Translated by Vivian Eden

### The ballad of alcohol valley

Only sharpen a knifeblade along its mate's hip.
In Alcohol Valley the sex knife spins on its tip.

Rock'n'roll cops push together straight ahead.
By the sweat of crimes – our daily bread.

Oh, girls of the Valley,
Barbies in the dangerous game room,
who will part your legs tonight,
what lullaby lower nylon lashes
over plastic eyes.

The Valley is a dream, a bad dream.
The moon is the nightlight of Dr Freud.

PS
About the meaning of dreams in the Valley:
a girl seen walking a dog – a sign she is lonely.
A girl seen walking without a dog – a sign
she forgot the dog at home.

### Poem for a daughter who is already born

On the day you were born the joyworkers warmed
their hands at the fire that was lit
by the match of your life.
Night after night I hypnotize myself with the voice of your breath
as if it were a lighthouse flashing for a sailor almost guzzled
by the sea's teeth.

### Ice Cream

"When I'm big," you say,
"I want to be an ice cream lady and a poet."

Here are scoops of ice cream that will slip through your fingers,
yellower than lemon, an orange grove in flame
and red squeezed from watermelon blood. This is
where poetry lives. So why do you need words.


### The sign of the bite

In the morning after the great chaos concert the faces emptied
like beer bottles.
Who turned to look saw that between the women's lips an apple
shuddered
and in the apple – the sign of the bite.
And love? Love was threaded like elastic in underwear:
what holds it up is
what exerts the pressure.


### A short history of vodka

I don't remember the name of the bar, at the end
Of the Metal Workers' Hall of Culture in Chiliabinsk.
I remember only the girl who every fifteen minutes
Came from behind the counter to collect the glasses into
A red plastic bowl.
She skipped from table to table, her high shoes
Clicking out the smell of heaps of loot,
A fur hat spread war snow on her forehead
And fumes of alcohol blurred her face furled like a white flag.
There is, said the man beside me, no woman who isn't beautiful
There is too little vodka.


### Blues for Elliot Sharp

His guitar has a severed neck.
He plays like someone sweeping plucked feathers
from the slaughterhouse floor. The feathers long for the body as
the flower in the pot licks, till it withers, the ground water
that flowed in its leaves.
Music is never the last wish
uttered through the victim's clenched lips
anticipating the chords from the rifle barrels.
It is the escape route through the rusty heart
of barbed wire fences.

### Testifying to Beauty

The most beautiful girl in the world used the pad of her finger to
wipe the dust off the label of a bottle in a wine shop in Bordeaux.
The fan of this movement is taught at archaeology schools
when eyes open wide to identify the year of Creation.
Inside the bottles all traces of the hand that squeezed the grapes
have vanished and from the grapes the scent
of the shady roofs of the vine leaves has been forgotten. In the leaves
nostalgia has shut down the wind turbines of the grains of sand, and
the sand
no longer covers the roots that crept through the earth like snakes
that shed their skin every season.
And the girl? Nine months, I guess from the brushstrokes on her body,
nine months Leonardo da Vinci sat between
her mother's legs and painted
her.

### Till when will we sleep after the whore

Till when will we sleep after the whore
and awaken before the milkman.
He who stays awake dreams the distance
between the baby and the victim,
and by the door lies the memory of the dead
like milk bottles brought by the milkman of death
from the battlefields.

[The Lebanese border, 1997]

### Transparent

Tayyib studies literature at Tel Aviv University.
He has a knapsack with a grammar book and a composition
about Mahmoud Darwish.
The knapsack is transparent because this summer
with any other bag
in the X-ray eyes of all policemen he is marked
as hiding a bomb.
"Even this," his father says, "Inshallah,
will soon come out in the wash," and hangs on
the timeline clothes from which a stain

of shame has been rinsed. But
life has to go to the market and he goes with it
to buy olives in vernacular Arabic and write
poems about them in literary Arabic.
Meanwhile, Tayyib is entirely visible. The taut skin
on his arms does not hide the knots of muscle,
the flexible cartilage in the space between
the bones and the blood vessels in which
the swimmer of despair can crawl drunken
to the shore where the lifeguards have hung
a black flag.


### 40

Forty years separate me from her.
I could have wandered in the desert,
longed for the flesh pot,
eaten quail God dropped
down from the clouds.
I could have passed by Mount Nevo,
been a spy,
seen a whore in Jericho.
I gave it all up for the war
in which the booty was the word "father."

# Jawad Yaqoob

## Translated by Saadi A Simawe and Chuck Miller

### The Only Choice

Ashes have collected in the heart and in the memory
. . . on the lips
ashes and a tear . . .

And now you are so close: a wound in my heart
I name you: a window in a wall.
But that wall has grown higher
until it has become a dungeon
with an iron gate
in the middle of quarantine.

For you
the poems lean towards sadness
and I am snatched by perplexity
waking up all night
collecting the killed stars
and drinking alone all the night
the wine of the long poems
and weep from the heart
without a wailing wall.

You, lady, usually come to me wet with longing
like fleeing birds, you come to me
and your face,
this sad swallow,
always takes me by surprise
pecking at the seed of my heart
and the poem cries . . .
but others can't understand.
You come to me at an hour after visitors have come and gone
all companions have left
you come when it is too late.

We are lovers in secret,
sending our sighs deep underground
yet we grow under the soil
yielding, like potato plants, our lives.

Would we at all be able to see
our own fruit ripening?

We are lovers
but why do I become lost on the road to you?
into the road of sorrows?
and why does the opposite wind become my only companion
toward your shores?
And why do the roads elongate and stretch away . . . ?
Sisyphus is free to choose:
to kiss both his rock
and his impossible summit.


## The Resurrections of Layla Al-Attar[1]

I dip a brush in tar
And colour all the sparrows in the house
And scream at the lovers of killing: Stop
Isn't it enough
that you have killed Layla al-Attar?

Tonight Ishtar is in sorrow
dripping hot tears.
Sadness in Baghdad's eyes
clouds all the ancestors' ziggurats.
And the ancient women of Ur and Uruk
mourning brothers and sons.
But the martyrs already in the other world
will be wearing red flowers
and singing with joy.

Who can erase from this world a homeland
its shape Layla al-Attar?

From the ashes of tragedy an Iraq rises
guarded by millions of lovers,
an Iraq with liquid black eyes
whose lips are dates,
a river of ebony flows down the back
to the waist.
An Iraq that dips the brush in endurance
and colours all sparrows with green and red
the painting waves with flowers

the two rivers[2] become a frame
and Layla al-Attar smiles again.

1    *Layla al-Attar is a prominent Iraqi woman artist who was killed in her house in the
1998 American bombing of Baghdad.*
2    *The two rivers are the Euphrates and Tigris.*

# S 'adi Yusuf

## Translated by Khaled Mattawa

### Good Morning, Fakhani

Good Morning!
Good Morning streets and rifles . . .
Good Morning red beret, sun glowing on the boy's head . . .
Good Morning to you, headquarters guard
to night's guns, night's secret
to the delicious weariness in your beautiful eyes
Good Morning to children in their uniforms
to the girls craving
and craving
coffee in sidewalk cafés.
To Umm Nabil . . .
smile!
Good Morning Umm Nabil . . . smile!
Good Morning Abu Ali's teahouse . . .
And to you who burn for the roaring of jet planes
at your guns . . .
Good Morning.
Good Morning to garbage workers
to the radio announcer
to the young men tired of debates
to the silence of Toledo
to the man who offered me
al-Shaghila[1] twice . . .
To the students passing their exams in cafés
Good Morning.
Good Morning to revolutions exploding
like fireworks in a manifesto's first draft
to the revolutionary in the café: Good Morning!
to the revolutionary in my heart: Good Morning
to my wife, Good Morning
Good Morning
Good Morning
Good Morning

1   Literally "The working people," a leftist Lebanese newspaper.

## Enemies

*a poem in three movements*

### 1 *Childhood*

Through cardamom flower beds,
through papyrus, through orchards of falling dates
we walk,
a stream trickling between forehead and mouth . . .
Air filled with the smell of wild boar
hangs to our clothes.
We clutch palm fronds
and our ancestors' rifles are handmade.
The wild boar swims on green clouds.
Morning crumbs are still under our fingernails,
and the eyes of our orphans search through cardamom flowers
through papyrus
through bilharzia
for driftwood tossed by passing ships,
and search those ships for a meaning to the sea.
A sailor waves
and we lift our muddied clothes:
Greetings, god of driftwood,
god of floating cans.
Seagulls rummage through garbage on the shore.
The wild boar rustles in the congested chest.
A spot of water reddens . . .
We piss blood
and laugh,
and the wild boar rustles through the papyrus.
I call to shore:
Aunt, my aunt, O aunt . . .
Where are our ancestors' handmade rifles?
The boar rustles in the mud.
We were orphans
searching for a meaning to the sea.
Things touched us, but we didn't learn.
Names touched us, but we didn't speak.
These blunt palm fronds are children's toys,
and the smell of bread,
and the roof of the hay hut by the shore.
Aunt, my aunt, O aunt . . .
These green fronds!
and the boar swims through green clouds
and a red spot appears on the water

between papyrus and children's feet.
The god of the sea disappears
and the last waves from his ship
pull us to driftwood and tossed cans.
The head spins,
the head with burned hair,
the head with burned eyes.
And the sun spins . . .
The sea-sun falls into the head aching under water,
and the wild boar leaves his hiding place in the green clouds
following the sun sphere aching into the water . . .
The wild boar rustles
between driftwood and tossed cans.
By the shore our orphans' eyes glare at pieces of bread,
and at the head aching under water.
The wild boar writhes in the red water.
Aunt, my aunt, O aunt . . .

### 2 Insurgency

A plane rains quails made of paper
a manna of words we do not comprehend.
We grab them happy and shivering,
a country we forget what to call . . .
We know that I.R.A.Q. are letters we pronounce,
but where can we see it.
Will it enter through the door of our reed hut some day?
Will it come carrying clay pots
filled with fresh buttermilk
or white butter?
A plane drops quails made of paper
and circles the date palms
draping them with words we do not comprehend . . .
Abdelhassan Ben Mubarak gathered ten pots
for the honeydew and the manna,
and Abdelhassan Ben Mubarak told us
"Tonight we'll eat."

The honeydew plane passes on the tops of the palms
like a black pig . . .
We are the poor youth,
walking the land of an I.R.A.Q. we do not know.
Tonight we'll eat . . .
Abdelhassan Ben Mubarak takes us all to the shore,
ten pots to his left side.

A plane like a black pig
circles the tops of the palms,
and Abdelhassan Ben Mubarak leads us naked to water.
He cries out to us

Tonight we'll eat.  Come to your senses.
The waters were rising
and the red tide was filled with fish.
A plane
like a shark
circled above the water,
and Abdelhassan Ben Mubarak, naked, led us into the water.
Tonight, we'll eat.
We carried pots for honeydew
and the red tide carried fish we craved,
and the fishermen on the other bank,
and the shark plane passed over the shore.
We fell into the warm water
naked
and alone
and we were carrying pots for the quails
and words we didn't comprehend,
and Ben Mubarak's I.R.A.Q.
The sides of the fish were soft against our scaly skin.
Abdelhassan Ben Mubarak shouted
*K.A.W.S.A.J.*
*K.A.W.S.A.J.*
shark
shark . . .
The black tail rose like an axe over the water,
and a plane like a wild boar,
like a shark,
passed over the water.
We, the poor youths, screamed.
We, the walkers of an I.R.A.Q. we do not know, screamed . . .
And we, the poor youths, hurried back to the shore,
the black tail like an axe hovering over the water,
and Abdelhassan Ben Mubarak screamed,
his flesh torn,
and the red water reddened and reddened,
and Abdelhassan Ben Mubarak fell
toward disfigurement,
and the shark rushed toward the white water . . .
a plane passing over an I.R.A.Q. we do not know.

### 3 Days of 1963

I sleep in Sibah.
The guard beyond the bars was kind.
He was ill,
withdrawn,
a stranger.
The poor youths roamed desert houses,
and houses in aggrieved towns.
They were carried in trucks that tossed them about,
chained two to two.
The pig-plane-shark watched over them.
Which I.R.A.Q. will rise in Sibah?
Last night "the station" was filled.
The youths sang until the wild boar screamed.
The wild boar rustled across the bars.
The wild boar has two fangs made of steel.
The river ran along the right corner of the station.
A long time ago a man came here searching for the Creator's tree.
A long time ago the poisoned water was a refuge.
Lovers hid in esparto grass.
Behind the palms on the other bank oil fumes rose.
The shark-oil tanker had the scent of wild boar,
the glimmer of the black plane.
We sing in the holding station:
*Where is the tavern girl?*
A gun smuggler runs a bar under his blanket.
Iranian workers sleep tonight in the square.
At midnight the village comes carrying flaming fronds,
and sacrifices of bread,
and offerings of dates.
Iranian workers sleep tonight in the square.
Oil fumes on the other bank . . .
behind the palms and the temples of Zara,
and the Iranian workers asleep in the square.
His visit was denied.

His wife will wrap her cape around her,
holding his clemency papers.
His wife sits in a corner, her eyes smiling.
He tries to look at her eyes.
A machine gun from the station roof watches him.
*Where is the tavern girl?*

I sleep in Sibah.

The wild boar was on "the station" roof.
And the poor youths roamed through houses in aggrieved towns.
They were in trucks
that tossed them about,
chained two to two.

[Baghdad, 1977]


## How L'Akhdar Ben Youssef Wrote His Last Poem

Seven days passed and he didn't write.  He read until his eyes hurt,
and at noon walked the park.
At night he walked up and down the sandy beaches of Oran.
His friend said:  You didn't sleep for six days . . .
He told her: Of all my friends, you're the only one who's remained.
He, at any rate, is an unbalanced character, even if he appears calm.
And because he's unbalanced, and because his mind is scattered, and
because he didn't sleep for six days . . . he couldn't write a poem.  Still,
he took down these notes fearing he'll forget them.

### Notes
– Do not turn your jacket over even if it's worn out.
– Look for your defeated ring in your victorious country.
– Do not live in the words of exile when the house becomes too small.
– Do not eat the flesh of your enemy.
– Do not drink the sweat on your brow.
– Do not bite the hand that feeds you flowers.
– A guest may have the house, but not the people of the house.
– He who asks shall receive anything, but love.
– In old age gray hair may look black.
– All betrayals begin with a woman.

Fine. Here is L'Akhdar Ben Youssef facing a task more complicated
than he imagined.  It's true that when he wrote a poem he thought
very little of what will happen to it.  Still, writing becomes easy when
one can concentrate on a thing, a moment, a shiver, a leaf of grass . . .

Now, however, he's confronted with ten commandments and he
doesn't know which to pick . . .
And more important than all of this, how to begin?
Endings are always open, beginnings are always closed.

*Don't Live in the Words of Exile When the House Becomes Too Small*

Waves gush between his hands.
He grabs a stone (suddenly), and turns it into a shell.

He remains listening;
a wind gust (constant), blows, blows, constantly.
He enters the elements.
All the sea holds becomes a giant wave.
All the earth holds becomes a giant wave.
And he enters the elements:
a clenched fist
a stone
and a face with embossed features.
Here he's in his familiar streets . . .
his steps quickened,
an oyster shell in his hand.

Is your breathing calmer now? Maybe you can still write. Since you
were twenty you often felt in danger when you started a poem. But
once you finish the first stanza you feel a power inside you, its origins
unknown to you . . . like a spring from hidden sources. You only feel
the muffled gush. It must be your belief then, I mean you L'Akhdar
Ben Youssef, it must be your belief that you are now among the lost.

*Do Not Turn Your Jacket Over Even If It Gets Worn*

A girl enters
the used-clothes
store.
She's thin.
Her eyes widen
the way a skirt widens in the wind,
and widen
to stare at her lover's jacket,
his red/black jacket
and its missing buttons.

He may have used a new metre here, or a no-metre. The issue is not
important. When L'Akhdar Ben Youssef is withdrawn from the world
he loses his bearings. This is why his wing remains tied to a string
dragging on the face of the earth.

*Search for Your Defeated Ring in Your Victorious Country*

No victor at Night's end, and no defeated.
Each struggles with his stumbling.
Each regrets his stupor.
Each walks to his own slaughterhouse foolish as a bee.
Search for your defeated ring in your victorious country.
That lost star . . .
maybe you'll find it.
And if you do,
you'll let go of it
at the end of the night.

Finally he remembered Al-Mutanabbi, an old myopic poet standing
in the sand looking for his lost ring. There are jewellers in the world,
and there are artists. On the Algerian rug black is balanced with red.
Between them is the colour of ash. And the yellow . . . why? The
yellow. *Jaune! Jaune!* Arthur Rimbaud or Tristan Tzara? Oh, how
close yellow is to green! Only the sea. Camus used to love the
yellowness of the wheat fields facing the sea near Tibaza . . . Tibaza,
ah Tibaza!

*In Old Age Gray Hair May Look Black*

An old man at fifty
squats in his room, occupied with lies and cigarettes.
Who will return to the toothless his milk teeth?
Who will return to the grayhead the hair of its youth?
Who can fill this empty head?
But in old age gray hair can look black
and a lie may hold the truth
and cigarette clouds can look like a sky raining
and in his toothless gums milk teeth may grow.
But in old age too
a man very old at fifty can fall
dead in his room
dressed in lies and smoke.

L'Akhdar Ben Youssef is still unbalanced, his mind still scattered
because:
He had not slept for six days.
He could not write a poem.
He didn't hesitate to publish everything he wrote.

[19/6/1476]

### Poetry

Who broke these mirrors
and tossed them
shard
by shard
among the branches?
And now . . .
shall we ask L'Akhdar to come and see?
Colours are all muddled up
and the image is entangled
with the thing,
and the eyes burn.
L'Akhdar must gather these mirrors
on his palm
and match the pieces together
anyway he likes
and preserve
the memory of the branch.

[26/3/1980]


### The Trees of Ithaca

1

Suddenly at sunset Adam surprised us,
and the world that lived within us was a glass palace.
Child of the moment,
Adam,
what is a moment?
And the twenty-five thorns pricking you are a crown.

\*


They were not many, but they were one contingent.
Their weapons stolen like the lives of small creatures.
They crossed national borders;
nations that had no meaning.
And turbulence began.
There are princedoms of smothered wells.
There are vast kingdoms
and royal republics.
There are Palestinians without a kingdom or a republic.

The gulf waters cool the pipes of poverty,
and at night village names flare.
We are farmers in Bedouin tents,
teachers who shuffle about in sandals,
merchants of confiscated goods.
We are not blind, we are not asking for bread or wine.
We turn in the earth the way a shepherd wraps his cloak around him.
But we love our dialect, and our intonation of the alphabet.
Let the continents come at us.
Let the Arab partisans come to us.
They crossed borders. These nations have no meaning . . .
Only village names flare at night.
We will wear them like camouflage uniforms.
We will hang them on our shoulders as rifles,
and shoot them with our first bullets.

And we will keep our names
Wael Zaitar, Ghassan Kanafani,
Majid Abu Sharar . . .

    *

Child of the moment,
kaffiyah of night,
do you realize that since you came, we have not known what to do?
Is it because we are still taken by that palace of brittle glass?
Even the solitude of remembrance failed us
before the walls and their holdings collapsed . . .
We are your cowardly brothers,
Adam.
Within your first steps we held the prison feast.
We invited you to the wolf's table
and you agreed to come, Adam,
so that you would know . . .
How glorious you are Adam!
You agreed to come so that you would know?
So that we would know?
But we, your cowardly brothers, celebrated
unavenged blood spilled on the kaffiyah of night,
and for every knife we planted in your sweet body we picked a rose.
You transgressed, Adam.
The party remained a prison party.
No chorus resounded at the wolf's table
as you had hoped,
and the world that lives within us is still a palace made of glass . . .

**2**

Like this, in twilight, Adam beguiled us
and the world that occupies us is a glass palace.
Child of the moment,
Adam,
what is a moment?
And the twenty-five thorns pricking you are a crown.

\*

Clumps of the Sports Complex leaven like dough in the acrid air
where cluster bombs scatter like the devil's rosary.
In Chatila the roofs fly off . . .
and family photographs and the faucets of scarce water,
and from the sea to the Sullam neighbourhood, to the museum,
bodies formed the battle lines.
In Alhambra we hold the festival of the poor in the thousand-star hotels.
This roaring coming from Khalda is our hoarded voice . . .
The revolutionary council is still in place
and Abu Iyad's building is spilled on the sidewalk
and we rummage on through the universe.
No drop, and no mirror.
With camouflage uniforms then, we go on;
with personal weapons and guns at the shore
we continue to rummage through the universe.
Weapons strapped to our flesh, give us our bread and our hands.
Give us the primal chant.
Yassir Arafat was sullen like a day riddled with explosions.
He knew the enemy had advanced
on the axis of the museum and Barbir.
The students who were fed up with their Northern universities
were blazing, as if they never left their bases.
Let it roar then, the primal chant.
And let us keep our names: Saad Sayil, Azmi Al-Saghir, Ali Fouda.

\*

Should we light the candle, Adam,
and briefly wear what we were accused of
and rise, pure as you were once . . .
An early morning penetrates trees and wind.
An early morning, you remember, Adam:
lemons in their greenness
and lettuce leaves in elemental adornment,

a summer for songs
for the accordion
for waves
for water you mixed with water . . .
I sigh for you Adam.
The summer was carried on a blue silver tray,
and the world was a child playing in a garden
like you, Adam.
But we, your cowardly brothers, came at you with tanks
with water from the sea
with missiles in the wind and snipers from another kingdom . . .
We, all of us, wanted to kill the summer that plays
and the child that tires . . .
to smash the landing of a falling wave
fearing it will rise again.
We wanted to kill the barbarity of loin and offspring
    every woman holds within her.
We wanted to kill what the night kaffiyah engraves on the face of the wind.
We wanted to kill you once, and once again, and a thousand times . . .
Oh, how happy we were with what we were doing!
How beautiful!
But the firing squad facing you was even more beautiful
Ah, Adam . . .
How cruel you were when you left us behind, your cowardly brothers!
Stones on the beach,
stumps on shifting sands,
you, murderer dressed in the victim's clothes . . .


   3
Like this, in darkness, Adam left us
and the world that lived within us is a palace of glass.
Child of the moment,
Adam,
what is a moment?
And the twenty-five thorns pricking you are a crown.


   *


Here we are, wearers of kaffiyahs wrapped like helmets.
To us the chirping of bullets,
and cedars falling like tears . . .
To us the harbour song
where young boys are submerged into war chants.
To us the twenty-one bullet salute and the new army trucks.

From the municipal stadium
and the Abu Shahla Square,
we march like a river of songs
"like a river of lions."
The Beretta rifle is polished in the early morning, and gleaming.
Which dew will gather on the balcony plants?
Which woman will say "No" ?
I love you like this
in the intensity of snubbing and quarrelling.
We smuggled our children tucked among our bodies . . .
The kaffiyah is a helmet,
and the face is a prophet's.
We go into the Hellenic sea to reclaim our souls.
And we will keep our names:
Laila Khaled, Mahmoud Darwish, and Al-Khidr . . .

*

He is building boats out of the ribs of speech
unfolding sails out of the scent of lemons
and bringing nearer cities that were ravaged by plagues
and raiders, and brothers, and history . . .

How long will it take him to cross the sea,
where there is no sea? How long will it take him to reach the earth,
where there is no earth?
How many young men will he need to conquer the known world?
A purple light spirals on the kaffiyah of night
and gun powder . . .
and this khaki outfit,
this great journey.
Who is he saving the dust of songs for?
Who is he leading away?
Yet . . . he's leaving
and the sails, thinner than a taste of air, fill up with wind.
And the boys between shadowy stern and prow
carried grass
flags
and small weapons . . .
Are you leaving, so suddenly, Adam?
The sea you cut through is cutting us,
leaving us prisoners, naked without Adam.
We do not know what to do.
You were the gift, the everlasting loom.

You were night, awakening, and certainty;
your aloofness held our yearning,
an assurance that the cowardly brothers will remain cowardly.
Why do you leave tonight, Adam?
Will you leave us prisoners
having been a captive yourself?


### 4

Adam did not reveal what he held secret.
And why speak when his eyes are conscience?
The seeds of intention, whenever he suppressed them,
burst like grass fed by deep roots.
This is God's earth.  If it were to shrink, let it.
Let it be the last foothold.
This is God's earth and he entrusted it
to an angel-child who walks on water.
This is God's earth, a stone of it will suffice . . .
I saw Al-Khidr
I was walking, the water lifting me rose higher
I wanted to go to the walls
I wanted only a door . . .
Al-Khidr said "Come, you have reached the gate.
Enter my garden."
I hesitated.
Al-Khidr said: "You didn't enter?"
I fell silent.
Al-Khidr said: "My son
          he who crosses the distance
          he who seeks water
          who roams this stone
          who pitches tents in the valley
          will enter the promised refuge."


### 5

Here in Africa's high noon . . .
here under the noon stars,
let us take a rest, Adam.
Let us drink some tea, and anise,
and bitter coffee.
Or let us chew (as if in dream) these beans.
It does not matter.
We have reached our twenty-fifth year, and we have become skillful
and wise . . .

The hazy trees of the Ithaca harbour appear in the distance,
Let us sit for a while...

[Paris, 31/12/1989]


## Three Bridges

You run alone, burdened
with bluish moss, forgotten and slow.
Waves glitter on you,
banks fall into you,
and in your abandoned silence
you carry them along with weeds,
and carry them far away.
Your chest remains naked, dewed,
burdened with gifts
green like water, like dim mirrors,
a branch, a hat, a dead cat,
a child's shoe, a condom.
    The weeds braid ribbons around them,
and you, careful stepper, carry them
and bend them
                    with your bending.
As the days pass they become your water.
Waves glitter on them,
banks fall into them.
And you return again: gifts and mirrors.

### *First Bridge*
I hid them under me.
Night brought out its stars,
soaked them, washed them, and let them swim.
There were three; they held their stars,
but didn't wash them
                    in water . . .
They waited.
I felt the wheels crush my backbone.
The three hid behind the shadow of my chest,
and I saw them running.
Iron exploded and my back sank
in the water. The stars fell upon me then.
And the river ran

and night laid its golden white palms
on the ruins of my chest.

### Second Bridge
The bridge leads to a small tree blossoming
with sparrows,
a princess listening out from her green balcony
for the sun's whispers.
There was a gate by her green waistline.
The river was a gate to her green waistline.
Princess:
Oh how the bridge worships you!
It barely recognizes the river.
What is this water, this wayfarer passing by,
this visitor passing by?
It barely recognizes the bridge.

### Third Bridge
Lend me your hands.
Lend me your rough hands
and let me feel
your heartbeat against my arm.
Lend me your hand.
Let me feel the wind scream in the sail.
Lend me a hand for vigour, a glance toward a lost stream.
In the days when we saw the world
with a flame thin as a dream,
our black eyes shone on nothing
except on the veins on your arms,
shone on nothing except the steps of those who
pushed through their stone souls
lunging toward you.
Today, we lend you a hand to find our garden.
If only you would lend me your wounded hand,
O bridge-tomb!
Our black eyes are heavy-lidded,
and my old boat is sailed by a blind captain.
But the garden remains the same.
Its red flowers have never seen
handkerchiefs waving goodbye.

Appointed hour in the midst of loss,
give me your rough hands to feel
your heart beat against my arms.

[Algiers, 1/4/65]

# The Boundless Poet: Fadhil al-Azzawi's *Auf einem magischen Fest*

by Daniel Reynolds
Grinnell College

In a course entitled 'Topics in German Culture', which coincided with a symposium at Grinnell College, 'Iraqi Culture and the Diaspora', the Iraqi poet Fadhil al-Azzawi visited a group of American students to discuss his German poems published as *Auf einem magischen Fest (At a Magical Celebration)*.[1] This visit offered the students (and the professor) in this class an unparalleled opportunity not only to speak with Dr al-Azzawi about his volumes of poems, but also to ask ourselves what it means to write German poetry, indeed, what it means to be German (or Iraqi, or American). The serendipity of Dr al-Azzawi's arrival, our good fortune to invite an Iraqi poet living in exile in Berlin since 1983 into a course on Germany's increasingly multi-ethnic make-up, offers an appropriate metaphor for the poems themselves. For this collection of verse presents many moments of chance encounters and fantastical dialogues, often crossing cultural boundaries and uniting poetic traditions.

It would be inaccurate to call Fadhil al-Azzawi's book of poems a collection of translations. Rather, the poems in this volume are adaptations, poems in German based on original verse in Arabic.[2] As al-Azzawi explained to the students of our German class, his goal is not to reproduce the poem in German in close approximation to its original structure in Arabic, but rather to rework the text into an entity with a new significance, one that speaks to an audience that reads German and calls on a different repertoire of cultural expectations and experiences. His aim in all poems, both their Arabic and their German incarnations, is to say something new.

These adaptations generate fascinating inter-cultural encounters that al-Azzawi, a poet from the multi-ethnic city of Kirkuk in northern Iraq and currently living in the multi-ethnic city of Berlin, deliberately evokes. For example, a poem entitled 'Stacheldraht' (Barbed Wire, 20), with its second line consisting of the word *"Konzentrationslager"* (concentration camp) or 'Asche' (Ash, 16) situates itself immediately in the Western reader's mind within the history of the Jewish Holocaust during World War II. But the knowledge that our poet lives in Berlin in exile, that he has been imprisoned in Iraq for nothing more serious than owning English-language books, reminds us that the meaning of that history is not confined to its European setting.[3] The cultural dynamics in al-Azzawi's poems are multi-directional. A poem entitled 'Lied im

Kerker' (Song in the Dungeon, 44) establishes an Arabian setting with the evocation of the name "Sultana" and the reference to "arabische Nächte" (Arabian nights), but in a volume of poetry that moves so freely from one locale to another, indeed from one timeframe to another, these specificities become fused with one another in a web of mutual correspondences.

The notion of correspondence calls to mind the French Symbolist poets, Baudelaire in particular. As Khalid al-Maaly states in his afterword to the volume, al-Azzawi belongs to the generation of Iraqi poets that follows the avant-garde free-verse generation. As al-Azzawi himself further explained to the class, poets of his generation turned to European modernist and pre-modernist movements for inspiration, borrowing from the Symbolists, the Expressionists, Dada and their contemporaries. The Symbolist tendencies (which, in the case of German poetry at least, never disappeared from the more radical modernist movements of the early twentieth century) are quite pronounced in this volume, but again, al-Azzawi does not naïvely mimic these traditions, he adapts them to create something distinctly new. A wonderfully playful example is his short poem 'Missverständnis' (Misunderstanding, 41), which I quote here in its entirety:

| | |
|---|---|
| Der Dichter stand auf dem Podium und stellte sich vor: | The poet stood at the podium and introduced himself: |
| "Meine Gedichte sind Vögel!" | "My poems are birds!" |
| die Vögel schwebten über unseren Köpfen und sangen: | the birds floated over our heads and sang: |
| "wir sind Gedichte!' | "We are poems!" |
| | |
| so kannst du sagen | so you could say |
| daß ich gestern in einem Café einen Vogel schrieb | that, yesterday in a café, I wrote a bird |
| und zuvor ein Gedicht verspeiste | and before that I dined on a poem |
| in einem | in a |
| Lyriklokal | lyric pub. |

The mutually referring images of poems and birds read here almost as a parody of the Symbolist doctrine of the self-contained, self-referential work of art, but al-Azzawi's sense of humour seems to be more about play than parody. The poet ultimately pokes fun at himself, asking not to be taken too seriously when he casts himself in a "lyric pub," the potential pretentiousness of which is now undermined by its ontological indeterminacy as a place somewhere between poems and birds.

This kind of humour is typical of al-Azzawi's poems, where a sense of lightness and wonder prevails over any images of gloom. But this levity is not to be mistaken for disengagement, as one might otherwise expect from a poet indebted to aestheticist art movements of late nineteenth- and early twentieth-century Europe. An example of the confrontation with the realities of a world where war, oppression, religious strife and exile are all too common, occurs in the poem 'Der Diktator und der Vogel' (The Dictator and the Bird, 51), wherein the dictator decrees how birds are to fly in his presence. The comic futility of the dictator's attempt to govern nature, while humorous, reminds us at the same time of the frequent attempt to control art, represented again in the image of the bird. Rather than focus on the brutality inherent in the situation, though, al-Azzawi's poem strikes a note of optimism that ultimately rests upon a more broadly historical, rather than a biographical, perspective.

The references to historical events signal themselves clearly in such poems as 'Stacheldraht' mentioned above. The poems 'Napoleons Pferd' (Napoleon's Horse, 17) and 'Kaiser' (Emperor, 52) do the same. But while 'Stacheldraht' remains sombre in tone, these two poems sound the same note of levity encountered in 'Der Diktator und der Vogel' or 'Missverständnis'. Napoleon's horse is discovered by the poet in a circus, being led by a clown; the emperor momentarily returns from the clouds, mounts a dinosaur, and departs, leaving *"uns mit dem Leben allein"* – leaving us alone with life. The transience of historical phenomena, their metamorphosis from present reality to future myth, provides a recurrent motif in these poems.

The ease with which al-Azzawi moves among historical time, autobiographical time and mythical time – often within the same poem – contributes to the magical quality of his lines. He peoples his self-referential poem 'Der Dichter und seine Gestalten' (The Poet and his Figures, 21) with a princess and a monster, but also with a retiree, a thief, and police. In 'Aus Gewohnheit' (Out of Habit, 14), the poet is on his way to the dentist's office in contemporary Berlin when he is visited by the tenth-century Arabian poet al-Mutanabi. The sequence of poems themselves in the volume represents a kind of time-travel, on multiple levels. Beginning with the most recent and more clearly autobiographical poems from the mid-90s, the volume concludes with the 'Abdullah Cycle' from 1974-1975, poems both about and addressed to a figure who resembles an ancient prophet in the desert. Drawing on both Arabian and European traditions of story-telling, the references to fairy tales, legends and myths locate the exile experience of cultural fluidity on a fantastic plane that augments rather than supplants the historical, political and personal notes so many of these poems strike.

While the poems reveal the pain that exile brings, the acceptance of life that these same poems convey cannot be described in terms of resignation or loss. As suggested by the title, celebration seems the more appropriate response. The middle section of the volume contains the eight-part 'Himmelfahrt ins Exil' (Ascension into Exile, 71-87), which presents the motif of exile as a metaphor for the poet's existence in any land: "*O du Wüste ewiges Weib der Propheten / ich kenne deinen Sohn / diesen zum Exil verdammten Zauberer / der uns zwischen Tod und Tod zum Leben führt*" (O you desert eternal wife of prophets / I know your son / this magician condemned to exile / who leads us between death and death to life; 74). The orphic mission of the poet as the mediator between the realms of life and death condemns him to exile, but not necessarily to isolation; rather, the poet in exile is called on to bear witness to the continuities of time and place. Al-Azzawi's boundary-crossing poems contain the creed by which he lives his life. While he now lives in Berlin, he has made poetry his home, and with this volume he invites us to join him for a magical celebration.

**Notes**

1    Al-Azzawi, Fadhil, *Auf einem magischen Fest*. Berlin: Das Arabische Buch, 1998. All English translations in this essay are my own.

2    In comments at the end of the volume Al-Azzawi acknowledges the assistance of Suleman Taufiq, Stefan Weidner and Heribert Becker in some of these translations.

3    This information is presented in the afterword of the volume by Khalid Al-Maaly, 149-153.

# Review

*Quartet of Joy*
Muhammad Afifi Matar
Translated by Ferial Ghazoul and John Verlenden
Fayetteville, University of Arkansas Press, 1997

*Quartet of Joy* (*Ruba'iat al-Farah*) is a long poem by contemporary Egyptian poet Muhammad Afifi Matar (1935- ). A few years ago it was translated by Ferial Ghazoul and John Verlenden, well-known translators, and published in a bilingual edition in 1997. After the publication of this translation, Matar's *Collected Poetic Works* was published in three volumes in 1998. Matar then won the prestigious prize for poetry from al-Owais Cultural Foundation. The fact that he was awarded this prize after the translation was published reveals how influential English translation has recently become on the literary standard in the Arab world. Whether or not a piece of literature is translated into English practically determines the artistic value of that work. At this early stage of globalization it is difficult to determine whether this phenomenon is enriching Arabic literary tradition. Already, one finds many influences of Western culture in Arabic literature. The four-part structure of Matar's poem, for instance, recalls the structure of the Western symphony. The content of these sections, entitled 'Earth Joy', 'Fire Joy', 'Water Joy' and 'Air Joy', blends the Islamic Sufi concept of the unity of being (*wahdt al-wujud*) with the ancient Greek belief that all objects are derived from four elements: earth, fire, water, and air. As the process of globalization continues, it is likely that art produced in different cultures will bear similar features. One can also predict that this current trend will cause languages as dissimilar as English and Arabic to lose some of the elements that keep these languages distinct, thus making it easier for translations to preserve the "original's mode of signification" (21), which, according to Walter Benjamin, is the litmus of good translation. Translators know very well that translating poetry is more difficult than translating prose. It seems to us that the source of this difficulty lies in the nature of poetic language. Poetry calls attention to its own imagery and rhythm, rendering the "meaning" of the poem subordinate. The 19th-century French poet Stéphane Mallarmé gave his friend Edgar Degas advice (which we know now to foreshadow Formalist studies of literariness): "You can't make a poem with ideas, you make it with words" (62). The primacy of rhythm and metre and imagery in the experience of poetry makes poetry closer to music than other literary genres. And since music is untranslatable, translators find themselves in a bind. The task of the translator becomes even more arduous when poetry is not only musical but is also saturated with philosophy and mysticism as is Matar's poem.

But Ghazoul and Verlenden rose to the challenge. Ghazoul, a native speaker of Arabic, is a professor of comparative literature and a well-known literary critic in English and Arabic. She has translated many literary works from Arabic into English and vice versa. Verlenden is a native speaker of English, a poet, and professor of creative writing. He studied Arabic while he was teaching English at the American University of Cairo. As the translators indicate in their Preface, this translation is the result of three renderings: first, Ghazoul translated the Arabic text literally into English; then, she reworded her literal rendering to bring it closer to idiomatic English without compromising the integrity of the Arabic text; and finally, the English poet-translator polished the poem while keeping it within the constraints Ghazoul had defined. "Our final version," the translators indicate, "is the outcome of dialectical insights and interlocking efforts, which were facilitated by the work site [The American University of Cairo]." Nothing less than these translators' qualifications would have sufficed in the translation of Matar's convoluted style. This team of wordsmiths was determined to capture the elusive spirit of the poem and to embed it into a foreign language without losing the poetry itself. The translated poem is therefore both Arabic and English in its essence. Its language is English, but its sensibility is clearly a creative hybrid of Arabic and English. One may argue that sensibility cannot be separated from language, and we would (to some degree) agree. Nevertheless a rift becomes evident each time an English reader understands the words in the translated poem but struggles with references to Islamic and Arabic culture. Aware of this cultural barrier, the translators appended to the translation two sections: 'Glossary' (pp. 65-67) and 'Explanatory Notes' (pp. 69-78). These sections assist the reader when he or she stumbles upon an unfamiliar image or allusion. But something crucial is lost when one turns away from the poem and toward the explanation. The flow of the reading experience is broken as the English reader seeks explanations for images that would, in most instances, be ingrained in the Arabic reader's mind.

One element that is not lost in translation is the story-line or the narrative substance, as Umberto Eco showed in his recent work *Experiences in Translation* (2001). He writes: "Neither story nor plot is a question of language. Both are structures that can be translated into another semiotic system" (30). But, as we have asserted, narrative structure is not the essence of poetry – words are. When we would try to locate the same line in the original Arabic and English versions of this poem, we found that our only guides were narrative structure and typography. We could not use words as guides because many words in Arabic have different connotations in English from those they have in Arabic.

In 'Second Prelude' of 'Earth Joy', for instance, the speaker declares: "I who am born of forty women,/I look out for the *ravings* of *memory*/ and the *defiance* of forms/for the earth is arched over/the harvests of death/and the decanters of aged thirsts" (p. 3). We have italicized three words that have strikingly dissimilar connotations in Arabic and English. The first word *ravings* does not convey the slant of the Arabic word *hathaian* which means something very close to the English *delirium*. The similarity between the two texts breaks down further in the second line, when the word *defiance* is used to refer to the Arabic word *jimuh*, which conjures the image of a wild horse neighing and lifting his front legs as he refuses to be mounted. The word *memory* does not capture the conscious effort in the Arabic word *tathakkur*, which is closer to *remembrance* or *recalling*. The words *ravings, memory,* and *defiance* do not raise problems in the English version, but when compared to the Arabic original, it is clear that the imagery has been altered. This problem raises the question: what would happen to the translation if we keep it as close to Arabic as possible? Can we retain "the original's mode of signification" (20) of which Benjamin writes, in the following translation of the same stanza?

I who was born of forty women,
I lie in wait for the delirium brought by remembrance
and forms, rearing as stallions
for the earth is arched over
the harvest of death
and decanters of aged thirst.

The following example illustrates how the symbolic order of the target culture holds more weight in the process of translation than does the particular meaning of a phrase in the original language.

Here is water, water, water!
Water is a portal whose locks
    night opens
for the passage of  creation:
        seas embracing seas,
        springs marrying springs;
        the river pulls out the wedding kerchief
        embroidered with dinars and bracelets.

Water is a portal whose locks
        dawn also opens:
        here is God saluting,
        dispatching trees and letters
        in lines and lines of scriptural space (p. 36)

The "closer" translation, which is, of course, inseparable from my own interpretation, would be this:

> Here is water and water and water
> Water is a portal night unlocks
> for the passage of all creations:
> here are the seas their arms around each other's waist
> here is the marriage of springs
> and the river drawing behind it, the wedding scarf
> embroidered with dinars and grass
> scattering rings and bracelets.
>
> Water is the portal dawn unlocks:
> here is God spreading His greetings:
>> trees
> and letters. The letters are birds filling space with writing,
> line after line. (p. 36)

In these examples we see a tension between the desire to preserve the meaning of the source text and the desire to create a poetic effect, when the particular signification is expressed in the target language. These two desires oppose one another, and the text that results from them has an identity distinct from the original. Nonetheless, the English/Arabic bilingual reader who reads both versions of Matar's poem will compare the two versions and wonder how the translator would justify employing certain English words that do not come close to their counterparts in the Arabic version. The key words here are *scriptural space*, which is a translation of the Arabic *al-kitabah*, that is *writing*. The Arabic refers to writing in general, and portrays the act of writing, whether scriptural or poetic, as a divine act. These crucial lines obliquely refer to the traditional quarrel between poetry and the Qur'an. It is well-known that the Qur'an in self-defence curses poets and poetry. Here Matar seems to assert that God is the source of both.

Other examples in which one can clearly see the divergence of the two texts for reasons of interpretation or the dictates of the target language follow:

> Are you, O tavern keeper,
>> ready to deflower the clay seals,
>> set the table with goblets,
> hunks of food,
>> bushel baskets of salted grass
>>> and olive (p.3)

In the Arabic original, the word *muhannatt* means *embalmed* or *mummified*, yet the word *salted* has been used instead of either. Did the word *salted* sound more poetic than *embalmed*?

The translated version also dilutes the climactic, lyrical and erotic moment that the original creates:

That was the forenoon prayer:
flows of creation stood in rows,
invigorated by collective ablution;
creation was under the profound space
      rising,
their steps and frames running parallel
      between two lines"
a horse for all, the earth
a dream for all, the horizon,
justice for all, the joy whose colours are aroused
in the fountains of birds, weaving and reweaving
heavens and serenity
laudation of
*Allah Akber*
from the resounding revelations
and the inspiration raised by the verdure
      of the living:
the turning of craned anxiety under the surfaces
      of matter;
*the rhythm of the pains*
of possible sculptures in the rock,
*of the mouth watering* with poetic stirrings
in the knot of the bosom amid the petals
of the raptures caused  by ripening pleasure
in the dropping fruit onto the down of grass (p. 55, italics added).

The italicized segments mark the places where we feel interpretation has come in the way of accuracy. In the original version of this section, there is no mention of *Allah Akber*. Matar used a word in Arabic that literally means "to utter God's greatness." This word emphasizes the action of uttering God's greatness, rather than the utterance itself. The translated version emphasizes the opposite. Similarly, the *rhythm of the pains* does not replicate Matar's elaborate birth conceit that follows the sexual encounter that has been implied since the beginning of the scene. If we replace *the rhythm of pains* with *the rhythm of contractions*, it becomes clear that the stone will soon give birth to sculptures. The original metaphor would be preserved.

These suggestions, of course, reveal a different interpretation of the original than is implied by Ghazoul and Verlenden's translation. Discrepancies between the original and the translation may not diminish the poetic quality of the English version, but we find that the translation definitely changes the theme and the vision of the poem. To some degree, this is the result of the inevitable process of the naturalization that the text undergoes when it is rendered in the language of the target culture. We assume that even the act of interpretation and the particular mode of signification are not free from their own culture and language. The following two lines from the above quoted stanza illustrate both the particularity of language and the limit of translation: "of the mouth watering with poetic stirrings / in the knot of the bosom amid the petals" erases the sexual implications of this poetic climax as it is conveyed in the original which literally reads like this: "What swells the lust of poetry [like milk in the mother's breast] in the knot [nipple] of the breast amid the petals." The line "of the raptures caused by ripening pleasure" is an image in Arabic of the intense pleasure that orgasm gives to the lovers (we think *raptures* is a printing error for *ruptures*) and that childbirth gives to the mother.

Ghazoul and Verlenden's translation is a unique model of translation that inevitably raises issues that face every serious translator. The extremely difficult examples we have discussed above indicate some of these issues, such as the compromise the translator has to make, the inevitable overlapping of translation and interpretation, and the primacy of the target language over the source language. The three issues are so interlocked that it would be impossible to discuss them separately. All three problems are enmeshed in the tyrannical nature of language and culture that caused the death of the author, according to Barthes and Foucault. If the author is really dead, the translator, murdered by two languages, is doubly dead.

*Saadi A Simawe and Carolina Hotchandani*

**Works Cited**

Benjamin, Walter, ' The Task of the Translator'. Trans. Harry Zohn in *The Translation Studies Reader*. Ed. Lawrence Venuti. New York: Routledge, 2000.

Eco, Umberto, *Experiences in Translation*. Toronto: University of Toronto Press, 2001.

# Biographies

## Poets

**Mahdi Muhammad Ali** has been living in exile since the late 1970s. Ali has published poetry in Iraqi and Arab literary journals. He lives in Damascus and he works as the editor of Iraqi journal *al-Thaqafa al-Jadida*. His poetry is rich with passion and nostalgia for the homeland.

**Sinan Anton** was born in Baghdad and left Iraq in 1996. Anton is a poet and translator. He has published poetry and translations in many Arabic and English journals. Anton is a doctoral student in Arabic at Harvard University.

**Fadhil Assultani** was born in a small town near the city of Hilla, south of Baghdad. He studied at the University of Baghdad, worked as a journalist, and taught in Iraq, Morocco and Algeria. He began writing poetry in the 1960s. He is widely read in English literature and has been working on a complete Arabic translation of Whitman. His poetry is characteristically modernist in its imagery and intimate rhythms. In addition to his publications in Iraqi and Arabic journals, he published a book of poetry entitled *Burning in Water*. He lives in London and works as the editor of the literature section of the Arabic daily *al-Sharq al-Awsat*.

**Fadhil al-Azzawi** was born and raised in Iraq's northern city of Kirkuk. Al-Azzawi published poetry, essays, fiction and literary criticism. He is one of the most innovative poets in the Arab world and has always been an iconoclast in politics and literature. He is widely read in English and German and his writing blends the Arabic literary tradition with Western modernism and postmodernism. At the University of Baghdad he studied English literature and joined the political left. He was sent to prison and there, he rebelled against the political tradition of the Iraqi left and became interested in existentialism and the literature of the absurd. Al-Azzawi, in his poetry and writing, has become an advocate of humanism as opposed to ideology. He has published many poetry books, several novels, and an important memoir on literary and political life in the 1960s. He lives now in Germany.

**Abd al-Wahhab al-Bayyati** (1926-1999) was a major Iraqi poet and a central member of *harakat al-sh'r al-hur* (free verse movement) of the 1950s. He published more than 20 books of poetry and essays on life in exile and the poetic experience. Al-Bayyati spent most of his life wandering from exile to exile. His poetry is characterized by modernistic concerns with the self, existentialism, Sufism, and the struggle with the absurd. His poetic style blends classical Arabic poetry with free verse forms and metres. Beginning in the 1960s he experimented with the use of the mask, invoking the Sufi masters of the Islamic Renaissance.

**Mahmoud al-Braikan** was killed in mysterious circumstances last year in his home in Basra at the age of 70. Al-Braikan was an important and inspiring figure of high modernism. Al-Braikan's poetry is innovative in terms of its new themes and stylistic techniques. He was a master of aesthetic ambiguity and presented a cosmic vision of humanity, portraying human life in its interactions with the environment in fresh and surprising ways.

**Abdula Sulaiman Abdula Beg (Goran)** was born in 1904 or 1905 in the town of Helebje. A contemporary of Faiq Bekes, he too was orphaned at an early age, rebelled against the prevailing social and political conditions and agitated on behalf of the Kurdish people. Unlike Bekes, who was a nationalist politically and a traditionalist poetically, Goran was an internationalist and a radical both politically and poetically. He abandoned the Arabic form of *roudh*, reverting to the old Indo-Iranic forms, and used Kurdish terms wherever possible, maintaining rhyme regardless of the rhythm. Goran is regarded as the founding father of modern Kurdish poetry, although some of his followers have abandoned rhyme altogether under the guise of modernism. Ironically, Bekes was more popular with the peasants and proletariat, whereas Goran was a favourite of the bourgeois nationalists, though on account of his poetic form rather than his political views.

**Faiq Abdulla Beg (Bekes)** was born in 1905 in Sitek village, near the city of Sulaimani. Orphaned at an early age, he was brought up in different cities and homes; he chose the pen name 'Bekes', which signifies aloneness. Bekes was a popular poet, using the vernacular form of Kurdish. His style is ultra-simple and to the point. He was politically active, and fearless in his criticism of the regime. In 1946, for instance, at a farewell ceremony for the local governor of Sulaimani, Bekes addressed the protesters with a poem titled 'My Twenty Seven Years', a reference to the British occupation of Iraq. His son, Sherko Bekes, keeps the family tradition alive.

**Sherko Faiq (Bekes Jr)** has all but abandoned rhyme, although his expressiveness and rhetorical energy more than make up for the lack of rhyme. Like his father, Sherko was banished to Southern Iraq for a while and lived in exile in Iran and Sweden, where he achieved some literary recognition. Following the liberation of Iraqi Kurdistan in 1991, he returned to the homeland, where he eventually became Minister of Culture, remaining in this position until the outbreak of the internecine struggle in 1994.

**Gzar Hantoosh** was born in the city of al-Diwaniyah, where he still lives. Early in his life, Hantoosh showed an interest in literature. He began publishing his poetry in the early 1970s in Iraqi and Arab journals. He published two books of poetry: *The Red Forest* and *The Happiest Man in the World*. As the selection in this anthology shows, Hantoosh's poetry builds upon folkloric episodes, characters and proverbs. His poetry depicts bizarre situations with a tone of bitter humour.

**Bulland al-Haydari** was born in Baghdad to a Kurdish family. He wrote in Arabic and was, for the most part, self-educated. In the 1950s, he became a central figure of the *Jeel al-Ruwwad* (the generation of the pioneers) which has dominated modern Iraqi and Arab poetic landscapes. In addition to two books of essays on art and literature, al-Haydari published nine poetry books. Although in exile for many years, al-Haydari continued his political activism in highly sophisticated poetry. In many of his poems, the speaker identifies himself with the Third World liberation movement. His poetic style is characterized by innovative metrical rhythms, vivid imagery, and quiet revolutionary themes. He died in London.

**Ahmed Herdi,** aged about seventy, has lived in the UK since the 1980s. His poem 'God's Freedom Lovers' is particularly noteworthy. Politics has been a dominant theme in his poetry.

**Fereydun Refiq Hilmi** was born in 1942. He speaks Kurdish, English, Arabic, Polish, German and some French. He has a doctorate in Systems Science, from City University, London, and has worked for various computer manufacturers in the UK. Dr Hilmi was in the first Kurdish Cabinet in South Kurdistan as Deputy Minister for Transport and Communication. His main interests are science and technology, politics, poetry (and the arts in general) and languages.

**Lamiah Abbas Imara** is an Iraqi woman poet born in the South to a Sabean (Mandaean) family. Imara studied at the prestigious High Teachers' Training College in Baghdad in the 1950s, where she met the emerging leaders of modern Iraqi poetry such as Badr Shakir al-Sayyab, S'adi Yusuf, and Nazik al-Mala'ika. During those years, she began publishing her poems. She published seven books of poetry in Baghdad, Beirut and California. Because of her identification with the left, Imara had to leave Iraq in the mid 1970s. Employing nontraditional images, her poetry depicts the theme of love and women's rights in connection with freedom and democracy in her country. She lives now in California.

**Muhammad Mahdi al-Jawahiri** was born to a family of writers and theologians in Iraq's sacred city of al-Najaf, the centre of political radicalism of the Iraqi Shi'at. Al-Jawahiri began writing poetry when he was very young. Early on, he rebelled against the religious tradition, moved to Baghdad, and joined the left. Although al-Jawahiri's themes and his revolutionary and nationalistic concerns are highly modernistic, he was influenced by the classical poetic tradition and his poetry may be considered neo-classical. His complete poetry, published in seven volumes, is considered a chronicle of the Iraqi and Arab struggle against Western colonialism. Many critics and readers consider al-Jawahiri the last great poet of the classical Arabic tradition and rank him with al-Mutannabi, Abu Tammam and al-Buhtari, the greatest poets of the Arab Renaissance (8th-13th centuries AD).

**Jamal Juma'h** was born in 1956 in the southern city of Imarah. He left Iraq in the late 1970s. In addition to his publication of poems in several Arabic journals, he has published five books of poetry: *People* (1987), *Painting with Cities* (1990), *The Book of the Book* (1990), *Footnotes and Supplements* (1991), and *Scandinavian Bezels*. He lives in Denmark.

**Fawzi Karim** was born in Baghdad in 1945. In 1968 he graduated from the University of Baghdad and published his first poetry book *Haith Tebda' al-Ashia'a* (Where Things Begin). He migrated to Beirut in 1969, where he published his second collection *Arfa'au Ydi Ihtijajan* (I Raise My Hand in Protest). He returned to Baghdad and published his third collection *Junun min al-Hajar* (Madness of Stone), and two books of nonfiction, one on exile and the other on the Iraqi author Admon Sabri. In 1978, he migrated to London where he still lives. In exile, he published three more books of poetry. His *Selected Poems* was published in 1995 in Cairo. In 2000 his *Complete Poetry* was published in Damascus by Dar al-Mada. In addition to his regular writing for newspapers on classical music and on painting, he edits his own quarterly *al-lahdha al-Shi'iria* (Poetic Moment).

**Abd al-Karim Kassid** was born and educated in the city of Basra. After many years of exile in Yemen and Syria, he moved to London, where he is now living. He taught in Iraq and Algeria and travelled in France; there he learned French, from which he translated three books of poetry and prose. He has published five books of poetry, the most recent of which appeared in 1990. Al-Kassid has worked as a journalist for many Arab journals in Baghdad, Damascus and London. His poetry is characterized by a blend of modernism, Sufism and references to Islamic and Arab history.

**Shakir Li'aibi** was born in 1955 in Iraq. Li'aibi is a poet, a writer and a painter. He earned an MA in Psychology and Science of Education from the University of Baghdad in 1977 and a Diploma in Art from the School of Art in Geneva in 1992. In addition to numerous articles on literature, art and culture in major Arab journals, Li'aibi has published more than six books of poetry, the first of which was *Fingers of Stone* ( 1976) and the most recent *There Are the Guards: My Sublime* (1993). He lives in Geneva and works in the Arab Emirates.

**Sami Mahdi** was born in 1940 and lives in Baghdad, where he works as the editor-in-chief of the official Iraqi daily *al-Thwara*. Once he published his first poems, Mahdi became recognized as an important poet who effectively blends lyricism with a strong sense of Arab nationalism. He has published several books of poetry, the most famous of which are *The Questions* (1979) and *Sunset* (1981).

**Nazik al-Mala'ika** was born in 1923 in Baghdad to a literary family. She studied literature at Higher Teachers' Training College in Baghdad and Princeton University. In 1956 she earned an MA in Comparative Literature from the University of Wisconsin. Al-Mala'ika is the most important woman poet and critic in the Arab world. Her central role in *harakat al-shi'r al-hur* (free verse movement) since the late 1940s is evident in her own poetry and in her critical writings and has left its mark on the modernist movement in Arabic poetry. In her second collection, *Shadhayah wa Ramad* (1949), she revolted against the traditional use of rhyme and the two-hemistitch line. Al-Mala'ika has published six volumes of poetry and three books of literary criticism. Her poetry is characterized by its intense lyrical romanticism and nationalism. Her latest poetry blends Sufism with romanticism and nationalism. She lives in Egypt.

**Dunya Mikhail** was born in Baghdad in 1964. Mikhail left Iraq in 1995. After earning an MA in Arabic at Wayne State University (Near Eastern Studies), she now teaches Arabic in Detroit. With highly sensitive and surprising poetry, Mikhail has impressively introduced a new genre in modern Arabic poetry, namely, the war poem. She writes about devastating wars within and against her country in a very intimate, child-like tone. Mikhail has published four volumes of poetry so far: *Bleeding of the Sea* (1986), *The Psalms of the Absence* (1993), *Dairy of A Wave Outside the Sea* (1995), and *Almost Music* (1997).

**Murad Mikha'il**, an educator, poet and writer, was born in 1906 in Baghdad where he earned his high school diploma and graduated from law school. He earned his PhD from the Hebrew University in Jerusalem, writing his dissertation on the *Cairo Geniza*. He was one of the Iraqi Jewish intellectuals who published many prose poems and managed to break from convention by varying the metre and the rhyme within a poem. He also served as the Principal (1931-1949) of the Jewish high school, *Shammash*, in Baghdad, where he taught students taking the English matriculation tests. After his arrival in Israel in the early 1950s and until his death, Mikha'il was engaged in teaching Arabic Literature in various Israeli educational institutions, writing in the Arabic newspaper *al-Yawm* as its literary editor, and delivering speeches on literary topics and Muslim civilization. His writing includes *al-Muruj wal-Sahara* (Baghdad, 1931), *Ta'rikh al-Adab al-'Arabi*, (Israel, 1965-69, 3 vols.) and *al-Hadarah al-Islamiyah* (Israel, 1967). The Biblical book *Song of Songs* influences his love poetry. The selection of poems translated in this anthology is from Mikha'il's collection of poems that he prepared two years prior to his death. His wife Shulamit published them under the title *al-A'mal al-Shi'riyah al-Kamilah lil-Duktur Murad Mikha'il*, with an autobiography by the author and a biography by Professor Sasson Somekh.

**Sheikh Mus Hasan Muhamad (Jigerkhwen)** was born in 1903 in Turkish Kurdistan, completing his education in the theological schools. He emigrated to Syrian Kurdistan where he eventually became a member of parliament. Following the 14th July revolution in Iraq, he left for Baghdad, where he was a lecturer in Kurdish literature at the university and a radio broadcaster. However, after the 8th February 1963 coup d'état by the Baath Party, he went into exile in Sweden, spending most of the rest of his life there. He died in 1984. Belonging to the generation of Faiq Bekes and Abdula Goran, he was a counterpart to the latter in the northern Kirmanji dialect.

**Sajidah al-Musawi** is an Iraqi woman poet, who writes in Arabic. No further information about her is not available.

**Awad Nasir** was born in the early 1950s and began publishing his poetry in the early 1970s in leftist newspapers and journals. He has published two collections of poetry and various essays on politics, culture and the arts. He left Iraq in the late 1970s and lives now in London. His poetry is characterized by a bold minimalism and by its concern with childhood and the homeland.

**Muzaffar al-Nawwab** was born in 1932 in al-Kadhimia, Baghdad. He attended Higher Teachers' Training College in Baghdad, where he studied Arabic literature and received painting lessons from prominent Iraqi painters such as Hafidh al-Duroobi and Fa'iq Hassan. He taught Arabic at several high schools in Baghdad. In the early 1950s, he joined the Iraqi left in its struggle against colonialism and monarchy. He was imprisoned several times and finally left Iraq in 1969. He emerged as a national poet of love and revolution after the outbreak of the Iraqi revolution against the British-installed monarchy in 1958. His early poetry, which was composed in the Iraqi southern dialect, was highly modernistic in its images, rhythms, and overall sensibility. In 1963, while in prison, al-Nawwab continued writing in dialect and began writing poetry in standard Arabic. His poems, in both the Iraqi dialect and standard Arabic, tend to be long. They are epic in their themes, collective voices, national narratives, and in their references to the golden days of Arabic and Islamic history. A singer with a powerful voice, al-Nawwab recites his poems in front of huge crowds. Though most of his poetry is not published, it is widely disseminated in cassettes and videotapes. He is the most popular poet in the Arab world, and divides his time now between Damascus, London and Tripoli.

**Salah Niazi** was born in the south of Iraq and studied Arabic literature at the University of Baghdad and at the University of London. Niazi wrote poetry in the spirit of TS Eliot but employed classical Arabic diction and adhered to the classical Arabic sense of balance. Since the late 1950s Niazi has published many poetry books, essays, criticism, and translations of Western classics. Niazi and his wife, Iraqi fiction writer Samira al-Mana, founded and edit *al-Ightrab al-Adabi*, a leading literary journal.

**Abdula Peshew** is a contemporary of the first generation of the followers of Goran's modernism. His poem 'Fratricide' shows him as remaining faithful to Goran's poetic formalism. If Goran and Bekes were in their time angry young men, then Peshew is now the angry middle-aged man of Kurdish poetry.

**Abd al-Rahim Salih al-Rahim** was born in 1950 in the city of al-Diwaniyah in the South, where he still lives and teaches at the University of al-Qadissiya. Al-Rahim has published two volumes of poetry. His poetry is characterized by an abiding yearning for the past and existential meditations on death.

**Yousif al-Sa'igh** was born in the northern city of Mousil in 1932 and now lives in Baghdad. Al-Sa'igh earned an MA in Arabic from the University of Baghdad. He taught at high schools and colleges. One of the most versatile Iraqi writers, al-Sa'igh has been writing poetry, fiction, plays, essays and autobiography. Since 1957, he has published, in addition to numerous essays, fourteen books. His complete poetry, *Poems*, was published in 1992. Since the early 1950s al-Sa'igh, like most Iraqi writers and artists, was inspired by the Iraqi left and joined the left to fight against Western colonialism and Western intervention in the Middle East. His writing is distinguished by its mastery of classical Arabic but is also experimental. More than any other Iraqi writer, al-Sa'igh, especially in his fiction and essays, is able to transform his anger and frustrations into hilarious satire and comedy.

**Aziz al-Samawi** was born and raised in the southern city al-Diwaniyah in 1941 and died in London last year. Beginning in 1957, Aziz wrote poetry in the southern Iraqi dialect. He published five books of poetry, literary essays, and poetry in standard Arabic. His poetry is known for its intense lyricism, which, following the tradition of Sufism, blends a love for the homeland with erotic love.

**Shakir al-Samawi** was born and raised in al-Diwaniyah, Iraq. He lives with his family in exile in Sweden. Al-Samawi is considered one of the major Iraqi poets and writers. Early in his life, he became involved with the Iraqi left and was imprisoned several times. Poet, playwright, essayist, al-Samawi has published five poetry books in the southern Iraqi dialect, three plays, and two books of essays on Iraqi culture and politics, philosophy and literature. His poetry is characterized by philosophical meditations, vivid imagery and effective rhythms.

**Sadiq al-Saygh** was born in 1936 in Baghdad. He graduated from Charles University, Prague in 1966 with an MA. He worked as editor-in-chief of three Iraqi literary and cultural journals: *al-Funoon* (art and culture), *Majalati* (children) and *al-Badeel* (Journal of Iraqi writers and artists in exile). Al-Saygh published his essays and poetry in many Iraqi and Arabic newspapers and journals. He also worked as a producer and performer in Iraqi TV and produced two documentary films for Czech TV. Al-Saygh published three volumes of poetry: *Ode To Unicorn* (1967), *A Home for the Soul* (1982), and *Where the Heart Is* (1997). He lives in London and publishes his essays and poetry in Iraqi and Arabic newspapers.

**Badr Shakir al-Sayyab** (1926-1964) was born in the village of Jaykur near Basrah. He was one of the leaders of the free verse movement in Arabic. Despite his untimely death, al-Sayyab left poetry so intense with its lyricism and so effective in its innovative rhymes, rhythms, and imagery that it has profoundly revolutionized the entire tradition of Arabic poetry. In the mid 1940s, al-Sayyab moved to Baghdad to attend the Higher Teachers' Training College, where he studied English, and was deeply influenced by John Keats, TS Eliot, and Edith Sitwell. There, he joined the left and suffered prison and exile. His poverty and mysterious tragic vision probably explain his identification with social outcasts such as prostitutes, with the homeless and the working class, evident in many of his poems. His profound sense of metaphysical alienation, on the other hand, probably led him to search for belonging in his memory of childhood, in mythology, and in near sexual unity with the landscape of his village Jaykur, his lost Eden. Al-Sayyab's complete poetry was published in two volumes in Beirut (1971-74).

**Sheikh Selman** was born in 1890 in the village of Azeban. He studied theology in the city of Sulaimani. Unlike the classical poets, he wrote very little love poetry, but published many critical pieces separately. His work is often characterised by patriotism. He translated the *Khayam Ruhaiyat* from Farsi into Kurdish, keeping the same form and style, thus rendering a great service to Kurdish literature.

**Hashim Shafiq** was born in 1950. He began publishing his poetry in the early 1970s in Iraqi, Arab, and international literary journals. He also published numerous critical articles on fiction and poetry. In addition to his literary and intellectual studies, Shafiq has published twelve books of poetry, the most recent of which appeared in 2001. He is the founder and director of the Iraqi House of Poetry in London. Shafiq's poetry has been translated into several European and Asian languages. His poetry is characterized by vivid imagery, sensitive rhythms, and high modernistic techniques.

**Ronny Someck** was born in Baghdad in 1951 and came to Israel as a young child. He has worked with street gangs, taught literature, and currently he leads creative writing workshops. With musician Elliott Sharp, he recorded three disks entitled 'Revenge of the Stuttering Child', 'Poverty Line', and 'Short History of Vodka'. He wrote a children's book entitled *The Laughter Button* and has published eight volumes of poetry, the most recent of which was entitled *Revolution Drummer*. His writing has been translated into 29 languages.

**Jawad Yaqoob** died last May, aged 36, after a long struggle with leukemia. After his death, his friends collected his poems and published them in one volume. His poetry carries an intense passion for life, friendship, and his homeland.

**S'adi Yusuf** (1934-) was born and raised in Basrah, a city famous for its rich literary history. Yusuf began composing free verse under the influence of al-Sayyab. In the 1950s Yusuf, like most Iraqi poets and writers, joined the Iraqi left. His identification with the Left led him to prison. In his poetry and prose, he persistently experiments with different styles and themes. He has appropriated forms associated with Western modernism. His poetry is subtle, quiet, and complex in its whispering rhythms. His interest in Iraqi folklore and Islamic and Mesopotamian mythologies lends his poetry originality and an appealing intimacy. In addition to many books of poetry, Yusuf has published fiction, essays, and translations. He lives in London.

**Sources Consulted:**
In compiling this biographical information about the poets, I have partially consulted the following sources:
Allen, Roger. Comp. and Ed. *Modern Arabic Literature*. (Ser. A Library of Literary Criticism). New York: Ungar Publishing Company, 1987.
Jayyusi, Salma Khadra. Ed. *Modern Arabic Poetry: An Anthology*. New York: Columbia University Press, 1987.
Meisami, Julie Scott, and Paul Starkey. Eds. *Encyclopaedia of Arabic Literature*. 2 vols. New York: Routledge, 1998.


# Translators

**Jenna Abdul Rahman** was born in Texas. She received a BA in Literature from American University, Washington, DC; an MA in English from the University of Maryland, College Park; and a PhD in Middle Eastern Languages, Literatures and Cultures from the University of Texas, Austin. She is the author of *The Image of Arabs in Modern Persian Literature* (University Press of America, 1996). She has taught in the US and the Middle East. Currently, she teaches English, ESL, and Peace Studies at Richland College in Dallas, Texas.

**Muhamad Tawfiq Ali** was born at the beginning of World War Two in the small town of Ruwandiz, in Iraqi Kurdistan. He received a scholarship to study civil engineering in the UK, where he has lived for most of his adult life. His interest in language led him to the study of linguistics and translation and he is a member of the Institute of Linguistics in London. Tawfiq Ali has translated between English and Arabic and Kurdish (Sorani), mainly on a voluntary basis and occasionally as a freelance writer; his volumes *Kurdistan's Immortal Poet* and *Selected Poems* were published in Arabic in 1990. He would like to express his gratitude to all those involved in the translation of Kurdish poetry published here.

**Saleh Alyafai** was born in Qatar. He is pursuing a degree in geography at the University of North Texas, Denton.

**Salah Ahmed Baban** was born in the city of Sulaimani in 1940. In 1949, the family moved to Baghdad. Baban received a scholarship to study mechanical engineering in Moscow. He returned to Baghdad in 1966. In 1971, he left for the UK, where he has resided ever since. He received a doctorate in structural engineering in 1975 and was appointed Research Fellow at the University of Birmingham where he remained until 1979. Besides his native Kurdish (Sorani), Baban has also mastered Russian and is fluent in English and Arabic, with smatterings of Turkoman.

**Ibtisam Barakat** is a Palestinian-American writer, poet and educator. Her work centres on healing the wounds brought about by political and social discord. Her writings have been published by Simon and Schuster, Bill Humanities Press, Pocket Books, the Loft Literary Center, Scholastic, Random House, *St. Louis Post Dispatch*, The Progressive Media Project, and others. Ibtisam was a delegate to the United Nations Conference on the Elimination of Racism, which was held in Durban, South Africa, August 2001. She leads Write Your Life seminars and speaks frequently about politics and writing.

**Carol Bardenstein** is an Assistant Professor of Arabic Language and Culture and of Comparative Literature in the Department of Near Eastern Studies at the University of Michigan. Her recent publications include 'Transmissions Interrupted: Reconfiguring Food, Memory and Gender in the Cookbook-Memoirs of Middle Eastern Exiles' (2002), 'Who's Who: Cross-Casting and Passing in Israeli and Palestinian Cinema' (forthcoming). She is currently completing a book entitled *Cultivating Attachments: Discourses of Rootedness in Palestine/Israel*, a comparative study of contested collective memories and symbols mobilized in the context of the Palestinian-Israeli conflict.

**Alex Bellem** is a PhD student in the Department of Linguistics at the School of Oriental and African Studies, University of London. She gained her MA in Linguistics from University College London and her BA in Middle Eastern Studies from the University of Manchester. Her research interests include phonological theory, Arabic linguistics and Arabic literature.

**Basima Bezirgan** is co-editor (with Elizabeth Fernea) of *Middle Eastern Women Speak* (1980). Bezirgan has translated Arab poetry and prose.

Currently she is the Cataloguer of the Middle Eastern section of the University of Chicago's Bergenstein Library.

**Melissa Brown** holds an MFA in poetry and a PhD in English, both from the University of Iowa. Brown has published poetry, translations, poetry reviews, and literary criticism. She is a writer and editor at Buckle Down Publishing, a publisher of educational materials based in Iowa City.

**Christina Coyle** has earned an MFA in playwriting. She lived in Yemen and now lives in Philadelphia.

**Terri DeYoung** is currently Associate Professor of Arabic Language and Literature at the University of Washington. DeYoung graduated from Princeton University in 1977 with a BA degree (cum laude) in Comparative Literature. She received an International Graduate Fellowship to attend the American University in Cairo, where she received an MA in Modern Arabic Literature in 1981. She was awarded a PhD in Near Eastern Studies from the University of California at Berkeley in 1988. She has taught also at Rhodes College in Memphis, Tennessee and at Yale University. Her book, *Placing the Poet: Badr Shakir al-Sayyab and Postcolonial Iraq*, won a Choice Award (given by the American Association of Research Libraries) in 1998. She has also co-edited, with Professor Issa Boullata of McGill University, a volume of essays in honour of Professor Mounah Khouri, *Tradition and Modernity in Arabic Literature* (1997). She has published more than a dozen essays and articles on medieval and modern Arabic literature.

**Vivian Eden** was born in the United States and has lived in Israel on and off since 1961. At the University of Iowa, where she received her PhD in Comparative Literature with a specialty in translation, she was a member of the staff of the International Writing Program. Her poems and translations have been published in Israel, England, the United States and elsewhere. Among her prose translations is the novel *Arabesques* by Anton Shammas. She is currently on the staff of *The International Herald Tribune - Ha'aretz* English Edition, where she edits a column of poetry in translation, 'Lines'.

**Abdul Kadir Said Ferhadi.** *MT Ali writes:* I had the pleasure of meeting the late Abdul Kadir Said Ferhadi in October/November 1993 and 1994 during my visits to Erbil in liberated Kurdistan of Iraq, where he was head of the Department of English at Salahedin University. He had graduated from a university in Iraq, in English literature. The University of North Wales, Bangor, conferred an MA in Linguistics on him in 1984. He wrote a cultural page for *The Kurdish Times Monthly*, under the title

*Kurdish Poetry in the 20th century.* I read the sad news of his death at a comparatively early age in the late nineties. Subsequently, his deputy Abdul-Hamid, who succeeded him, also died. In appreciation, I dedicate the selection of Kurdish poetry in *MPT* 19 to both of them, who served with such devotion under the difficult circumstances.

**Elizabeth Fernea** is Professor Emeritus of English and Middle Eastern Studies at the University of Texas at Austin. A well known author and filmmaker whose work focuses on Middle Eastern women, Fernea has authored several books on Middle Eastern societies. Her first book, *Guests of the Sheiks: An Ethnography of an Iraqi Village* (1965), is a classic study of the social status of women in a southern Iraqi rural community. Her most recent book is entitled *In Search of Islamic Feminism* (1998). Fernea has produced six documentaries on the Middle East, particularly on women and family. Fernea has also translated poetry from Arabic into English.

**Ferial J Ghazoul** received a PhD in Comparative Literature from Columbia University, 1978. She has been teaching in the Department of English and Comparative Literature at the American University in Cairo since 1979. She was co-founder and is an editor of *Alif: Journal of Comparative Poetics* (1981-present). She has participated as a judge in a number of contests and is a member of several professional associations: Cavafy Awards for Poets, Nour Awards for Literary Works by Arab women, and others. In addition to numerous articles on Arabic literature, she has authored and translated *The Arabian Nights: A Structural Analysis* (1980), *Saadi Youssef* (1989), *The View from Within* (1994), *Nocturnal Poetics* (1996), *Quartet of Joy* (1997), and *The Palestinians and Comparative Literature* (2000).

**Carolina Hotchandani** studied English literature at Brown University and Oxford University. While living in Providence, she wrote for the *Providence Journal*. Currently she lives in Iowa City, where she writes poetry and prose.

**Emily Howard** writes and teaches poetry. She lives in Chicago.

**Hussein Kadhim** teaches Arabic language and literature at Dartmouth College. He is the co-editor of *Edward Said and the Post-Colonial* (New York: Nova Publishers, 2002). He recently completed a book tentatively entitled *The Poetics of Anti-Colonialism in the Arabic "Qasidah"*. He is currently working on a book tentatively entitled: *Abd al-Wahhab al-Bayyati and the Poetry of Social Realism*.

**Mustapha Kamal** was born in Morocco. Kamal earned his PhD in Arabic from the University of California at Berkeley. He is a professor of Arabic at the University of Illinois at Chicago. He has published articles on Arabic literature and translations of Arabic literature.

**Sadok Masliyah** is Branch Chief at the Middle East School of the Defense Language Institute in Monterey, California. He received his PhD from UCLA in Near Eastern Languages and Literatures. He has published numerous studies on Iraqi literature and culture. His English translation of the Iraqi novel *Nzulah u-Khait el-Shitan* (Tenants and Cobwebs) by Samir Naqqash is expected to be published in 2004.

**Khaled Mattawa** is the author of two books of poetry, *Zodiac of Echoes* (forthcoming from Ausable Press), and *Ismailia Eclipse* (The Sheep Meadow Press, 1996). He has translated three volumes of Iraqi poetry, the latest of which, Saadi Youssef's *Without An Alphabet, Without A Face* is forthcoming from Graywolf Press. Mattawa is an assistant professor of English at the University of Texas, Austin.

**Richard McKane** is a British poet living in London. He has published four books of poetry and has translated numerous literary works from Turkish and Russian.

**Christopher Merrill's** most recent books are *Only the Nails Remain: Scenes from the Balkan Wars* (nonfiction) and *Brilliant Water* (poetry). He directs the International Writing Program at the University of Iowa.

**Chuck Miller** is a teacher and writer. He has authored ten books of poetry and fiction. Raised in Illinois, Chuck has worked in Europe and Asia. Poetry, according to Chuck, should inform us directly of the most crucial situations.

**Farouk AW Mustafa** is Ibn Rushd Professorial Lecturer, Department of Near Eastern Languages and Civilizations; and Associate Director, Center for Middle Eastern Studies, University of Chicago. His pen name is Farouk Abdel Wahab.

**Raghid Nahhas** was born in Syria and lives now in Sidney, Australia. He is the Editor-in-Chief of the Arabic-English literary journal *Kalimat* (Words). He translates from Arabic into English and vice versa.

**Najat Rahman** is Assistant Professor of Arabic Literature at James Madison University. She has a PhD in Comparative Literature from the University of Wisconsin-Madison and was recently a Fulbright Scholar in Beirut, Lebanon. Her research interests include poetry, translation and aesthetics. She has written on Mahmoud Darwish (*Islamic Masculinities*, Zed Press), Rashid Al-Daif (*Cross-Cultural Poetics*) and Amin Maalouf (*Al-Jadid*). Forthcoming are articles on Assia Djebar (in Dr Rose Mezu Ure's book, *A Literary History of African Women's Writings*) as well as selected poetic translations of Darwish (*Flyway*).

**Daniel P Reynolds** is Assistant Professor of German at Grinnell College, where he has been teaching since 1998. He earned his PhD from Harvard University in 1996 in Germanic Languages and Literatures, and studied as an undergraduate at Georgetown University and the Eberhard-Karls-Universität, Tübingen, Germany. Among his research endeavours are articles on Rainer Maria Rilke, Günter Grass, and most recently, Bernhard Schlink. He is writing a monograph on German metafiction. His translation of 'Sorotchintzy Fair', a German adaptation of a tale by Nikolai Gogol, appeared in 1990 by David R Godine Publishing.

**Ralph Savarese** teaches American literature and creative writing at Grinnell College. His poems have appeared in *Sewanee Review, American Poetry Review, The Beloit Poetry Journal, Graham House Review, Seneca Review*, and many other journals. A former student of Slavic languages and literatures, particularly Polish, he has lived in Eastern Europe and translated numerous modern and contemporary Polish poets.

**Saadi A Simawe** is Associate Professor of English and current Chair of the English Department at Grinnell College. He teaches African American literature and literary theory. In addition to many articles in Arabic and English, he published a novel in Arabic entitled *Al-Khuruj min al-Qumqum* (London, 1999), collaborated with Ellen Doré Watson in translating Palestinian poetry for *MPT* No. 14, 1988, edited the *Arab Studies Quarterly* special issue on *Modern Iraqi Literature* (No. 19, 1997) and edited *Black Orpheus: Music in African American Fiction From The Harlem Renaissance to Toni Morrison* (2002).

**Ellen Doré Watson** is Director of the Poetry Center at Smith College and is Translation Editor of *The Massachusetts Review*. She has translated a dozen books from Brazilian Portuguese, including *The Alphabet in the Park: Selected Poems of Adélia Prado*, which was supported by a National Endowment for the Arts Translation Fellowship. She has worked with Saadi Simawe before, on a large group of contemporary Palestinian poems for *MPT* No. 14. Watson's own poetry has been published widely and received many awards. Her most recent collection is *Ladder Music* from Alice James Books.

**Liz Winslow** is a writer and translator. Her translations of Dunya Mikhail and Mahmoud Shukair have been published in *Banipal, Mizna* and *Poetry International,* and her fiction has been published in the *Louisville Review, Blue Mesa Review,* and *Phoebe.* She currently lives and works in Las Vegas.

**Salaam Yousif** is Professor of English at California State University at San Bernardino. He has published articles on Iraqi literature and culture.

# Oded Halahmy Foundation for the Arts inc.

The Oded Halahmy Foundation for the Arts is a non-profit cultural organization created to fund original artistic expressions of peace and hope in the Middle East, the United States, and around the world.

We are very pleased to announce the publication of Professor Saadi A Simawe's anthology of contemporary Iraqi poetry, published by *Modern Poetry in Translation* (*MPT* 19).

The Foundation launched its first series of grants this year; they include funding a series of prominent writers from the Middle East, man of whom have never had the opportunity of appearing in print in English for the reading public. Other grants will support innovative artistic expressions of peace in drama, music, and in the visual arts, encouraging all forms of art as a means of fostering a dialogue for peace.

"May there be peace in Iraq, the Middle East, and around the world."

*Oded Halahmy*
President

Oded Halahmy Foundation for the Arts, Inc is a 501 (c) (3) organization. Contributions are tax-deductible as allowed by law in the United States.

# *MPT* Back issues

**MPT (New Series) No 1**

BONNEFOY, plus Pasolini, Emmanuel, Larbaud, Cassou, Celan, Cabral de Melo Neto, Miljkovic, Sepehri, 4 German poets (Volker Braun, Bernd Jentzsch, Kurt Bartsch, Thomas Brasch), Inan Diu';
+ essays: Trans-textual Readings, German Poetry in Recent English Translations

**MPT (New Series) No 2:**

FRANZ BAERMANN STEINER (bi-lingual number featuring a single poet translated & introduced by Michael Hamburger)

**MPT (New Series) No 3:**

KAMIEŃSKA, plus Musiał, Piechowicz, Czekanowicz, Maj, Lars, Borun-Jagodsinska, Szymborska, Vasovic, Belev, Stratanovsky, Preil, Dor, Anghelaki-Rooke, Davetas, Zanzotto, Bellezza, Ray, Hocquard, Polet, Hauge, Nordbrandt, Sylvester, Parra;
+ translators of poetry: Michael Bullock;
+ essays by Bilbija, Longinović, Du Val, Hocquard
+ reviews

**MPT (New Series) No 4:**

THE JERUSALEM INTERNATIONAL POETS FESTIVAL: Alkalay-Gut, Amichai, Araidi, Back, Bargouti, Berggren, Berinsky, Bernstein, Christensen, Eden, Ghanyim, Grobman, Haddad, Halter, Kirsch, Kosman, Kushner, Levin, Lichman, Magrelli, Masalha, Molina, Or, Pey, Ravikovitch, Rubin, Shir, Silk, Someck, Turkka, Vernikova, Zarchi, Zisquit;
+ essays by Sandbank, De Haes, Felstiner;
+ translators of poetry: Robert Friend;
+ in memoriam: Gabriel Preil

**MPT (New Series) No 5:**

GALICIAN TROUBADOURS plus Pessoa, Breyner, Cernuda, Alberti, Aurora Araujo Story, Rivera, Sereni, Saba, Norwid, Kamieńska, Harasymowicz, Martinaitis, Haavikko, Aspenström, Sjögren, Hessler, Heine, Ausländer, Augustin, Teuschl, Gumilev, Bunin, Aizenberg, Jelloun, Qasmi, Niazi;
+ Adam Czerniawski interviews;
+ reviews

**MPT (New Series) No 6:**

BRAZIL: M de Andrade, O de Andrade, T de Almeida, CD de Andrade, G de Almeida, Meireles, Ivo, Faustino, de Lima, Mendes, de Moraes, Cabral de Melo Neto, Quintana, Ricardo, Prado, Filho, Bandeira, Ferreira

Gullar, Fiorani;

+ Poswiatowska, Dropkin, Faiz, Rafiq, 9-13th-century Arabo-Andalusian poems, Magrelli, Cosma, Anghelaki-Rooke, Patilis, Chouliaras, Runeberg, Tegnér;

+ essays: Boase-Beier;

+ reviews: Kirkup, D Robinson, Pynsent, Treece;

+ opinions: Sulyák

## MPT (New Series) No 7:

WELSH: Dafydd Johnston, Gareth Alban Davies, Menna Elfyn, Donald Evans, Bobi Jones, Dewi Stephen Jones, Huw Jones, R Gerallt Jones, Emyr Lewis, Gwyneth Lewis, Alan Llwyd, Iwan Llwyd, Elin Llwyd Morgan, Mihangel Morgan, Gerallt Lloyd Owen, Gwyn Thomas;

+ translations by R S Thomas, Gerwyn Wiliams;

+ essays: T Arfon Williams, Joseph P Clancy, Dafydd Johnston, Professor M Wynn Thomas;

+ reviews: Katie Gramich, Richard Griffiths;

+ letter: Dannie Abse

## MPT (New Series) No 8:

FRANCE plus Germany, Greece, Italy; Bonnefoy, Guillevic, Deguy, Dupin, Jaccottet, des Forêts, Roubaud, Jacob, Apollinaire, Baudelaire, Deschamps, John Du Val on translating *fabliaux*;

+ Trakl, WD Jackson on Heine, Elytis, Magrelli, Montale, Neiger, Someck, Pagis & more

## MPT (New Series) No 9:

FILIPINO POETRY (Cebuano literature, poetry of the West Visayas, English and Taglish poetry);

+ Bolivia, China, France, Germany, Greece, Italy & more

## MPT (New Series) No 10:

RUSSIAN POETRY: Akhmatova, Aranzon, Aygi, Bukharaev, Khlebnikov, Khodasevich, Ivanov, Rein, Tarkovsky, Tsvetayeva, Voznesensky, Zugman & others;

+ Peter Levi on translating poetry

+ reviews, articles

+ a feature on Joseph Brodsky

## MPT (New Series) No 11:

PERU & RUSSIA: *Peru* – Ribeyro, Watanabe, Verastegui, Mora, Varela, Chocano; *Russia* – Krylov, Pushkin, Turgenev, Oleinikov, Vvedensky, Vinokurov, Mark, Papadin, Tychyna;

+ Argentina, France, Germany, Greece, Hungary, India, Japan, Italy,

Poland, Sweden, Uruguay
+ James Kirkup as Translator

**MPT (New Series) No 12:**
DUTCH & FLEMISH POETRY: Ghyssaert, van Bastelaere, Spinoy, Jansma, Boskma, Barnard, Oosterhoff, Van hee, Hertmans, Gerlach, van den Berg, Nolens, Enquist, Komrij, van den Bremt, ten Berge, Bernlef, Kopland, Herzberg, Claus, Kouwenaar, Jellema;
+ a checklist of Dutch and Flemish PostWar Poetry compiled by Theo Hermans

**MPT (New Series) No 13:**
GREECE: Anagnostakis, Angelakis, Aslanoglou, Calas, Cavafy, Chionis, Elytis, Embiricon, Fokas, Galanaki, Ganas, Gatsos, Gougouris, Ioannou, Karyotakis, Karouzos, Kondon, Patrikios, Seferis, Sikelianos, Stamatis, Vayenas, Vlavianos;
+ poetry from Italy, Spain (including Lorca), Mexico, France, Germany, Ireland, Holland, Poland, Sweden, Korea, Vietnam, Iraq, Jordan, Palestine
+ reviews

**MPT (New Series) No 14:** ISBN 0-9533824-0-0
PALESTINIAN AND ISRAELI POETRY: Taha Muhammad Ali to Ghassan Zaqtan; Yehuda Amichai to Natan Zach

**MPT (New Series) No 15:** ISBN 0-9533824-1-9
CONTEMPORARY ITALIAN POETRY: Sixteen contemporary poets, chosen by Luca Guerneri, introduced by Roberto Galaverni
+ nine of the older generation poets.
+ **A Pushkin Portfolio** A Pushkin lyric, translated by thirty poets and translators, introduced by David Bethea
+ Daniel Weissbort on Ted Hughes as a translator of Pushkin
+ Antony Wood on 'Can Pushkin be Translated?'.

**MPT (New Series) No 16: Guest Editor: Norma Rinsler** ISBN 0-9533824-2-7
GERMAN AND FRENCH POETRY: Goethe, Novalis, Heine, George, Morgenstern, Rilke, Ringelnatz, Trakl, Czechowski, Kirsch, Cohn, Kunert, Enzensberger, Sebald, Hahn, Labé, Belleau, Jodelle, Valéry, Jacob, Apollinaire, Cendrars, Cassou, Bekri.
+ poets from the Netherlands, Norway and Sweden
+ reviews

**MPT (New Series) No 17: Guest Editor: Stephen Watts** ISBN 0-9533824-7-8
MOTHER TONGUES: NON ENGLISH-LANGUAGE POETRY IN ENGLAND: Azad, Begikhani, Blatny, Bukaraev, Calderara, Ceylan, Chandan, Cohn,

Czerniawski, de Dadelsen, Dyson, Ebrahimi, Enciso, Farhi, Farooqi,
Fried, Gömöri, Grigorieva, al-Haidari, Hardi, Határ, Jelinek, de Jésus,
Karbassi, Khoi, Kinsky, Knopfli, Korkmazel, Macedo, Masoliver, Nasser,
Naz, Palandri, Pomeranzev, Prigov, Prokofiev, Rana, Rivera-Reyes,
Sebald, Serrano, Simonovic, Tabachnikova, Taufer, Thomas, Tirmazi,
Vadji, Vernitski, Vishniak, Lian;
+ essays by Ranja Sidhanta Ash, Martin Orwin, Aydın Mehmet Ali
+ an Introduction to Somali poetry
+ Turkish-speaking women's writing in London
+ Bengali and Hindi poets

## MPT (New Series) No 18: ISBN 0-9533824-4-3
EUROPEAN VOICES: Apollinaire, Atxaga, Bonnefoy, Braun, Camões, Cavafy,
Celan, Cliff, Dizdar, Ekström, Enzensberger, Fritsch, Goethe, Heine,
Kaddour, Kolbe, Kunze, Leyvik, Machado, Mallarmé, Verlaine, Malroux,
Mayakovsky, Montale, Nordbrandt, Pasternak, Pavese, Poswiatowska,
Pushkin, Quasimodo, Réda, Saba, Schiele, Simic, Snoek, de Sousa,
Suied, Svenbro, Szabó, Twardowski, Ungaretti, Ursachi, Ursu, Valéry,
Wat, Yashin, Zanzotto;
+ ten lyrics from the Greek Anthology
+ three Polish poets, three Russian poets
+ translators of poetry: Peter Viereck
+ reviews

## MPT (New Series) No 20: Guest Editor: Valentina Polukhina
ISBN 0-9533824-8-6
RUSSIAN WOMEN POETS: Akhmadulina, Alaverdova, Anserova,
Avvakumova, Barskova, Bek, Berezovchuk, Boroditskaya, Boyarskikh,
Chizhevskaya, Chulkova, Den'gina, Derieva, Dolia, Ermakova,
Ermoshina, Esrokhi, Fanailova, Gabrielian, Galina, Glazova,
Gorbanevskaya, Gorlanova, Grigoryeva, Grimberg, Ignatova, Iskrenko,
Ivanova, S Ivanova, Kabysh, Kapovich, Kekova, Khvostova, Kildibekova,
Kossman, Kovaleva, Krylova, Kudimova, Kulishova, Kunina, Lavut,
Lazutkina, Lisnianskaya, Litvak, Martynova, Miller, Milova,
Mnatskanova, Morits, Negar, Nikolaeva, Nikonova, Pavlova, Petrova,
Petrushevskaya, Postnikova, Ratushinskaya, Retivova, Sedakova, Shats,
Shcherbina, Shvarts, Stepanova, Sukhovei, Sulchinskaya,
Tkhorzhevskaya, Ushakova (Nevzvgliadova), Vlasova, Voltskaya,
Zubova;
+ interviews: Svetlana Kekova, Yunna Morits, Vera Pavlova, Olga
Sedakova, Evelina Shats, Tatyana Shcherbina and Tatyana Voltskaya
+ essays by Tatyana Voltskaya, Aleksei Alekhin, Tatyana Retivova,
Dmitry Kuzmin
+ Bibliography by Valentina Polukhina